"The Internet has seamlessly interconnected customers, suppliers, and the workforce, and b-webs are effectively blurring all traditional roles and changing how we think about infrastructure. *Digital Capital* is a breakthrough—a must-read to understand the dynamics of how this new economy will unfold."

—Craig Conway, President and CEO, PeopleSoft, Inc.

"*Digital Capital* is an insightful guide to the rules of engagement in the new economy. Its explanation of collaborative business webs—the emerging market models for value creation—should be required reading for anyone who wants to reach the digital customer."

—Michael S. Dell, Chairman and CEO, Dell Computer Corporation

"Exciting and compelling, *Digital Capital* concisely captures important new thinking on Internet business models and how to apply them today."

—Larry Downes, Coauthor, *Unleashing the Killer App*

"The seminal book on business webs and how they can help move your business units into the new, new economy. Every business leader should read this book!"

—Robert Eaton, Former Chairman, DaimlerChrysler

"With a surgeon's precision, Tapscott, Ticoll, and Lowy define and explore new business models and opportunities coming to light in the emerging virtual 'Agora.' *Digital Capital* is the guide to the new world of Internet work."

—William T. Esrey, Chairman and CEO, Sprint Corporation

"One of the most important challenges facing today's executives is the need to disaggregate and reaggregate their firms to harness the power of business webs. *Digital Capital* presents an actionable blueprint for meeting this challenge. If you have any responsibility for the future of your business, read this book."

—Durk Jager, Chairman and CEO, Procter & Gamble

"Simply a must-read. *Digital Capital* provides real out-of-the-box insights, and, even more, excites and captivates you."

> —Jeff Papows, Former CEO, Lotus Development Corporation, and Author, *Enterprise.com*

"*Digital Capital* is an insightful and recommended read for anyone wrestling with the impact of e-business and the pace of change. Our business literally exploded with the b-web thinking outlined in this book."

> —Peter Schwartz, Chairman and CEO, Descartes Systems

"*Digital Capital* provides clear insight into responding to the new economy. Working with the authors, our Corporate Foreign Exchange division embodied the ideas behind this book in its e-business strategy, and is now ready to participate successfully in many business webs."

> —Alan Stewart, Deputy Chief Executive, Thomas Cook Holdings Limited, and Chairman, Global and Financial Services, Thomas Cook Group

"*Digital Capital* is the guidebook for any business leader who wants to win in the e-business world. Well-written and provocative, this book provides us with the first practical navigation system for what the authors coin as 'b-webs'—the new platform for winning in the twenty-first century."

> —Noel Tichy, Professor, University of Michigan, and Coauthor, *The Leadership Engine* and *Every Business Is a Growth Business*

digital
capital

harnessing the power
of business webs

DON TAPSCOTT

DAVID TICOLL

ALEX LOWY

NICHOLAS BREALEY
PUBLISHING

LONDON

First published in Great Britain by
Nicholas Brealey Publishing in 2000

36 John Street
London
WC1N 2AT, UK
Tel: +44 (0)20 7430 0224
Fax: +44 (0)20 7404 8311

1163 E. Ogden Avenue, Suite 705-229
Naperville
IL 60563-8535, USA
Tel: (888) BREALEY
Fax: (630) 898 3595

http://www.nbrealey-books.com

ISBN 1-85788-209-1

British Library Cataloguing in Publication Data
A catalogue record for this book is available from the British Library.

Printed in Finland by WS Bookwell

contents

preface

The industrial age was an age of giants, megacorporations that did everything from soup to nuts. The information age is bringing forth a new business form: fluid congregations of businesses—sometimes highly structured, sometimes amorphous—that come together on the Internet to create value for customers and wealth for their shareholders. We call these systems business webs, or b-webs.

Many other names have been given to networks of collaborating companies, such as outsourcing services, virtual corporations, extended enterprises, *keiretsu*, business ecosystems, and swarms. In our view, each of these names refers to a precursor, or special form, of b-web, the increasingly universal business platform. B-webs challenge traditional approaches to management and business strategy, and perhaps ultimately even the roles of business and government. B-webs are the mechanisms for the accumulation of digital capital, the knowledge- and relationship-based currency of the new economy. To succeed in the digital economy, every employee, entrepreneur, and manager must embrace a new b-web strategy agenda. This book is, we hope, a significant attempt to shed light on the b-web phenomenon—to describe it, and to provide the beginnings of a strategic approach to developing and implementing innovative, competitive strategies for creating value in a world of b-webs.

The book has four parts:

- Chapter 1 is an overview of the b-web phenomenon, including the driving forces and main implications for business strategy. We also introduce two core frameworks: the elements of digital capital and a new five-part taxonomy of business models.

- Chapters 2 through 6 provide strategy concepts for each of the five types of b-web: Agoras, Aggregations, Value Chains, Alliances, and Distributive Networks.

- Chapters 7 and 8 describe the changing dynamics of digital capital: human capital (people) and relationship capital (marketing).

- Chapters 9 and 10 describe how to design b-web strategy and harvest the benefits.

Thank you for taking the time to consider our ideas. We hope that you find this book useful as you define and redefine your strategies for the digital economy. Please join us in a dialogue about these issues—or just contact us—at digitalcapital@actnet.com or http://www.actnet.com.

Don Tapscott
David Ticoll
Alex Lowy

origins

This book draws on the insights from a multimillion-dollar research project conducted by the Alliance for Converging Technologies, a consulting and research firm we founded with Paul Woolner in 1994. We are deeply thankful to the companies—and the many individuals within them—that have sponsored our series of research programs.

By 1996, just after the publication of *The Digital Economy*, the early online communities—people-to-people networks on the Net—had become very popular. We developed a view that e-community, or Web-enabled collective action, also applied to the world of business. We investigated a concept that we initially called the e-business community; later on, we chose the term *business web* to describe this emerging heir to the industrial-age corporation. A series of case studies uncovered a collection of then-obscure (and still privately held) companies, such as eBay and E*Trade, as well as the story behind the story of emerging leaders such as Cisco.

We initially investigated some 170 potential b-webs and reported on 28. As we looked at these 28 embryonic success stories and began to reverse engineer their business strategies, we noted patterns that traversed industry boundaries. These patterns ultimately resolved into the taxonomy that we employ in this book. At first, we saw four "types" of b-web: Agora, Aggregation, Value Chain, and Alliance, on the two axes of value integration (low to high) and economic control (hierarchical versus self-organizing). Then, while working on this book in 1999, we concluded that one of the sub-types, which we had included under Value Chains, required its own box, and defined the Distributive Network as a new element of the taxonomy.

Each of the five business "types" has always existed to some degree. But until the Internet lowered transaction costs, Alliances—despite achievements like the development of language and science—were too inefficient and slow to be recognized as models for creating economic value. Now that Alliances have gone mainstream, the axes of the taxonomy make sense.

The origins of this book go back to the leaders and thinkers in business and strategy whom we have cited—and many others whom we have not mentioned. We single out two who helped us set off on our unique path: Ronald Coase and James Moore. We also thank Verna Allee, Charles Fine, Ravi Kalakota, Tom Malone, Chuck Martin, Doug Neal, Nicholas Negroponte, Carl Shapiro, Hubert Saint-Onge, and Hal Varian. Riel Miller, who brought Coase's work to our attention in 1994, was to our knowledge the first to tackle the implications of the Net for Coase's theory of the firm.

This book would simply not have happened without the dedication and quality focus of our associates at the Alliance for Converging Technologies. Natalie Klym was our trusted partner throughout, functioning as editorial coordinator, researcher, and a leading contributor to chapter 4 (Value Chains). Dave Cosgrave was a valued researcher and leading contributor to chapter 3 (Aggregations). Key Alliance contributors of research, analysis, dialogue, and insight were Andy De, Mike Dover, Darcelle Hall, Phil Hood, Alan Majer, Michael Miloff, and Paul Woolner. Other Alliance contributors of invaluable research were Jennifer Akeroyd, Rob Haimes, David Lancashire, Ed McDonnell, Chris McRaild, and Nicole Morin. From New Paradigm Learning Corporation, Bill Gillies provided thoughtful editorial support, while Jody Stevens and Antoinette Schatz provided valuable editorial advice and research support.

Having said all this, as authors we take full responsibility for the content of this book.

Kirsten Sandberg, senior editor at Harvard Business School Press, provided incisive advice on how to improve this book; we appreciate the dedication and principles she applied to the editorial process. Jane Judge Bonassar managed the book through production and saved us from many sins. We extend our thanks to all the other participants in the creative and diligent Harvard team. Wes Neff of the Leigh Bureau, our literary agent, helped provide the wherewithal that we needed to take time out of our day jobs to do this project.

Most important, we would like to thank our families. Every thoughtful book project eats into precious family moments—evenings, weekends, and holidays, and even weeks at a time. Heartfelt thanks to our spouses, Ana Lopes (Tapscott), Tracey Macey (Ticoll), and Julia Mustard (Lowy), and to our children, Andre Lowy, Benjamin Lowy, Alex Tapscott, Nicole Tapscott, and Amy Ticoll.

Part I
introduction

1 value innovation through business webs

THE MP3 STORY

"We record anything—anywhere—anytime," proclaimed Sam Phillips on his business card. Phillips was a white man who wanted black musicians to feel comfortable at Sun Records, his two-person recording studio in segregation-era Memphis, Tennessee. In July 1953, a shy-looking eighteen-year-old named Elvis Presley came by the studio and paid Phillips $3.98 to record his version of "My Happiness." The young man took home the sole copy of his vinyl disk. Although Elvis hung around the studio persistently after that, Phillips only twigged his potential a year later, when he launched the future star's career with a haunting cover of "That's All Right." Then, after 1½ years of working his way up the hillbilly circuit, Elvis finally cut his first RCA hits.[1]

If Elvis were trying to break into the music business today, then he would not need to wait 2½ years to get national distribution. Instead, like thousands of others, he could use MP3, which fulfills the bold claim on Sam Phillips's business card. MP3 really does record—and distribute—any music, anywhere, anytime. It does so free and unmediated by agents and record companies.

Through Elvis's career and beyond, an oligopoly of industrial-age record companies and broadcast networks like RCA and CBS controlled the music distribution business. Today, their dominion is in tatters. While partisans quibble about its profitability, convenience, sound quality, or long-term prospects, the MP3 phenomenon has rent forever the rule book of this $38 billion industry.

The Fraunhofer Institute, a German industrial electronics research company, released MP3 in 1991 as a freely available technical standard for the compression and transmission of digital audio. The user "business case" for MP3 is simple: Buy a CD burner for three hundred dollars, and you can download and save an entire pirated Beatles collection on two CDs. At this point, you've made back your hardware investment, and now you can build the rest of your music library for the cost of the blank CDs.

Viscerally appealing to youngsters in the Net Generation demographic, MP3 attained critical mass in 1998, when it whirled through the Internet almost overnight. Millions of technology-literate kids and teenagers, high on music, low on cash, and sold on the mantra that "information wants to be free," used the Net to freely create and share MP3 software tools and music content. MP3 shows how internetworking and critical market mass can drive change with breathtaking speed. Piracy cost the music industry $10 billion in 1998; at any one time, more than half a million music files were available on the Internet for illegal downloading.[2] While the recording industry scrambled to deal with this hurricane of music piracy, most people were not even aware that all this was going on!

MP3's success is the product of an Internet-based alliance—a business web—of consumers, businesses (content and software distribution sites like MP3.com, and technology manufacturers like Diamond, maker of the Rio MP3 player), and content providers (musicians). It exemplifies how business webs have risen to challenge the industrial-age corporation as the basis for competitive strategy.

MP3 meets our definition of a business web (b-web): a distinct system of suppliers, distributors, commerce services providers, infrastructure providers, and customers that use the Internet for their primary business communications and transactions. Without such an Internet-enabled system, MP3 would almost certainly never have succeeded—and certainly not as fast as it did.

Though the MP3 b-web is an informal, grassroots phenomenon, it has shaken the foundations of an entire industry. Most other b-webs emanate from businesses, rather than college and high school students. They have identifiable leaders who formally orchestrate their strategies and processes. But no matter where they come from, b-webs provide challenge and opportunity to every business. They are the only means for accessing and increasing what we call digital capital, the mother lode of digital networks.

Simply put, digital capital results from the internetworking of three types of knowledge assets: human capital (what people know), customer capital (who you know, and who knows and values you), and structural capital (how what you know is built into your business systems). With internetworking, you can gain human capital without owning it; customer capital from complex mutual relationships; and structural capital that builds wealth through new business models.

This book shows business leaders how to form and build reserves of such digital capital by harnessing the power of business webs.

DRIVING FORCES OF THE DIGITAL ECONOMY

The question facing leaders and managers is not just "What is driving change in the economy today?" It is "What should I *do* to respond to all these changes?" This book is intended to help answer the second question. But before doing so, we will quickly describe the forces that drive the new economy, forces that are leading to the inevitable rise of the b-web.

The industrial economy depended on physical goods and services. Mass production addressed the problems of scarcity and the high costs of mobilizing raw materials, fabricating and assembling goods, and delivering them to their destinations. In the new economy, many offerings (like software and electronic entertainment) are nonphysical and knowledge-based, whereas the value of "physical" items (like pharmaceuticals and cars) depends on the knowledge embedded in their design and production.

Consequently, the economy shifts from scarcity to abundance. We can reproduce and distribute knowledge products like software and electronic entertainment for near zero marginal cost. Knowledge-intensive physical goods also become cheaper. Self-evident in the case of computer chips, this principle even applies to natural resources. Satellite imaging quickens the hunt for mineral resources. Ocean fisheries collapse, but the applied science of aquaculture fills markets with fish. Everywhere, knowledge yields new abundance.

Network economics drive the interlinked phenomena of increasing returns and network effects: Many (but by no means all) knowledge-based goods obey a law of increasing returns: once you have absorbed the cost of making the first digital "copy" (e.g., of a piece of software or an electronic publication), the marginal reproduction cost approaches zero—resulting in huge potential profits. Certain goods also display network effects: The more widely they are used, the greater their value. The more people who buy videodisc players, the more manufacturers are motivated to publish titles; this in turn makes the players more valuable to the people who own them. In such situations, those who control the standards can make a lot of money. Other examples include PC operating systems, the Web, and word processing software.

As MP3 illustrates, hurricanes of change can hit hard, and without warning. To prepare for such events, managers in every industry must learn to lead and change in "Internet time."

Space and time have become elastic media that expand or contract at will. Global financial markets respond to news in an instant. Nonstop software projects "follow the sun" around the world each day. Online auctioneers host millions of sessions simultaneously, with worldwide bidding stretched over a week instead of the moments available in a traditional auction gallery.

The new economics of knowledge, abundance, and increasing returns precipitate long-term deflationary trends. Networked computing cuts the cost of doing business in every industry, which inevitably means better deals on just about everything. There is a lot of room for growth well into the twenty-first century, in both rich and poor countries. And growth with little or no inflation is the best kind.

In this world of abundance, attention becomes a scarce commodity because of three factors. First, no person can produce more than twenty-four hours of attention per day. Second, the human capacity to pay attention is limited. Third (a result of the first two and exacerbated by the Internet), people are inundated with so much information that they don't know what to pay attention *to*.[3] To capture and retain customer attention, a business must provide a pertinent, attractive, and convenient total experience.

Industrial-age production, communications, commerce, and distribution were each the basis of entirely different sets of industries. Now, these activities implode on the Net. Industry walls tumble as companies rethink their value propositions. Car manufacturers reinvent their offering as a service-enhanced computer-communications package on wheels. Publishers confront today's Net-based periodical and tomorrow's digital paper; with the Web, all businesses must become publishers. Who will move in on your markets—and whose markets should you move in on?

To win in such an economy, you must deliver much better value at a much lower price. But no single company can be a world-class, lowest-cost provider of everything it needs. Another key transformation comes to the rescue: the driving forces of the digital economy slash transaction costs—the economic underpinnings of the integrated industrial-age enterprise. The twentieth-century enterprise is giving way to the b-web, driven by the disaggregation and reaggregation of the firm.

DISAGGREGATION AND REAGGREGATION OF THE FIRM

Why do firms exist? If, as Economics 101 suggests, the invisible hand of market pricing is so darned efficient, why doesn't it regulate *all* economic activity? Why isn't each person, at every step of production and delivery, an independent profit center? Why, instead of working for music publishers like Sony and PolyGram, doesn't a music producer auction recordings to marketers, who in turn sell CDs to the street-level rack jobbers who tender the highest bids?

Nobel laureate Ronald Coase asked these provocative questions in 1937. Some sixty years later, several thinkers, seeking to understand how the Net is changing the firm, returned to Coase's work.[4]

Coase blames transaction costs (or what he calls the cost of the price mechanism) for the contradiction between the theoretical agility of the market and the stubborn durability of the firm. Firms incur transaction costs when, instead of using their own internal resources, they go out to the market for products or services. Transaction costs have three parts, which together—and even individually—can be prohibitive:

- *Search costs.* Finding what you need consumes time, resources, and out-of-pocket costs (such as travel). Determining whether to trust a supplier adds more costs. Intermediaries who catalog products and product information could historically reduce, but not eliminate, such search costs. Music distributor Sony, through its Epic Records label, hires a stable of producers and marketers, cuts long-term deals with artists, and operates its own marketing programs—all in the name of minimizing search costs for itself and consumers.

- *Contracting costs.* If every exchange requires a unique price negotiation and contract, then the costs can be totally out of whack with the value of the deal. Since Sony owns Epic Records, it does not need to negotiate a distribution deal when Epic signs a new artist like Fiona Apple.

- *Coordination costs.* This is the cost of coordinating resources and processes. Coase points out that with "changes like the telephone and the telegraph," it becomes easier for geographically dispersed firms to coordinate their activities. Industrial-age communications enable big companies to exist. Sony's internal supply chain includes finding and managing talent, and producing, marketing, and distributing recorded music.

Coase says that firms form to lighten the burden of transaction costs. He then asks another good question. If firm organization cuts transaction costs, why isn't everything in one big firm? He answers that the law of diminishing returns applies to firm size: Big firms are complicated and find it hard to manage resources efficiently. Small companies often do things more cheaply than big ones.

All this leads to what we call Coase's law: *A firm will tend to expand until the costs of organizing an extra transaction within the firm become equal to the costs of carrying out the same transaction on the open market.*[5] As long as it is cheaper to perform a transaction inside your firm, says Coase's law, keep it there. But if it's cheaper to go to the marketplace, don't try to do it internally. When consumers and artists use the Net as a low-cost marketplace to find one another and "contract" for tunes, the Sonys of the world must face the music.

Thanks to internetworking, the costs of many kinds of transactions have been dramatically reduced and sometimes approach zero. Large and diverse groups of people can now, easily and cheaply, gain near real-time access to the information they need to make safe decisions and coordinate complex activities. We can increase wealth by adding knowledge value to a product or service—through innovation, enhancement, cost reduction, or customization—at each step in its life cycle. Often, specialists do a better value-adding job than do vertically integrated firms. In the digital economy, the notion of a separate, electronically negotiated deal at each step of the value cycle becomes a reasonable, often compelling, proposition.

This proposition is now possible because the Net is attaining ubiquity (increasingly mobile through wireless technologies), bandwidth, robustness, and new functionality. The Net is becoming a digital infrastructure of collaboration, rich with tools for search transactions, knowledge management, and delivery of application software ("apps on tap").

Call it hot and cold running functionality and knowledge. This explosion, still in its early days, is spawning new ways to create wealth. A new division of labor that transcends the traditional firm changes the way we design, manufacture, distribute, market, and support products and services. Several examples illustrate the success enjoyed by companies that employ this new division of labor.

- MP3.com is a Web-based music distributor that uses, but does not control, the MP3 standard and that offers legal, non-pirated music. In September 1999, it listed 180,000 songs from 31,000 artists, ranging from pop to classical to spoken word. Music downloads are free and nearly instantaneous. Fans also purchased 16,000 CDs online for a typical price of $5.99.

- Global Sources is a b-web that provides manufacturers, wholesalers, and distributors with access to products from 42,000 Asian makers of computers and electronics, components, fashion items, general merchandise, and hardware.

- The GE Trading Process Network (GETPN) enables companies to issue fully documented requests for quotations to participating suppliers around the world via the Net, and then to negotiate and close the contract. Through a partnership with Thomas Publishing Company, a publisher of buying guides, GETPN provides an even bigger transactional database for manufacturing procurement.

Consider James Richardson, owner of a two-person industrial-design firm in Weston, Connecticut. In 1998, he received a contract to design and build a running-in-place exercise machine. He set out to find manufacturers of membrane switches, essentially pressure-sensitive circuits printed on Mylar polyester film. Richardson first went to the Thomas Register Web site. Then he explored other sites on the Internet. He found dozens that listed products and described the companies that made them, their delivery schedules, and whether the products met international quality standards. Then he hunted up assemblers, who described their quality levels. Richardson produced a set of engineering drawings on his computer and e-mailed them to a list of prospective suppliers. A few weeks later, his chosen suppliers were mass-producing the exercise machine. Richardson had set up a virtual factory without leaving his office or investing any of his own money.[6] *He created a new business model by using internetworking to cut transaction costs.*

Adrian Slywotzky defines a business model as "the totality of how a company selects its customers, defines and differentiates its offerings (or response), defines the tasks it will perform itself and those it will out-source, configures its resources, goes to market, creates utility for customers, and captures profits. It is the entire system for delivering utility to customers and earning a profit from that activity."[7] He points out that companies may offer products or they may offer technology, but these offerings are embedded in a comprehensive system of activities and relationships that represent the company's business design. Slywotzky emphasizes activities and relationships, both of which are changing dramatically.

In this ever-changing tapestry, which thread should you grab first? Our research and experience suggest that you should begin with disaggregation—and its natural complement, reaggregation. Richardson's story shows that because the Net cuts transaction costs, a company can create value through a disaggregated business architecture. The challenge facing today's manager is to turn disaggregation from threat to opportunity.

Webster's defines the verb *disaggregate* as "to separate into component parts," and *reaggregate* as "to cause to re-form into an aggregate or a whole." These themes apply both to the transformation of the value proposition and to the design of new organizational structures for enhanced value creation. In the digital economy, Coase's law goes into overdrive. On the one hand, the discrete value-creating activities of firms, even entire industries, become easier and cheaper to disaggregate out to the open market. On the other, the coordination tools of the digital infrastructure enable firms to expand massively in highly focused areas of competency. In this book, we describe how companies like eBay and Cisco Systems provide models for doing both these things simultaneously.

Disaggregation enables entirely new kinds of value, from entirely new kinds of competitors. As a result, relegating digital technologies to nifty Web-site designs or superficial cost-saving initiatives are potentially fatal errors of an industrial-age mind-set. Disaggregation should begin with the end-customer's experience—the value proposition. It breaks out that experience—as well as the goods, services, resources, business processes, and organizational structures that make it possible—into a set of logical components. Effective strategists honestly face the many weaknesses inherent in industrial-age ways of doing things. They redesign, build upon, and reconfigure the components to radically transform the value proposition for the benefit of the end-customer. Planners must imagine how networked digital technologies enable them to add new forms of value every step of the way, to each component part. Then, they creatively reaggregate a new set of value offerings, goods, and services, as well as the enabling resources, structures, and processes.

The *Wall Street Journal*, founded in 1889, spent its first century as an aggregated collection of content (news, listings, advertising), context (the physical newspaper), and infrastructure (printing, physical distribution), bundled into a single tightly integrated offering. With the arrival of the Internet, the *Journal*, working with partner companies and even readers, disaggregated these elements into separate component parts, and then reaggregated them into an entirely new value proposition. The old value proposition was a physical package of yesterday's news, delivered to your doorstep or newsstand. The new one is a twenty-four-hour customizable information service, increasingly available anywhere—at the point of need. Subscribers can use the online *Wall Street Journal Interactive (WSJI)* to track their personal stock portfolios, set up the "newspaper" to present the stories they care about the most, join online discussions, and access the Dow Jones Publications Library to research just about any business topic. For Internet time, the *WSJI* value proposition may not be quite up to snuff: Avid readers note that some "current" news stories are as much as twenty-four hours old (and more on weekends)!

Disaggregated from its physical wrapper, the content is now available through a variety of electronic contexts, including the publication's own *WSJI*, and a variety of third parties like a Microsoft Web channel, the PalmPilot wireless network, and mobile phones. These services share an underlying delivery infrastructure—the Internet—but each enables a different shade of customer value. The *Journal's* own Web site posts the entire contents of the printed newspaper and much more, which the serious reader can customize. Microsoft and PalmPilot provide quick, though sometimes perforce superficial, news updates for desktop and mobile users, respectively. The *Journal* redefines and enhances its value proposition to meet a particular set of customer needs. A specific cast of players—not only Microsoft and Palm Computing, but also network companies like BellSouth—participates in the b-web that supports a specific distribution context. All collaborate and compete in the creation of value, with an eye to the changing needs and expectations of the digital end-customer.

In the digital economy, the essence of the value proposition itself is destabilized. But so is the structure that enables the creation of value—the vertically integrated firm. The *Wall Street Journal* can no longer rely on its own printing presses and delivery trucks to mass-produce its daily information feed. To get the new, customized message out, it must now form partnerships with Microsoft, Palm Computing, and many others.

The reaggregation of the value proposition leads companies to change in other important ways. The *Journal* adds content to the Web site that readers of the print edition never get to see. It learns how to present and customize this content for Internet users. Microsoft and Palm extend their mandates from technology to information services. While intensifying its focus on its core competencies, each company uses partners to broaden its range of customer attractions. This is the payoff of reaggregation for the digital economy.

POPULAR APPROACHES TO
BUSINESS-MODEL INNOVATION

We present here a brief tangent to our main focus: popular approaches to business-model innovation that turned out to be forerunners of the b-web phenomenon.

The first stage of innovation was the vertically integrated industrial-age corporation, with supply-driven command-control hierarchies, division of labor for mass production, lengthy planning cycles, and stable industry pecking orders. Henry Ford's company—the first archetypal industrial-age firm—didn't just build cars. It owned rubber plantations to produce raw materials for tires and marine fleets for shipping materials on the Great Lakes. Hearst didn't just print newspapers; it owned millions of acres of pulpwood forest. IBM's most profitable products during the Great Depression were cardboard punch cards, and the company built and sold clocks until well into the 1970s.[8] Mania for diversification reached an absurd peak in the conglomerate craze of the 1970s, when companies like ITT Industries poured billions into building Rube Goldberg-like corporate contraptions that simply did not hang together.

It took sixty years for the global business environment to converge with the potential implicit in Ronald Coase's insights. As the twentieth century unfolded, the accelerating progress of computer and communications technologies peeled back transaction costs at an ever-increasing rate. In the late 1970s, the vertically integrated mass-production manufacturing company went into crisis. North American companies had become dozy, fat, hierarchical, and bureaucratic in the twenty-five years after World War II. They gradually awoke to a U.S. defeat in Vietnam, an oil price shock instigated by a Middle Eastern cartel, and frightening competition from Japan and other Asian countries. Japanese manufacturers shook the ramparts of the industrial heartland—steel and automotive. Customers flocked to their innovative, reliable, and cheaper products. In 1955, American-owned companies built 100 percent of the cars sold in the United States. Thirty years later, their share had dropped below 70 percent.[9] And other industries, from textiles to computers, felt the same heat.

Managers responded with innovation in two business dimensions: process and structure. *Process* innovations included concepts like agile manufacturing, total quality, supply-chain management, and business process reengineering (BPR). These techniques helped fend off the challenges of offshore competition, cost, and customer dissatisfaction. They remain vitally important in their updated forms of today. But the techniques did not attack the core issues of value innovation and strategic flexibility. BPR's single-minded focus on cost cutting often led to forms of corporate anorexia that did more harm than good.[10]

Structural (business model) innovations were important forerunners of the b-web. Popular approaches to business model innovation included the virtual corporation, outsourcing, the concept of the business ecosystem, and the Japanese *keiretsu*.

At the height of their crisis of self-confidence, North American managers and strategists stumbled across the *keiretsu*. It struck terror in their hearts. *Keiretsu* members in automotive, electronics, banking, and many other industries had suddenly emerged as global samurai. Rooted in centuries-old fighting clans, a *keiretsu* is a semipermanent phalanx of companies bound by interlocking ownership and directorates. *Keiretsu* battled aggressively with one another and on the international front, drawing strength from a strong us-versus-them mind-set. *Keiretsu*, along with cartels, were not just a strategic option for Japanese companies. They defined the business environment: The Japanese Fair Trade Commission estimated that over 90 percent of all domestic business transactions were "among parties involved in a long-standing relationship of some sort."[11] The strength of *keiretsu* also proved to be their downfall. Their tight, permanent linkages—the very opposite of an agile business structure—help to explain Japan's economic difficulties during the latter half of the 1990s.

Ironically, now that the *keiretsu* have been increasingly discredited in Japan, they have become fashionable in Silicon Valley as companies in all sectors discover the power of strategic partnering via the Internet. Proponents like the industry analyst Howard Anderson have not developed a new view of the *keiretsu*. Rather, they use the term as a pop epithet to describe partnerships ranging from loose associations to corporate conglomerates like AOL/Time Warner.[12] In our view this application of the term is not helpful and obfuscates the much more important underlying dynamics of the business web.

Though in part a response to the *keiretsu*, the North American virtual corporation was a fundamentally different idea. Proponents mystically described it as "almost edgeless, with permeable and constantly changing interfaces between company, supplier, and customers. Job responsibilities will regularly shift, as will lines of authority—even the very definition of employee will change as some customers and suppliers begin to spend more time in the company than will some of the firm's own workers."[13] Other proponents depicted the virtual corporation as good, but elective, business medicine. But in Japan, *keiretsu* are like oxygen: Breathe them or die. Also, a virtual corporation is a temporary, opportunistic partnership: "Complementary resources existing in a number of cooperating companies are left in place, but are integrated to support a particular product effort *for as long as it is economically justifiable to do so.*"[14] *Keiretsu* relationships, on the other hand, are institutional and permanent. As we describe in this book, b-webs are, in one sense, more like *keiretsu* than virtual corporations. They are not merely good medicine, but part of the "air" of the digital economy. And a b-web—like the now twenty-year-old Microsoft software alliance—can go on for a very long time. However, unlike a *keiretsu*, a b-web is not necessarily a permanent arrangement, nor does it need to use ownership to integrate its participants.

Outsourcing was a less ambitious idea than the virtual corporation: Pick a non-core activity and contract it out to a supplier who can do it more cheaply or better than you. Outsourcing is often a way to unload a problem function—like transportation or information technology. But outsourcing relationships can be tough. Outsourcer and outsourcee often perceive that they are in a zero-sum financial game, and they lack openness or trust. Such a mind-set characterized supply-chain relationships in the automotive industry for years.

More fundamentally, in a world of b-webs, outsourcing is dead, not because big firms will take over all business functions, but rather the opposite. Managers will no longer view the integrated corporation as the starting point for assigning tasks and functions. Rather, they will begin with a customer value proposition and a blank slate for the production and delivery infrastructure. Through analysis, they will parcel out the elements of value creation and delivery to an optimal collection of b-web partners. The lead firm in a b-web will want to control core elements of its digital capital—like customer relationships, the choreography of value creation and management processes, and intellectual property. Depending on the particulars, partners can take care of everything else.

None of these models—*keiretsu,* virtual corporation, or outsourcing—fully reflected how the world was changing by the mid-1990s. Then, with blazing insight, James Moore announced the business ecosystem, "an economic community supported by a foundation of interacting organizations and individuals—the organisms of the business world."[15] The ecosystem includes customers, suppliers, lead producers, competitors, and other stakeholders, who "coevolve their capabilities and roles, and tend to align themselves with the directions set by one or more central companies."

Moore's ecosystem metaphor illuminated the workings of the personal computer industry and others like it, in which many companies and individuals innovate, cooperate, and compete around a set of standards. Bill Gates, the Henry Ford of the information age, pioneered and popularized ecosystem management techniques that have become common principles for b-web leadership: *Context is king. Ensure voluntary compliance with your rules. Facilitate independent innovation. Harness end-customers for value creation. Go for critical mass fast.* Moore's ecosystem metaphor, though powerful, has limitations. It evokes a natural world in which biology and animal instinct rule, instead of human thought, judgment, and intentional actions. Animal instinct may be a big part of business life, but it does not explain everything.

By the mid-1990s, only a handful of corporations had made genuine progress toward any of these popular approaches to business model innovation. Two factors stood in their way. For industrial-era firms, all these approaches required too much of a break from established management cultures. And even the most advanced information technologies of the time—client server computing and electronic data interchange (EDI)—reinforced a centralist, hub-and-spoke business architecture. These technological systems had to be custom built, and at great expense. The Internet's universal-knowledge utility did not yet exist.

At this point in the mid-1990s, the sense of anticipation was nearly palpable. The worlds of business and communications were on the eve of revolutionary changes. It was as if the air had gradually become saturated with a combustible mix of gases; the tiniest spark would set off a vast explosion. The explosion came with the creation and discovery of the World Wide Web—a revolutionary new medium of human communications based on a few simple lines of software code. By the end of the decade, the Net was driving over $160 billion in transactions per year, most performed in and by b-webs.[16]

WHAT IS A B-WEB?

If the corporation embodied capital in the industrial age, then the b-web does the same for the digital economy. In b-webs, internetworked, fluid—sometimes highly structured, sometimes amorphous—sets of contributors come together to create value for customers and wealth for their shareholders. In the most elegant of b-webs, each participant focuses on a limited set of core competencies, the things that it does best.

Business webs are inventing new value propositions, transforming the rules of competition, and mobilizing people and resources to unprecedented levels of performance. Managers must master a new agenda for b-web strategy if they intend to win in the new economy.

As stated earlier, a b-web is a distinct system of suppliers, distributors, commerce services providers, infrastructure providers, and customers that use the Internet for their primary business communications and transactions. Several b-webs may compete with one another for market share within an industry; for example, the MP3 b-web competes with the SDMI (Secure Digital Music Initiative) b-web launched by the Recording Industry Association of America (RIAA) in December 1998.

Three primary structures of the b-web universe are internetworked enterprises, teams, and individuals; b-webs themselves; and the industry environment (figure 1-1). Internetworked enterprises, teams, and individuals are the fundamental components of b-web collaboration and competition. Typically, any single entity participates in several—sometimes competing—b-webs. Microsoft leads its own b-web and also participates, for better or worse, as a licensed developer in the competing Java b-web. Meanwhile, its fierce competitors, IBM and Oracle, contribute applications to Microsoft's b-web and (in IBM's case) sell Windows-compatible personal computers. An industry environment (e.g., the software industry) is a distinct space where several b-webs compete.

How do you tell a b-web when you see one? Look for nine features, which are also key design dimensions for an effective and competitive b-web (table 1-1).

1. *Internet infrastructure.* The participants in a b-web capitalize on the Internet's ability to slash transaction costs, using it as their primary infrastructure for interpersonal communications and business transactions. If you scratch a business exchange on the Net, then you will likely find a b-web. Spot ways that the Net can cut transaction costs, and you'll find b-web opportunities.

2. *Value proposition innovation.* A b-web delivers a unique, new value proposition that renders obsolete the old way of doing things. MP3 doesn't just let fans play cheap tracks. It infinitely expands the music community, making tunes almost as easy to share as the printed word. B-webs deliver wildly diverse forms of value, ranging from liquidity in financial markets to restaurant supplies, computer operating

FIGURE 1-1   Three Phases to B-Webs

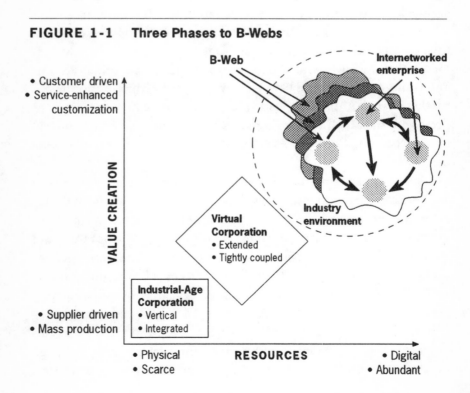

systems, and *X-Files* fan clubs. End-customers don't always pay for these outputs. Often, third parties such as governments, advertisers, and volunteers subsidize the creation and delivery of customer value.

3. *Multienterprise capability machine.* Leaders of b-webs increasingly prefer a market model of partnership to the "internal monopoly" of a build-or-acquire model. Relying on b-web partners helps maximize

TABLE 1-1   Nine Features of a B-Web

Feature	Description
Internet infrastructure	B-webs use the Internet as their primary infrastructure for business communications and transactions.
Value proposition innovation	A b-web delivers a unique, new value proposition that renders the old way of doing things obsolete.
Multienterprise capability machine	A b-web marshals the contributions of many participating enterprises. B-web leaders rely on partners to maximize return on invested capital.
Five classes of participants	A typical b-web structure includes five types—or "classes"—of value contributors:
	Customers, who not only receive but also contribute value to the b-web.
	Context providers, the interface between the customer and the b-web. A context provider leads the choreography, value realization, and rule-making activities of the system.
	Content providers design, make, and deliver the "intrinsic" forms of value—goods, services, or information—that satisfy customer needs.
	Commerce services providers enable the flow of business, including transactions and financial management, security and privacy, information and knowledge management, logistics and delivery, and regulatory services.
	Infrastructure providers deliver communications and computing, electronic and physical records, roads, buildings, offices, and the like.
Coopetition	B-web participants cooperate *and* compete with one another.
Customer-centricity	Rather than making, then selling, b-webs focus on customer value. They build mutual relationships and respond to individual customers at the point of need.
Context reigns	The context provider manages customer relationships and choreographs the value-creating activities of the entire system. Such b-web leaders get the captain's share of the spoils.
Rules and standards	Key participants know and adhere to the b-web's rules of engagement.
Bathed in knowledge	B-web participants exchange a variety of data, information, and knowledge.

return on invested capital. For example, in 1999 eBay facilitated $3 billion in auction sales via a $200 million technology and marketing system, with profit margins that exceeded Wal-Mart's. Traditional distributors like Sony sign artists to exclusive long-term deals; MP3.com's agreements are nonexclusive, and artists can end them at any time. While a traditional corporation defines its capabilities as its employees and the assets that it owns, a b-web marshals the contributions of many participating enterprises. The advantages—cost, speed, innovation, quality, and selection—typically outweigh the risks of partner opportunism. And it's much easier to switch from a non-performing partner than it is to drop a weak internal business unit.

4. *Five classes of participants.* A typical b-web's structure includes five types, or classes, of value contributors:

- *Customers,* who not only receive but also contribute value to the b-web (e.g., MP3.com's music consumers).

- *Context providers* facilitate the interface between the customer and the b-web. A context provider leads the choreography, value realization, and rule-making activities of the system (e.g., the company MP3.com).

- *Content providers* design, make, and deliver the intrinsic forms of value—goods, services, or information—that satisfy customer needs (e.g., musicians who distribute through MP3.com).

- *Commerce services providers* enable the flow of business, including transactions and financial management, security and privacy, information and knowledge management, logistics and delivery, and regulatory services (e.g., Cinram International, which burns CDs for MP3.com on a just-in-time basis).

- *Infrastructure providers* deliver communications and computing, electronic and physical records, roads, buildings, offices, and the like (e.g., CERFnet and Exodus Communications host MP3.com's Web servers).

5. *"Coopetition."*[17] Since participants cooperate and compete with one another, b-webs demand coopetition. Issuers of stocks, mutual

funds, and other financial instruments have always cooperated by sharing press releases and other information, while competing for investor dollars. As financial markets shift to the Internet infrastructure, these processes accelerate and gain millions of new participants. Sometimes, as in the Wintel b-web, coopetition can be nasty. Its b-web participants, including the U.S. government, won a court case accusing Microsoft of using its control over the operating system context to deal itself unfair advantages in the applications content arena.

6. *"Customer-centricity."* Effective b-webs function as highly responsive customer-fulfillment networks. Instead of building goods and services to sit in warehouses in accordance with an inventory plan, they closely monitor and respond to individual customers—at the point of need. MP3.com has a tool that reviews customers' past selections and, based on their preferences, suggests other music that they might like. Members of a traditional supply chain, such as in the auto industry, tend to focus only on the next link to which they ship their products. Well-choreographed b-webs encourage all participants to focus on the *end*-customer: Cisco product assemblers Solectron and Celestica increasingly ship goods directly to consumers' homes. And, recognizing their own self-interest, these customers often willingly contribute knowledge value to such b-webs. Amazon devotees write book reviews and get virtual recommendations from other readers who share their reading preferences.

7. *Context reigns.* The context provider typically manages customer relationships and choreographs the value-creating activities of the entire system. By defining, piloting, and managing the context, a b-web leader gets the captain's share of the spoils. The company MP3.com, having branded itself with the name of the popular MP3 standard, has levered this advantage into a market leadership position. Within its own b-web, MP3.com defines the core value proposition and is lead manager of the customer relationship, the competitive strategy, the admission of participants, the rules of engagement, and the value exchanges. Other sources provide content and other services; MP3.com plays a limited role in defining the specific day-to-day details of the content that its customers see.

8. *Rules and standards.* Participants must know and adhere to the b-web's rules of engagement. Voluntary adherence to open standards and technologies minimizes dependence on the proprietary methods of individual b-web participants; the MP3 standard has attracted dozens of companies, including Amazon.com, Yahoo!, and America Online (AOL). Some rules can't just be voluntary. Stock markets have tough rules about disclosure and compliance; if you break some of these rules, the government might put you in jail. The context provider often originates rules and monitors compliance. But rules—and enforcement—can come from anywhere, including government, key customers, and suppliers.

9. *Bathed in knowledge.* Participants in a b-web use the Internet to exchange operational data, information, and knowledge instantaneously among all participants who "need to know"—sometimes in depth, other times to a limited degree. In addition to music, MP3.com offers personal playlist management, musician biographies and tour schedules (as well as links to *their* Web sites), industry news, message boards, online forums, and the preference-based selection tools mentioned above. Knowledge sharing is also important in a negative sense. In the baseline definition of a b-web, participants evidently share operational data, such as product information. But they do not necessarily share strategic or competitive information with one another.

B-WEB COROLLARIES

Everyone seems to agree that the new world of Internet commerce works differently. New modes of operation mean new rules, and several authors have offered up lists. Instead of rules, we would like to suggest corollaries of the b-web phenomenon: some obvious propositions, logical deductions and inferences, and natural consequences to consider as you ponder the implications of this new corporate form.

We are in uncharted territory. Unlike the traditional industrial corporation, b-web structures and processes are highly malleable. Creative business-model architects like the leaders of MP3, Priceline, Linux, and Cisco have already seized on the b-web to create arrestingly new and competitive value propositions and organizational designs. In 1999, the MP3 phenomenon took another leap into the unknown when a company called Napster.com (quickly sued by the RIAA) launched a free service to let users seek and share tunes directly from one personal computer to another. Who knows where all this will end up? The first twenty years of the new century will be a golden age of business model innovation, which will set the course for decades to come.

Exceptionally high returns on invested capital (the capital resources at a firm's disposal) can occur. A b-web requires less physical capital (stores, warehouses, and inventory) than do traditional firms, meaning lower fixed costs and higher operating margins. The b-web's leaders can leverage the capital assets of partners, but need to carry none of the associated liabilities. For such reasons, by our calculation, for several years Cisco's return on invested capital was about twice Nortel's. Moreover, firms in b-webs can exhibit exponential returns to scale where revenue growth is exponential, while costs grow at a modest linear rate. Amazon.com expects to increase revenues in new markets like toys and auctions by leveraging the relationship (brand, customers) capital and structural (business processes, technology) capital it amassed as an online bookseller. The company's high market capitalization of its early years assumed both high returns on invested capital and exponential returns to scale.

Industrial-age businesses (like supermarkets) often put customers to work doing physical labor (like picking and delivering their own groceries). In b-webs, where customers mainly contribute information and knowledge, *customers have more power than ever before.* They have the power of choice, because a move to a new supplier is only a click away. They have the power of customization, as new technologies increase their expectations that vendor offerings will match their unique needs and tastes. They have power coming from near perfect information: If Tide stops washing whiter than white, everyone will find out faster than fast. And customers have collective power. MP3 illustrates how customers can go "out of control" and change the course of an industry. Customers gain both tangible (cost, quality) and intangible (information, control, relationships) benefits while themselves contributing ever more value to the b-webs in which they participate. All of this means that to attract and retain customers, sellers must build trustworthy, two-way relationships that deliver real value.

Disaggregation leads to "disintermediation" and "reintermediation"—
the elimination and replacement of physical-world agents and other
intermediaries between producers and customers. New, low-cost,
knowledge-value-enhanced intermediaries like MP3.com have placed
music distributors under siege. But, for the time being at least, the
old intermediaries will not simply fold up their tents and disappear.
Rather than a single "killer app" intermediary in each space, we see a
growing variety of intermediation models, each offering a distinct
form of value added. To acquire music, you can go directly to the Sony
site, an alternative like MP3.com, an online distributor like Amazon.
com, or any of the traditional physical-world options. For a music
publisher or musician, each of these intermediaries is an element of
the b-web distribution channel mix. Each has a place, depending on
the customer's situation and needs of the moment. So, although some
individual intermediaries may be gasping for air, as a species, intermediaries are alive and well—in fact, busily mutating and multiplying.
We (apologetically!) propose a neologism to describe this phenomenon: *polymediation.*

The b-web poses a challenge to asset-based models of market control. As
the world shifts from physical to digital distribution models, it is obvious that assets like music stores become less relevant to controlling markets. But big, capital-heavy assets are also losing clout in other, less obvious places. Sometimes, as in telecommunications, the pace of mergers
and acquisitions camouflages this deeper industry challenge. The value
and performance of a telecom company have traditionally depended
on physical capital (wires and rights-of-way) and physical capital metrics (return on assets). With the emergence of wireless networking, such
physical assets decline in relative value. A wireless network—whether for
voice or data—can be cheaper to set up and run, and more flexible, than
a wire-based one. Such networks will empower both customers and content providers with new kinds of flexibility and choice. Customers will
be able to choose among a variety of competing service providers. Meanwhile, a galaxy of services, comparable to those on the Internet itself, will
emerge for the new wireless communications infrastructure. Constella-
tions of converging customer and content provider power will squeeze
the economics of telecom even more. The result will be a competitive

commodity market for mobile communications, in which network assets become less relevant than customer choice and value-added services. As we describe in chapter 6, this type of analysis applies to several other asset-oriented industries.

Proponents of b-webs tout big ideas of business excellence as good medicine. Take a dose of the virtual corporation, process redesign, or knowledge management, and your company will feel better in the morning. Whether b-webs seem attractive or not, ignoring them is perilous. *Unlike other big ideas, b-webs are inevitable.* The MP3 b-web arose spontaneously, not because a manager read an illuminating book on business strategy. *The b-web is emerging as the generic, universal platform for creating value and wealth.* Like the corporation itself, the b-web concept is descriptive, not prescriptive; it will come in many different flavors, shapes, and sizes. Management practices—and everyday life—in a b-web will take many forms. Some b-webs will be wonderful places to work and do business, while others will be nasty and brutish. Some will succeed, others will fail. There is no single path to b-web success. Approaches that seem vitally important in most situations will be irrelevant, even counterproductive, in others.

To paraphrase Mao Tse-tung, *the b-web revolution is not a tea party!* A b-web is a market space in which organizations both collaborate and compete with one another. The competition is often aggressive, sometimes wicked, and even unfair. Consider how Microsoft's treatment of its b-web partners landed it in court. At the same time, collaboration and partnerships are critical to the performance of most b-webs. Cooperation with competition—*coopetition*—is a b-web theme song.

B-webs breed internetwork effects, a form of digital fusion among business entities. Physics describes how the fusion of hydrogen atoms releases energy. Under conditions of critical mass, a chain reaction occurs, with explosive results. Internetwork effects can display similar critical mass. MP3 experiments on the Net began in 1995–1996 and required vast amounts of energy just to keep moving. At a certain point in 1998, MP3 achieved critical mass of users and market momentum, took a quantum leap, and began to grow exponentially. In physics, fusion has a dark side—the release of terrible, destructive forces. Similarly in business, the internetwork effect blasts the bastions of the old economy.

DIGITAL CAPITAL

Former Citibank chairman Walter Wriston observed that information about money has become almost as important as money itself. Since this prophetic statement, new business models that deploy digital capital have wreaked havoc in the financial services industry, challenging the very existence of traditional banks, stockbrokers, and insurance companies. When intellectual capital moves to digital networks, it transforms entire industries and creates wealth in entirely new ways.

Digital capital adds new dimensions to the three kinds of intellectual capital described by knowledge-management thinkers Leif Edvinsson and Hubert Saint-Onge: human, structural, and customer.[18] One explanation for the high valuations of Internet stocks is the market's growing recognition of digital capital.

Knowledge-management theory describes *human capital* as the sum of the capabilities of individuals in the enterprise. It consists of skills, knowledge, intellect, creativity, and know-how. It is the capability of individuals to create value for customers. The IBM stock of human capital includes the knowledge and experience of technology developers and consultants and the creativity and moxie they apply to innovation; the expertise of its sales people in closing deals; and the brain and determination of its CEO Lou Gerstner. A problem with human capital, as the saying goes, is that "it rides down the elevator every night." More than one IBM brain has made off to Hewlett-Packard, Sun, or a Silicon Valley start-up.

The key shift in the digital economy is that the enterprise's human capital now extends to people across the b-webs in which it participates. MP3.com's human capital is internetworked. It includes the Net awareness and creativity of the 31,000 musicians who use it as a distribution channel; customers' willingness to set up their own "My MP3" home pages; and their involvement in personal playlist management, message boards, online forums, and preference-based selection tools. Sometimes, customers even participate in the design and creation of products. Users created the entire Linux operating system. The Java b-web depends on the design contributions of many different business partners and customers. When human capital becomes internetworked, participants share knowledge and commitments, dwarfing what was possible in the old economy. We describe the challenges and opportunities of choreographing internetworked human capital in chapter 7.

Customer capital is the wealth contained in an organization's relationships with its customers and, according to most thinkers, its suppliers. It is IBM's brand equity, its depth (penetration) and breadth (coverage) in customer accounts, the trust of its customers, its deals with universities to seed IBM technology in the experience of future decision makers, the willingness of CIOs to share their plans with its sales force, and its customers' reluctance to switch suppliers. It also refers to relationships with Intel (which manufactures microprocessors for IBM personal computers), contract manufacturers that assemble its products, and software developers.

When internetworked in your b-web, customer capital becomes relationship capital. In the digital world, customer capital intensifies into profoundly reciprocal linkages. It is also multidirectional, involving all b-web participants—customers and providers of context, content, commerce services, and infrastructure. Dynamic two-way relationships replace the concept of the brand as a one-way image that a vendor defines through print and broadcast media. Old marketing mind-sets become obsolete, as we describe in chapter 8.

Structural capital consists of the codified knowledge and business processes that enable an enterprise to meet market requirements. Because structural capital does not reside in the minds of individual people, it helps mitigate the human capital brain drain. IBM's structural capital includes software development methodologies, project management tools, and development platforms for designers, analysts, and programmers. It includes sales management systems, product descriptions, training courses, and marketing databases. And it includes business processes for manufacturing, customer support, and myriad other functions.

The digital extension of structural capital consists of, first, networked knowledge, processes, and tools available at the point of need and, second, new b-web business models that change the rules of market leadership. "MP3 shock," which combined networked knowledge, processes, and tools with new business models, quaked the industrial-age music business. Similarly, the Linux b-web ambushed Sun and Microsoft, mobilizing a volunteer army to create a new computer operating system that anyone can get for free. A major focus of this book is the transformation of structural capital that occurs in the digital economy.

B-WEB TAXONOMY

Not all b-webs are equal. We have investigated many hundreds and have written more than two hundred case studies. A number of distinct patterns emerged, with direct bearing on competitive strategy. Central to our analysis is a new typology of business models (figure 1-2).

The typology applies to the physical business world almost as well as to the digital world. However, its digital application has some key differences.

First, organizations often shift the basis of competition from one type to another as they move from the physical world to a b-web approach. A traditional full-service broker works (at least in theory) as a Value Chain, expertly tailoring advice to each individual investor. An online broker like Charles Schwab or E*Trade shifts the model to an Aggregation of advisory information and investment services, available to their customers for picking and choosing.

Second, business model innovation becomes the basis of competitive advantage. Innovators like eBay, Cisco, and Priceline develop new ways to create and deliver value. In the process, they dramatically change the playing field and the rules of the game.

Finally, in the physical world, one of the types of business models—the Alliance—is rare and primitive. In the world of b-webs, however, Alliances, including innovation collaboratives like Linux, become highly visible as powerful and dynamic drivers of change.

FIGURE 1-2 The B-Web Typology

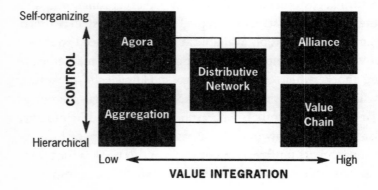

Dimensions of Differentiation: Control and Value Integration

Business webs differentiate along two primary dimensions: control (self-organizing or hierarchical) and value integration (low or high).

Economic control. In our analysis, control is about economics. Some b-webs are *hierarchical*; they have a leader who controls the content of the value proposition, the pricing, and the flow of transactions. General Motors designs and leads the integrated supply networks to produce preconceived products (e.g., the Cadillac Catera). Retailers like Amazon.com and Wal-Mart function hierarchically, taking responsibility for product selection, pricing, and customer satisfaction. Other b-webs *self-organize*. The market and its dynamics define the value and price of goods and services. Open-source software follows no management-imposed blueprint, because the product evolves through an organic development process open to all programmers. In stock exchanges and other types of auctions, the participants, not a single leader, drive content and price. Anyone can sell anything on an eBay auction (with the exception of prohibited items like weapons, animal parts, and other contraband!). Trading activity in the stock market continually responds to internal and external forces, whether a crisis of confidence in Asia, a speech by the chairman of the U.S. Federal Reserve, or a stampeding herd of institutional investors.

Value integration. Some b-webs focus on high value integration, that is, facilitating the production of specific product or service offerings (like cars, computers, consulting services) by integrating value contributions from multiple sources. We define *value* as the benefit that a user gains from a good or service. IBM achieves high value integration by taking contributions from many suppliers and turning them into a computer. Other b-webs focus on selection (low value integration); that is, providing a basket of choices rather than a single integrated solution. Ingram Micro, a leading wholesaler of computer hardware and software, does not alter the product offering. It focuses on distributing high-tech products, not making them. It currently offers products from more than 1,500 manufacturers. In between high and low value integration lie services like Instill, a restaurant industry supplier, which aggregates online catalogs from food producers, but also manages part of the restaurant supply chain, reducing inventory and minimizing stock outs.

Five Types of B-Webs

These two parameters—economic control and value integration—define the fundamental characteristics of five basic types of b-web: Agora, Aggregation, Value Chain, Alliance, and Distributive Network (table 1-2). As we describe later, each type also has subtypes. Agoras, for example, include open markets, sell-side auctions, buy-side auctions, and exchanges.

TABLE 1-2   Key Features of B-Web Types

	Agora	Aggregation	Value Chain	Alliance	Distributive Network
Main theme	• Dynamic pricing	• Selection and convenience	• Process integration	• Creativity	• Allocation/ distribution
Value proposition	• Liquidity— converting goods into a desirable price	• Optimization of selection, organization, price, convenience, matching, and fulfillment	• Design and delivery of an integrated product or service that meets a specific set of customer needs	• Creative collaboration in aid of a goal shared across a community of contributors	• Facilitate the exchange and delivery of information, goods, and services
Customer role	• Market player	• Buyer	• Value driver	• Contributor	• Sender/ recipient
Knowledge focus	• Timing • Market intelligence	• Market segmentation • Supplier offerings • Fulfillment	• Innovation • Supply-chain management	• Community • Creativity • Standards and roles	• Network optimization • Visibility and transparency
Key process	• Price discovery	• Needs matching	• Product design • Supply-chain management	• Innovation	• Distribution
Examples	• Yahoo! classifieds • eBay • Priceline • AdAuction • NASDAQ • MetalSite • FreeMarkets	• Amazon.com • Chemdex • HomeAdvisor • Webvan • E*Trade • Travelocity • WSJI	• Cisco Systems • Dell Computer • General Motors • Celestica • Bidcom	• America Online • NetNoir • Linux • MP3 • Wintel	• Enron • UPS • AT&T • Wells Fargo • Internet

Typically, a b-web is recognizable as a single, specific type. At the same time, as with most such models, every real-world b-web blends features of several types. Business design entails crafting a competitive b-web mix that draws on the many shades of this typology.

Agora. The agora of ancient Greece was originally the assembly of the people, convoked by the king or one of his nobles. The word then came to mean the place where assemblies gathered, and this place then evolved to become the city's center for public and especially commercial intercourse.[19] We apply the term to markets where buyers and sellers meet to freely negotiate and assign value to goods (figure 1-3).[20]

An Agora facilitates exchange between buyers and sellers, who jointly "discover" a price through on-the-spot negotiations. Price discovery mechanisms in Agoras include one-to-one haggling, multiparty auctions, and exchanges. Examples include eBay, an Internet-based consumer auction, and Freemarkets, an innovative online business procurement site.

Typically in an Agora, many participants can bring goods to market, or decide what the price should be. Because sellers may offer a wide and often unpredictable variety or quantity of goods, value integration is

FIGURE 1-3   Agora

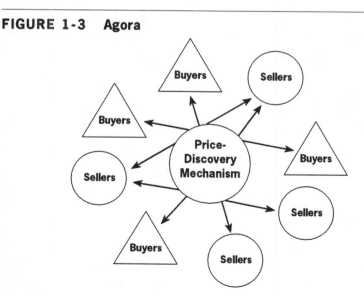

low. Internet Agoras offer significant benefits: many more sellers with a wider variety of products (benefiting buyers) and many more buyers to push prices up (benefiting sellers); convenience, low distribution and marketing costs, lots of information about all aspects of the deal; and entertainment—the thrill of the chase.

Aggregation. In an Aggregation b-web, one company—like Wal-Mart—leads in hierarchical fashion, positioning itself as a value-adding inter-mediary between producers and customers (figure 1-4). The lead aggre-gator takes responsibility for selecting products and services, targeting market segments, setting prices, and ensuring fulfillment. The aggrega-tor typically sets prices and discount schedules in advance. An Aggrega-tion offers a diverse variety of products and services, with zero to limited value integration. Retailers and wholesalers are prime examples of Aggregations.

HomeAdvisor, Microsoft's Web context for home buying, not only offers half a million listings, but also provides real-time mortgage cal-culators, crime and school statistics, maps covering every U.S. metro-politan area, live e-mail updates, and loan qualification—all made pos-sible through partnerships with b-web content providers. HomeAdvisor offers a total solution—from searching to financing—under one vir-tual roof. By bundling real estate information and services around a mortgage offering, it captures this profitable portion of the financial services industry away from banks and other lending institutions.

E*Trade has aggregated many companies to create a virtual brokerage

FIGURE 1-4   Aggregation

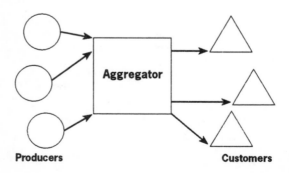

firm, charging one-tenth the fees of a traditional broker. Its dozens of content and service providers include stock quote services (Reuters, Quote.com), news (Reuters, PR Newswire, Businesswire), proprietary issuers (Robertson, Stephens), research (Briefing.com, InvesTools), market trends and projections (Baseline Financial Services), and personal financial tools (Quicken)—to name but a few. Internet delivery reduces customer costs; more important, customers gain intelligence that was formerly only visible to the high priests of the investment industry.

Value Chain. In a Value Chain, the context provider structures and directs a b-web network to produce a highly integrated value proposition (figure 1-5). The output meets a customer order or market opportunity—from an individual's buying of a Jeep with custom trim or Procter & Gamble's manufacturing of 20,000 case lots of Crest, to EDS's implementation of an electronic commerce infrastructure for one of its clients. The seller has the final say in pricing. It may be fixed (a tube of toothpaste), somewhat negotiable (the Jeep), or highly negotiable (the EDS deal).

Cisco Systems makes networking products—such as routers—that shuffle data from one computer to another over the Internet or corporate computer networks. The company sits at the top of a $12 billion Web-enabled Value Chain. It reserves for itself the tasks of designing

FIGURE 1-5   Value Chain

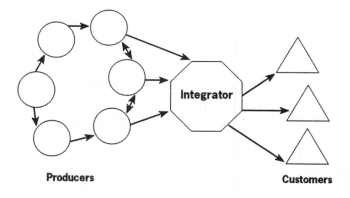

Producers   Customers

core technologies, coordinating processes across the b-web, marketing, and managing relationships. Other b-web participants do just about everything else, including most manufacturing, fulfillment, and on-site customer service.

Alliance. An Alliance, the most "ethereal" of b-webs, strives for high value integration without hierarchical control (figure 1-6). Its participants design goods or services, create knowledge, or simply produce dynamic, shared experiences. Alliances include online communities, research initiatives, games, and development communities like the PalmPilot and Open Source innovation initiatives. The MP3 phenomenon is an Alliance.

FIGURE 1-6 Alliance

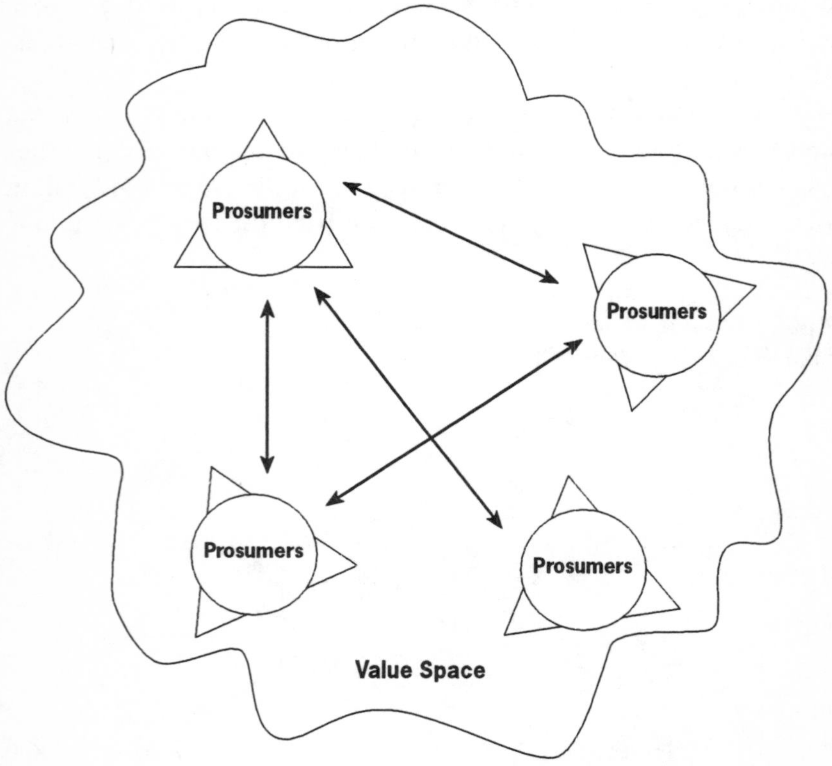

Alliances typically depend on rules and standards that govern inter-action, acceptable participant behavior, and the determination of value. Often, end-customers or users play a prominent role in value creation, as contributors to an online forum or as designers (e.g., of PalmPilot software or of the next piece of encoding in the Human Genome Pro-ject). Where products come from an Alliance, the end-customer often handles customizing and integrating the solution.

Alliance b-webs often enjoy network effects. The more customers who buy PalmPilots, the more developers who decide to create applica-tions. The value cycle is continuous and accelerating: As the value increases, usage mushrooms, and the applications market grows.

Smart managers appreciate the power of Alliance b-webs. They will-ingly sacrifice some control over product evolution for the extra momen-tum that hundreds or even thousands of contributors can provide.

Distributive Network. The fifth type of b-web to have emerged from our research thus far is the Distributive Network (figure 1-7). These are the b-webs that keep the economy alive and mobile.

In addition to the roads, postal services, telephone companies, and electrical power grid of the industrial economy, Distributive Networks include data network operators, the new logistics companies, and banks. These networks play a vital role in ensuring the healthy balance of the

FIGURE 1-7   Distributive Network

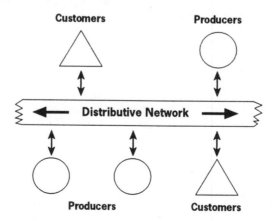

systems that they support. Like the human blood system, Distributive Networks neither create nor consume their essential cargo. But when these services fail, their host systems can die. And when a Distributive Network clots, its host can turn severely ill.

Distributive Networks, in their purest forms (which is not always how you find them), service the other types of b-webs by allocating and delivering goods—whether information, objects, money, or resources—from providers to users. Along with Alliances, Distributive Networks often evince network effects: The more customers who use a Distributive Network (e.g., a telephone network), the more value it provides to all its customers.

In relation to our two axes of b-web analysis—value integration and nature of control—Distributive Networks are "pure" hybrids. Their value integration is both high and low. It is high, because Distributive Networks must vouchsafe the integrity of their delivery systems, often a critical performance metric, for example, in a bank or a courier company. The value integration of Distributive Networks is also low, because their outputs can be diverse and unpredictable; from one day to the next, you can't foresee with certainty the pattern flow of cash through the banking system, or the flow of packages through UPS. Control of a Distributive Network's value is both hierarchical (tight network management is critical) and self-organizing (the continuous fluctuation of supply and demand determines value and price, as in electrical power and financial capital systems).

In the following chapters, we present business model innovation strategies for the five types of b-webs: Agoras, Aggregations, Value Chains, Alliances, and Distributive Networks.

Part II

the new models

of wealth creation

2 agoras

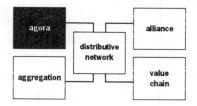

Do you buy or sell—anything? Then chances are, you already participate in at least one Agora, a real or virtual place where buyers and sellers come together to collectively discover the price for a good or service. The Net turns Agoras into boundless meeting places, radically transforming their dynamic pricing mechanisms and opening up more efficient—and exciting—markets. Now, the price of anything could be negotiable. And goods that traditionally sold through a local Agora like a flea market or classified newspaper ad now move through global auctions and exchanges.

THE INNER LIFE OF AGORAS

On September 24, 1998, a nearly unknown company called eBay blew the then-slumping Web initial public offering (IPO) market wide open. With revenues of only $33.5 million for the first half of the year, the online consumer-to-consumer auction achieved a first-day market capitalization of $1.8 billion.

eBay tapped into marginal economic activity—collectibles, flea markets, and garage sales—and created a megaenterprise. Hosting a shared space in which buyers and sellers connect and do business, eBay captures millions of transactions that would otherwise occur on people's front lawns, in quaint estate auctions, through classified ads, and other non-retail channels—as well as in traditional retail stores. Indeed, without an eBay, many items would still be in attics collecting dust.

The core value proposition of eBay—like that of any Agora—is *liquidity*: the ease of converting assets into cash. Agoras achieve liquidity by matching buyers and sellers and facilitating price discovery, whereby buyers and sellers cooperate and compete to arrive at a mutually acceptable deal.

Agoras, whether classified ads or spot markets, historically served a special distribution function for goods of uncertain or volatile value. Prime examples are unique, distressed, or perishable items and commodities for which supply and demand fluctuate continually. These goods are unsuited to traditional fixed-price models (there is no list price); their value had to be resolved—or discovered—through direct negotiation between producers and consumers. As Charles Smith, author of *Auctions: The Social Construction of Value*, says, "The transaction is the means to the price rather than the price a means to the transaction."[1]

An auction or exchange community requires a critical mass of buyers and sellers who wish to exchange the same good during the same period and use the same mechanism to communicate and conduct price discovery. This is not as easy as you might think. It is why physical-world transactions tend to be fixed-price retail or one-on-one haggles. As eBay illustrates, the Net is a hothouse of relationship and human capital that enables these conditions to flourish almost spontaneously.

Economists say that auctions and exchanges like eBay are efficient and rational because they attune pricing to fluctuations in supply and demand. But negotiating every transaction is impractical and expensive. *Agoras tend to prevail where the transaction costs of negotiating are lower than the range of uncertainty about the final price.*

Typical operators—what we call context providers—of Agoras are not intermediaries who take possession of goods for resale. eBay (figure 2-1) is a neutral third party, facilitating negotiation and transactions between customers (buyers) and content providers (sellers).[2] Its core value contribution is creation, management, and regulation of the mechanisms for setting prices and allocating goods.

FIGURE 2-1 eBay Value Map

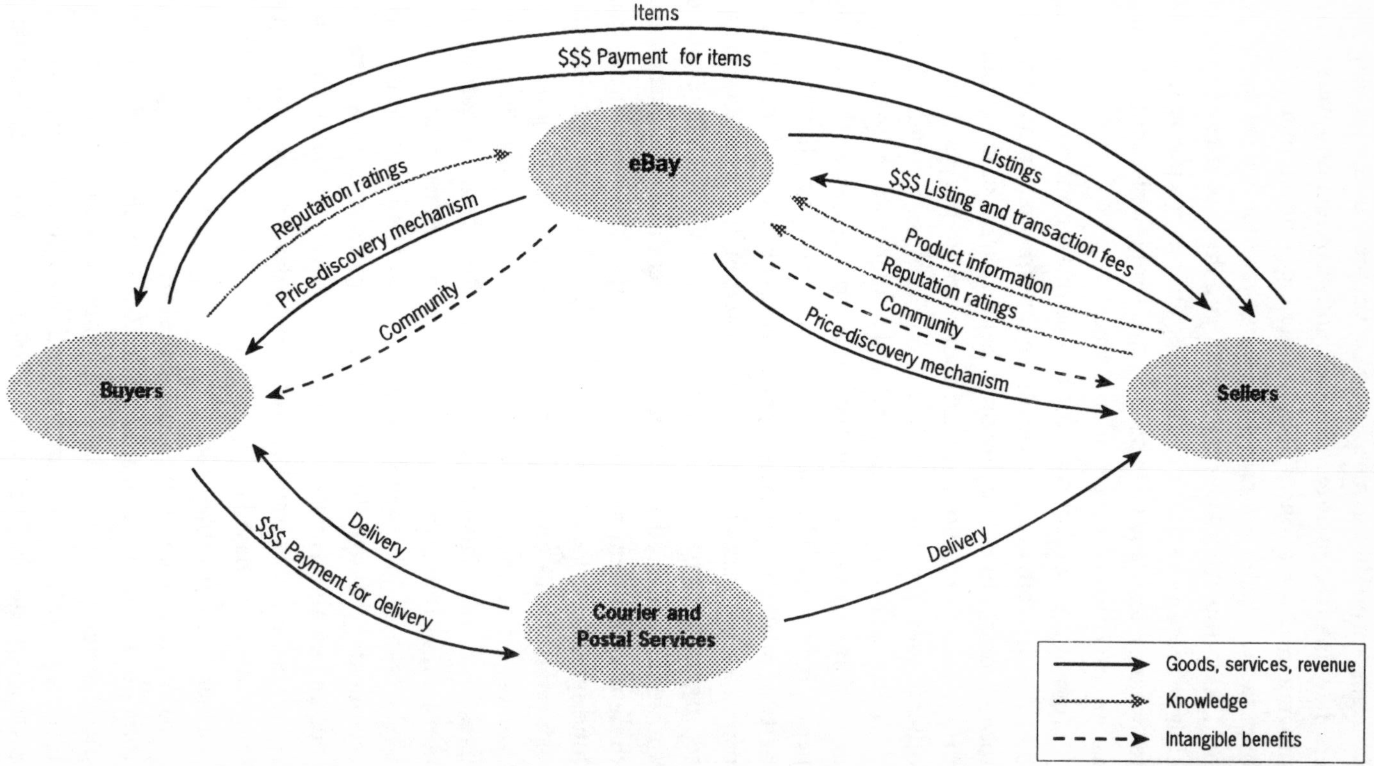

Sellers

eBay

Buyers

Courier and Postal Services

Listings

$$$ Listing and transaction fees

Product information

Reputation ratings

Community

Price-discovery mechanism

Items

$$$ Payment for items

Reputation ratings

Price-discovery mechanism

Community

Delivery

Delivery

$$$ Payment for delivery

Goods, services, revenue

Knowledge

Intangible benefits

Agoras work like games. Some are simple one-on-one haggles. Others, like financial markets, involve multiple layers of buyers and sellers moving in all directions. The pace can range from slow and deliberate to hyperactive. Rules are critical. They govern the nature of the playing field, its boundaries, player eligibility, and the processes of competition. eBay referees an exciting, casino-like game to determine who wins and for what price. Many eBay participants simply write off their purchases as the cost of an evening's entertainment.

Agoras are not just ways for people to act on their preferences—as they do when buying groceries in the supermarket. Instead, people often rely on Agoras to help figure out what they want to do. Unsure whether they really want a good, or what they ought to pay for it, buyers look to other bidders for cues.

Trust (of other participants) and authentication (getting what you expect) are big issues in an Agora. Newspaper classifieds are risky from beginning to end: The publisher takes no responsibility for the authenticity or quality of the goods or the trustworthiness of the parties to the transaction. Meanwhile, high-end auction houses like Christie's and top financial markets like the New York Stock Exchange assure trust and authenticity and vouchsafe the completion of transactions. But even these markets deny accountability for the true value of a good. If, in hindsight, the price paid seems too high or low, that's just too bad. And you can't go back on a deal: Buyer beware, all sales are final.

eBay's trust mechanism, and one of its secret weapons, is the Feedback Forum, designed to weed out deadbeat bidders and sellers. After every transaction, participants can write one-line reviews of one another's performance. Some regulars have accumulated thousands of positive comments. Through this grassroots mechanism, these isolated individuals and small businesses have built enduring global brands in cyberspace. Instances of fraud do occur, but eBay provides a small financial warranty, a fee-based escrow service, and authentication services for high-end product categories.

The Feedback Forum, already the largest public repository of customer opinions in the world, is eBay's core human capital asset. Imagine if General Motors or IBM could publish a continually renewed collection of individual customer endorsements for every one of their product categories. The Feedback Forum is a knowledge asset that draws and binds buyers and sellers; copycats will have trouble replicating the sheer volume of feedback that eBay has accumulated.

With the exception of commodity exchanges and stock markets, most traditional Agoras have been limited by time and space—fundamentally by the *transaction costs* incurred in negotiating price, and the time and effort entailed in doing so. And, in an industrial-age economy of scarcity, buyers and sellers often preferred the predictability of fixed prices.

Agora agent and broker fees are pure transaction costs. Stock exchanges have several layers of intermediaries, each of whom must be paid off. In 1997, U.S. securities exchanges made $1.8 billion, while brokers and dealers made $161 billion.[3] A floor trader at the New York Stock Exchange makes his or her money from the *spread*—the difference between the price that an investor and the trader pay for a stock, typically between 0.3 and 1.4 percent.[4] Now, electronic communication networks (ECNs) bypass exchanges entirely. Joshua Levine, founder of the Island ECN, argues with some exaggeration, "I can replace the NYSE trading floor with one $20,000 computer and do a much better job than they do, and charge somewhere between one one-thousandth and one one-hundredth of what they charge."[5]

eBay has capitalized on the logic of low transaction costs to spin a nearly perfect b-web: Its customers, whether sellers or buyers, take on most of the work, cost, and risk. Although the company deals entirely in physical products, it enjoys the following benefits:

- *Zero inventory costs:* The sellers acquire and stock their own goods.

- *Zero product merchandising and marketing costs:* The sellers select the products and design, create, and download their own product sales pitches, photos, and snappy ad copy to the eBay Web site.

- *Zero distribution costs:* The buyers and sellers arrange and pay for shipping.

- *Near zero product liability:* It's an auction, so—buyer beware!

- *Near zero editorial content development:* The users create over 99.9 percent of the site's massive content.

- *Near zero marginal growth costs:* Every new customer requires only a bit more space on eBay's computer and a small increment in customer-support services.

- *Near zero revenue risk:* Of the sellers, 85 percent provide eBay with a credit card balance in advance to cover the company's auctioneer fee.

This structural and relationship capital enables eBay to instantaneously replicate its business-model innovations and bring them into the lives of millions of buyers and sellers around the world.

Low transaction costs drive Agora growth. Investment strategist Jeffrey Ricker measured the relationship between stock market trading costs and volume, and found that "a 1 percent decline in trading cost causes a 2.5 percent increase in volume."[6] It should come as no surprise that—unlike many Internet start-ups—eBay is *very* profitable, cash-rich, and free of debt. Founded in 1995, the company facilitated some $350 million in live auction sales during its first three years. By 1999, transaction volumes had soared to $3 billion, yielding eBay commission fees and other revenues in excess of $200 million.[7]

Price Discovery Mechanisms

Four fundamental *price-discovery mechanisms* define the basic options for Agora b-web strategy. As we will describe, Agora business-model innovation often revolves around new and inventive approaches to price discovery.

1. An *open market* is set up for one-to-one negotiations—haggling—between buyer and seller. These negotiations tend to work best for unique goods, each of which is of interest to a limited market. The simplest form of Agoras, open markets, include business negotiations, real estate and car sales, bazaars, flea markets, garage sales, and classified ads. Monster.com, with over 300,000 job listings, is a global open market that enables employers and prospective employees to connect with one another.

2. A *sell-side auction* is a one-seller-to-many-buyers competition. The seller may specify the timing, the minimum bid, and a reserve price. There are several types of sell-side auctions based on different sets

of rules. Most of the action on eBay uses the *English* (or Yankee) auction format, in which bidders compete openly and the highest bid wins. In a *sealed* auction, participants submit their one best bid, which remains hidden from the others. In *Dutch* auctions, typically for multiple identical items like flowers, the seller specifies the minimum unit price and the quantity available. Bidders submit a price that is equal to or higher than this amount. The highest bid gets first rights to the goods, but all winners pay the same price. The *second price* (also known as a Vickery) auction, which takes sealed bids, is a new variation on the English auction.[8] Here, the highest bidder wins, but pays the second highest price.

3. *Buy-side auctions* enable a buyer to receive bids from several sellers. They work best when the buyer's budget is high relative to the cost of bidding and there is market competition among sellers. The most common buy-side auction is a *request for quotation* (RFQ). Each bidder provides one best quote as a sealed proposal. Structurally, sealed-bid reverse auctions tend to favor sellers, since they are not forced to compete with one another in real time. Sometimes, however, a perverse, blind poker logic comes into play, when a supplier decides to "buy" the business by bidding below cost. In this case, the other bidders lose the deal for the wrong reasons. As we explain in the following pages, FreeMarkets Inc. tackled this problem and figured out how to shift corporate purchasing to an open-bid online auction setting.

4. *Exchanges,* such as stock and commodities markets, are the most advanced and complex form of Agoras, typically trading goods whose supply and demand are both high and in continuous flux. They work as a series of multiple auctions, in which many players simultaneously trade various goods in different volumes using fast-paced bid-and-ask mechanisms. Sellers and buyers frequently switch roles. The same items may be sold and resold day in and day out, with continually fluctuating spot markets that make the price of a commodity or security from one moment to the next. Exchanges enable businesses to manage continuous fluctuations in supply and demand. Much of the action is—and must be—visible to all, but many deals happen behind the scenes. Exchanges deal in fluid, uniform, and divisible goods like commodities, securities, and financial

instruments. As we describe in this chapter, financial market-type exchange models and innovations (like OptiMark) will move into a wide variety of new markets, from semiconductors to telecommunications bandwidth. We expect to see Securities and Exchange Commission–type regulation in the wake of these market transformations.

Every Agora has its own quirks: What seems essential in one would ruin another. These features—outgrowths of the Agora exchange process itself—can define the core culture of the participating community, even an entire industry like fine art or the oil business. To outsiders, these cultures can seem weird and impenetrable. Consider the peculiar lingo and habits of the global securities industry or even a Dutch flower auction.

Agoras seemingly maximize logical choices about what to buy and how much to pay for it, because buyers and sellers are face to face and compete in their own self-interest. They ought to exemplify economists' theories about rational pricing. Of course, they don't. Whether for stocks, Coca-Cola memorabilia, coffee futures, or cars, buyer and seller decisions depend on fashion, transitory events, social norms and pressures, personal passions, and beliefs. Over the long run, statistical means and equilibriums may seem economically rational. But daily choices and moves often fluctuate on news, gossip, and rumor—sometimes mildly, other times wildly.

The Power of Exchanges

Arguably, exchanges are the most sophisticated and powerful market mechanism of all. Open markets and auctions usually price unique transactions, but a robust exchange defines the universal spot price for a good. Exchanges work best for commodity-like goods: those in high demand, available in volume from a variety of producers, and relatively undifferentiated.

Exchange markets for many types of goods have emerged and thrived over the past century. Besides financial instruments, exchanges deal in a variety of commodities, from oil to wheat to orange juice and coffee.

Michael Fix, CEO of Industry to Industry (a new Agora player backed by the World Economic Forum), points out that exchanges have deep roots: "Village traders started asking farmers what the price of corn would be six months from now. The same skill set soon played out for other related commodities, resulting in a market for futures. Eventually the ultimate market emerged—the stock market."

Because commodities have wide use and impact, markets have developed a variety of derivative tools that build on the mathematics of exchange. What is the value of a futures contract? Corn wholesalers can protect themselves by purchasing a contract that guarantees their ability to buy a ton of corn for $120 next July. If the price escalates, then the wholesalers win. If it falls, then they can still sell the corn.

Other commodity derivatives such as swaps emerged and took on lives of their own as investment instruments. Consequently, commodity exchanges gained tremendous power. They have become global forces, setting prices through supply and demand. The most efficient exchanges, like agricultural exchanges, demolish producer monopolies and ruthlessly drive prices downward. Inefficient ones—like the oil market in the sway of global cartels—keep prices above natural levels.

Many commodity exchanges have been electronic for a long time. Now, two kinds of changes are happening. First, these markets will move to the Internet (as stock exchanges are already doing). Second, entirely new kinds of goods will be traded in exchange-type markets. This second transformation deserves exploration.

Michael Fix argues that a shift to online auctions and ultimately to exchanges drives the huge growth projections for business-to-business b-webs. As has already happened with financial instruments and bulk commodities, markets for complex goods will change:

> [Markets will become] fluid and increasingly global, while gradually diminishing the number of expensive intermediaries who do no more than match buyer and seller. Buyers and sellers will want to choose a transaction model that enables them to do business in the most transparent and efficient manner possible. The Internet expands the number of buyers and sellers—across borders and industries. It turns inventory losses into profits.[9]

AN AGORA IN YOUR FUTURE

eBay clearly represents opportunity. But does it threaten anyone? The company itself thinks not, arguing that the original owners of items in eBay's ever-changing online attic might never otherwise sell their cheap or unusual possessions. The Internet's new reach lets these sellers find buyers for goods such as wall hangings from someone's favorite—now demolished—restaurant in Singapore.

Jupiter Research estimated that newspapers would lose $200 million in print classified revenue to the eBay phenomenon by the end of 2000. Other types of Web sites could also reduce newspaper classified ad revenue. Local city guides like sidewalk.com, as well as independent classifieds, draw audiences to their classified listings.[10] The damage could get worse, as eBay sets up local sites for big-ticket items like used cars, furniture, and perhaps even homes. Perhaps the local media ought to respond with auctions of their own.

eBay has trained millions of consumers in the logic and methods of auction-based price discovery, wherein the buyer can set the value of a good. These b-web participants—and the global market culture as a whole—are turning toward variable pricing. eBay habitués are not just stay-at-homes with limited discretionary dollars. They also include managers, professionals, procurement officers, and executives who will bring eBay's lessons into business buying and selling.

Now, online auctions and other Agoras are visibly plowing across the b-web landscape. Facilitated by the Internet, the resurgence of negotiated transactions between buyers and sellers is challenging pricing habits and value-allocation models in one industry after another.

Using services like Autobytel.com, car buyers force dealers to compete against one another by e-mailing lowest-bid proposals. Electric utilities— barely emerging from monopoly status—trade power through online exchanges. In-demand professionals bypass headhunters and employment agencies to auction their know-how to the highest bidder. ECNs and online brokers challenge the existence of core economic institutions like the New York Stock Exchange. Meanwhile, individual investors and day traders have not only booted their full-service brokers, but also gained power over institutional investors in the pricing dynamics of the stock market itself. This is particularly true with Internet stocks, for which institutional investors currently hold only 22 percent of shares, compared with 62 percent of Fortune 50 companies. The share turnover rate for Internet stocks averages 52 days, compared with 333 for Fortune 50 companies.[11]

Because of their multifaceted and dynamic nature, Agoras present nearly unlimited opportunities for business-model innovation. Some

Agora operators, like Onsale, simply bring auctions to traditional retail goods. Others, like OptiMark, with its new approach to conducting block trades, are out to transform the core trading architecture of the stock market. Priceline, another innovator, has designed new ways to engage in dynamic buying and selling, increasing the range of goods susceptible to variable pricing.

Despite the near elimination of transaction costs, variable pricing will not take over completely. Why haggle over the price of a Mars bar or, for that matter, an IBM laptop? Just choose the most convenient seller or the one who offers the best price. On the other hand, how about loading a smart card with the credits you bought in the Mars bar futures market? Maybe you'll save a bundle when you stock up next Halloween!

If the value of a good is uncertain, or the purchaser is flexible within a category (any state-of-the-art laptop will do), or the deal is big enough—then a variable-pricing opportunity exists. These criteria cover a surprisingly big territory. Any business that conducts large-scale selling or buying should consider how variable pricing could change its marketplace. Those who already compete in a variable-priced market as a seller, broker, or agent should beware. Business web innovation will likely change the rules of the game, potentially disintermediating you or a big chunk of your business.

To spot opportunities for an online Agora, look for the following conditions:

- *An existing industrial-age Agora whose poor cost-performance frustrates participants.* Before eBay, lovers of Beanie Babies, Coca-Cola memorabilia, and such had to do business at costly flea markets and collectors' conventions—or communicate via back-page classifieds in specialty magazines.

- *A hot new market intrinsic to the Net.* AdAuction assembled a media buyer community for "surplus" Web ad space. Then, once it had achieved critical mass, the company branched out from the $2 billion Web advertising space into billboards, print, and other offline media—a $200-plus billion market.

- *Buyer frustration with costs of big-ticket goods.* Priceline's price-offer mechanism enables consumers to gain influence in the pricing of travel, cars, and loans. Other online car buyer markets help consumers force dealers into competitive bidding.

- *Regulatory intervention.* The state electrical power industry has formed a b-web around the Internet-based California Power Exchange for one primary reason: They had no choice.

ELEMENTS OF AGORA B-WEB DESIGN

Time, Place, or Space

Commodity exchanges and stock markets have made huge investments in network infrastructure, creating instantaneous global markets. But most industrial-age Agoras face restrictions of time and space. Hagglers often require direct, face-to-face contact. Auctions typically gather participants in one place at the same time. Bidding sessions are short—a $50 million van Gogh might get fifteen minutes; most goods sell in seconds. These time and space barriers limit the number of buyers to those who show up. Limited buyer numbers tend to force prices down—in other words, less liquidity. Low liquidity keeps sellers away, so buyers may fail to get the goods that they desire. In this world, certain goods (like the previously mentioned Singapore restaurant wall hangings) have tiny markets and rarely sell at any price.

The Net, as we said earlier, turns time and space into elastic media, which Agoras can compress or expand to meet the needs of any design. Time is now infinitely scalable. eBay auctioneers or Yahoo! classifieds participants can take a week or more not just to display their wares, but also to arrive at a price in a suddenly global marketplace. Other markets—like securities—gain liquidity, precision, and dynamism from nanosecond transaction pacing.

Product Offering

In theory, an Agora b-web can provide just about any content—goods, services, or information. The challenge is to design an Agora to minimize negotiation costs and simplify the participants' experience. As the Internet lowers the transaction costs associated with real-time price negotiation, more types of goods become candidates for innovative Agora business models. Manufacturers, distributors, and retailers auction overstocked items and remnants through Onsale, eBay, and Amazon. com. The California Power Exchange auctions electricity and transmission facilities by the hour.

eBay has globalized markets and improved liquidity, price efficiency, and search costs for over 1,600 categories, from the sublime to the ridiculous. Every day, tens of thousands of people proffer close to three million items for sale. Many people have quit their day jobs to become full-time auction sellers on eBay. Thousands more significantly supplement their incomes. Meanwhile, dozens of small and not-so-small businesses have shifted to eBay as a major—sometimes the only—channel to their customers.

For buyers, eBay provides entertainment, with something for everyone. Want to treat your niece to a Millennium Princess Barbie ($30)? A vintage Mercedes for yourself ($100,000)? Need a sixteen-person software engineering team (a 1999 offering)? How about a human kidney (bidding reached $5.6 million before eBay pulled the plug)? Name it, you might just bag it (maybe for a steal) somewhere on eBay.

One common business-model innovation is to change a good's price-discovery mechanism to one that is more efficient (table 2-1). A photographer stands to make more money auctioning his or her used camera through eBay than haggling with readers of classified ads. Industry auctions like MetalSite and eSteel replace the time-consuming process of faxing and phoning dealers in search of buyers.

Few consumers will haggle over the price of a chocolate bar, but as Priceline has shown, some will bargain for a basket of groceries. Imagine sending your weekly shopping order (conveniently stored in your Netphone) as an RFQ to your grocery service. Using software, your online grocer automatically optimizes your order based on your stated preferences and its weekly specials. It may even negotiate directly with suppliers on the collective behalf of five hundred customers who want ground beef this week, shifting the Agora up the supply chain.

Information about Products and Traders

The New York Stock Exchange (NYSE) describes itself as an information marketplace. In Agoras, information is arguably more valuable than the goods themselves—because price decisions depend on how much information one has, compared with everyone else in the Agora—and on how one interprets it. NYSE market insiders, who have asymmetrical access to information compared with the bulk of investors, enjoy unique, sometimes potentially illegal, advantages.

One form of information, which we call *product knowledge*, describes the qualities of goods on sale, including strike price, trading volumes, features, risk/return analysis, marketplace news, and the trustworthiness of the seller. Widely available product knowledge improves liquidity by attracting informed participants.

In the stock market of the 1980s, typical retail investors gained product knowledge from personal experience and newspapers filled with

TABLE 2-1   Transforming Pricing Models

Context Provider	Products	Sellers	Buyers	Old Mechanism	New Mechanism
eBay, Amazon.com	Collectibles and consumer products	Consumers, small businesses	Consumers, small businesses	Direct haggling	Online auction
Priceline	Airline tickets, hotel rooms, cars, loans, groceries	Airlines, hotels, car dealers, mortgage lenders, grocers	Consumers	Fixed price	Consumer price offer
Onsale	Wholesale/retail overstocks and remnants	Onsale (as liquidator)	Small and medium business	Fixed-discount pricing	Auction
W. R. Hambrecht & Co.	IPOs	Stock issuers	Investors	Fixed price	Dutch auction
FreeMarkets	Business procurement	Business product and service vendors	Corporations	Sealed fixed-price bid	Live buy-side auction
MetalSite, eSteel	Prime and surplus metals	Steel manufacturers and distributors	Manufacturers and fabricators	Phone, fax haggling	Online auction and haggling
California Power Exchange	Electrical power and transmission	Power generation and distribution companies	Power companies, large power users	Phone, fax haggling	Online exchange
ECNs (Island, Archipelago)	Securities	Brokers, day traders	Brokers, day traders	Floor trader matches orders and pockets spreads	Direct electronic order matching for a fee

yesterday's news. Full-service brokers serviced lucrative clients with occasional proprietary research and personal advice. Discount brokers tapped into customer discontent. They made no pretense of providing product knowledge or advice, but at least they were cheap.

Then the Internet, the infinite information environment, smashed these information monopolies. Online brokers like E*Trade shifted the product knowledge resource from the broker's human capital to the more predictable and comprehensive structural capital of networked intelligence. Many investors now know more about their favorite stocks than the average full-service investment adviser. Online transactions accounted for 37 percent of all retail, or small-investor, trades in the first half of 1999.[12]

Another form of information, which we call *trader intent*, describes the plans, goals, and constraints of buyers and sellers. Plexus Group, a financial research firm, has measured what happens when the market discovers trader intent for a big trade like a two-million Intel share deal. The price of a major stock will surge in response to a buy order, or slide in response to a sell order—on average, by 101 basis points (i.e., by 1.01 percent). A small-cap stock will vary more, by 449 basis points.

In an ideal Agora, buyers and sellers would have (1) complete, accurate, and up-to-date product knowledge, and (2) total control over who may learn their trader intent. The idea is this: I could share my trader intent with you—but control how you use it. I could even retract it, wiping it from your memory. If you were a trustworthy piece of computer software, then retracting my trader intent information would indeed be feasible. Industrial-age Agoras deploy information poorly, whether in disseminating product knowledge or in protecting trader intent.

OptiMark: Protecting trader intent. OptiMark's electronic stock trading system is a digital black box that aggregates orders and then automatically matches and executes them every ninety seconds. By placing and executing orders without displaying them publicly, the system keeps trader intent confidential. It essentially provides a safe structural mechanism for matching traders' human capital (the knowledge of their personal intentions). Powered by supercomputers, OptiMark's system can process billions of operations per second. The company touts its unique exchange mechanism as the first to optimize trades among all possible participants.

OptiMark's software works like an electronic confessor. Investors describe their trading objective through the user interface. At regular intervals, the application compares all its buy and sell orders. When it finds a match, it closes the deal. If appropriate matches cannot be found, then OptiMark returns an unexecuted trade, with no one the wiser. OptiMark says its system works like a rock that lands in a pond, but makes no ripples.

The system actually increases liquidity, particularly when large numbers of people play. A large order does not require an exact match, because the OptiMark system can assemble fills from hundreds of parties. These individuals would almost certainly never find one another in the industrial-age stock market. More matches mean more deals, which mean better liquidity.

A second OptiMark innovation is the language it uses to communicate trader intent. Traditional electronic trading systems (like the NYSE) use simple, limited jargon: "Place a limit order to buy 10,000 shares of AT&T at $50," or "place a market order to buy 5,000 IBM." When speaking to one another on the phone, human traders can convey more subtle and complex objectives: "Sell whatever you can at the current bid, then see if you can unload another sixty thousand without dropping the price more than fifty cents. If you get a good price, then I might try to get you fifty thousand more." Even this information doesn't specify all possibilities: Is there a price at which the seller would part with 500,000 shares? How many shares would the customer sell at twenty-five cents below market?

OptiMark enables users to communicate complex preferences by defining goals along dimensions of price, volume, and satisfaction. You can state that you will be 100 percent satisfied to sell 50,000 shares at $37.00, and 90 percent satisfied at $36.75.

NASDAQ began using OptiMark at the end of 1999. Such models for protecting trader intent will eventually transform commodity markets ranging from electrical power to air travel. They potentially disintermediate several layers of market insiders, while simultaneously reducing self-dealing and increasing customer control. Versions of this concept will no doubt extend to auctions of unique goods, as well as haggling-oriented markets like real estate.

Community and Critical Mass

In Aggregations and other types of b-webs, community is often merely a new kind of marketing tool, a "sticky"(Web jargon for something that attracts and retains customer attention) device to capture customer attention. But in an Agora—especially an auction or exchange—community is a central functional design element. The participants have implicitly agreed to engage in a self-organizing group process to discover the price and allocation of goods, that is, the "social construction of value."[13]

To self-organize, participants must communicate with one another directly or indirectly (e.g., through eBay's automated mechanism for displaying the current bid). For the market to endure, the core participants must develop ongoing relationships. They share product knowledge; develop consensus views on price, the allocation of goods, and rules and norms of behavior; and publicize and (if they can) discipline those who commit infractions. Because of the need for voluntary, collective participation, an Agora business is much tougher to construct than traditional retail.

Communities thrive when participants recognize that they share interests. In some Agoras—like the stock market or even a consumer auction like eBay—participants recognize their common interests. eBay's community extends well beyond the site's own online forums. Many thousands of participants have developed enduring, independent relationships with their eBay contacts. By contrast, when was the last time that you befriended a sales clerk at a department store? As Robert Kagle of Benchmark Capital (an early eBay investor) has said, "eBay gives back to America what Wal-Mart took away."[14]

An Agora manifests community—indeed, provides its community with an "experience." The venue—be it the eBay Web site, the floor of the NYSE, the hall at Christie's, or a flea market—has a consciously staged atmosphere of its own. The context provider, like eBay or the NYSE, choreographs the process, defining the rules and the language. When visiting a retail store, the customer merely takes in what the seller has designed. But in an Agora, customers themselves help to shape the experience. Agoras generate relationship capital when their protocols, procedures, and culture provide customers with the tools they need to join in constructing value.

Rules Guiding Community Behavior

In the charged, risk-laden atmosphere of an Agora, trust depends on the rules of the game—and the norms of compliance. But physical Agoras crudely manage time, space, choice, and information access, providing many temptations and opportunities for insiders.

Creators of digital Agoras articulate the rules explicitly so that they can be written into software. Then, the software enforces the rules with consistent, unerring logic. Until the late 1990s, market makers at NASDAQ and the NYSE enjoyed unique insider advantages, including direct access to, and knowledge of, exchange transactions. New rules from the U.S. Securities and Exchange Commission ordered NASDAQ to give individual customers access to the same information. Day traders came onto the scene, using network-based trade-matching services to operate on a more even footing with the market makers.

Similarly, the California Power Exchange is wresting the flow of transactions away from the old boys' club of utilities insiders. They are losing the monopolist's ability to cut sweetheart deals for megawatts and distribution services that have artificially pushed up the prices paid by corporate and consumer customers. Power prices have plummeted by 50 percent and more.

DIGITAL BUSINESS MODELS

Agora b-webs exist in three market environments: business-to-business, business-to-consumer, and consumer-to-consumer. The four price-discovery mechanisms (open market, sell-side auction, buy-side auction, and exchange) work differently in each of these market contexts. We have already covered consumer-to-consumer markets in the earlier eBay discussion. Here, we describe Agora innovations in business-to-business and business-to-consumer markets.

Business-to-Business

Compared with the amateur slant of consumer auctions, industry Agoras do serious business. They're also *big* business, with enormous growth potential. In 1999, Forrester Research estimated that business-to-business auctions would net $52.6 billion by 2002, compared with $19 billion for consumer auctions.[15] eBay single-handedly put online auctions on the map. But in its first year of operation, one local business-to-business sectoral Agora—the California Power Exchange—transacted more than the volume of all consumer-to-consumer Agoras combined, which suggests that Forrester's projection may be much too low.

Business-to-business Agoras are hard to build, particularly for manufactured goods in specialized industry markets like textiles, auto subassemblies, and computer chips. The purchasers are fewer, individual needs tend to be unique, and timing windows are short. Habits, relationships, and processes bind market participants to the past. Agoras will flourish in business-to-business endeavors, but achieving critical mass in each market will take time.

Business-to-business sell-side auctions. Industry sell-side auctions began as liquidation channels, mostly for manufacturer surplus and secondary products, in high-volume, fragmented markets ranging from paper goods to industrial equipment. FastParts.com describes itself as a semiconductor commodity exchange. In reality, it works like a collection of simultaneous auctions with a bit of last-minute haggling thrown in. Buyers anonymously compete to set a price, and then haggle with an individual seller before closing the deal. FastParts guards the identities of sellers (i.e., their relationship capital)—they could be equipment manufacturers (such as PC companies), contract manufacturers, component manufacturers, or distributors. The seller could be an overstocked plant dumping surplus goods, or a well-heeled distributor selling from a catalog. Anonymity protects sellers from buyers who might try to turn a one-time deal into an everyday low price. Similarly, the seller can only guess the buyer's identity and strategy. FastParts, as the trusted context provider, handles fulfillment, escrow, and payment and makes its money from a "small" transaction fee. The playing field is as level as it could possibly be.

The real action in business-to-business auctions to date has been private, because both sets of intermediaries—say, wholesalers auctioning surplus goods to retailers—prefer to keep end-customers ignorant about price cuts in the channel. As end-customers become more savvy, they may demand the right to participate directly in such auctions, to the detriment of retail intermediaries.

Ingram Micro, the $30-billion-plus electronics distributor, has been operating a private auction of surplus wholesale goods on its Web site since 1996. The "millions per quarter" that its AuctionBlock raises is a tiny fraction of Ingram's total revenues—and the company loses money on the goods sold. But where Ingram formerly realized only fifteen to twenty cents to the dollar on large-lot surplus sales, it now gets three times as much. Typical buyers, small and midsize Ingram-registered dealers and resellers, bid on slightly obsolete computers, printers, and the like. Because the Internet auction format lowers transaction costs, the lots can be economically broken down to small sizes, providing good deals for dealers and higher prices for Ingram. In a word: liquidity.

In late 1999, Ken Jenkins, Ingram's auction business manager, told us that auctions were becoming a positive cash flow contributor. In true b-web style, Ingram had begun to capitalize on its Agora business-model innovations in a couple of ways. First, suppliers like 3Com paid commissions to Ingram to help them auction excess inventory, such as obsolescent model PalmPilots. Second, in what Ingram called the Affinity Project, Ingram was taking over the back rooms of major customers like CompUSA, handling everything from shipping to customer service. As part of this initiative, Jenkins's group supported the liquidation of surplus goods, transferring the company's online auction capabilities to other companies—for a fee. Jenkins also told us that like FastParts, Ingram might eventually put some categories of products through a more dynamic exchange mechanism.

Business-to-business buy-side auctions. True buy-side auctions—in which sellers compete in real time to offer a customer the lowest price—are rare. A more common buy-side auction is the request for proposal (RFP), or, more technically, a sealed-bid auction. The customer issues a set of requirements, and each aspiring supplier submits a sealed bid. The buyer reviews the bids and makes a choice. The RFP model is not the fairest and most effective way to conduct procurement or arrive at a price. Buyers often find it difficult or impossible to state their requirements with precision; as a result, no two bids offer truly comparable goods and services. Once the quotes come in, buyers must choose between apples and oranges.

Buy-side auctions on the Net typically reproduce the traditional RFP process. Many government sites publish RFPs via the Web. Proposals arrive as traditional sealed bids, and the agency sorts through the competing offers in the usual manner.

FreeMarkets turns the RFP process upside down and empowers the customer. The company has worked with General Motors, Procter & Gamble, United Technologies, and the State of Pennsylvania, among others. The company claims that customers achieve significant savings over what they expect to pay, often from incumbent suppliers. FreeMarkets facilitated procurement of more than $1 billion in industrial goods and services in 1999. Based in Pittsburgh, it concentrates on commodities and components for heavy industrial manufacturing.

The FreeMarkets price-discovery process zeros in on a half-day bidding event that resembles a typical live auction. The difference is that sellers (instead of buyers) bid against one another, and the winner is the lowest (rather than the highest) bidder. Sellers see one another's bids, but not their identities. The buyer sits with the FreeMarkets team, which facilitates the process via the Net and by telephone. The whole process happens over a private Web site, enhanced by FreeMarkets proprietary software.

For such a process to work, all competitors must tender comparable bids: apples to apples. FreeMarkets makes most of its money from its consulting services to help buyers and sellers in constructing comparable bids. It works with the buyer to prepare a clear and complete request for proposal and a comprehensive response format. It then works with vendors to make sure that their responses comply. In the process, FreeMarkets conducts a comparative benchmark on current and potential suppliers.

At the end of the day, the lowest bid doesn't always win. For example, if the second-lowest bidder is an incumbent, then the customer might decide that the cost of switching would be higher than the savings on the price. Even in these situations, the incumbent usually bids a competitive price. FreeMarkets CEO Glen Meakem comments that his reverse auction threatens incumbents, who are

> *living the life of Riley, making big margins without your customers' knowing about it. Once they have access to all the available information, you may retain the business, but you're going to take a haircut on pricing. . . . On the other hand, if an incumbent supplier is very good, it has a chance to consolidate business. The buyer uses this very analytical approach and finds out.*[16]

FreeMarkets converts a procurement process that relied on industrial-age structural capital (knowledge and business processes in a collection of disparate RFQs) to one that draws on digital structural capital (networked intelligence available at the point of need, producing a set of comparable RFQs). FreeMarkets customers have used the system for basic commodities—like coal—to precision machined parts and even the outsourcing of a machine shop. The company advises that its offerings work best for big-ticket purchases for which the supplier market is highly competitive.

The FreeMarkets approach may work for special-event procurements, but what about access to goods or services on the fly? Could digital auctions work in your everyday supply chain? ShoeNet, a b-web for the shoe industry, has done just that. Anne Perlman, CEO of auction solution provider Moai Technologies, points out that in a fashion-driven industry like the shoe business, retailers and designers sometimes need to respond quickly, as they become aware of shifts in consumer taste. At other times, their products are more predictable and commodity-like.

In either case, routine procurement can incorporate a reverse auction. Perlman explains:

> Shoes have twenty-two distinct attributes—that's how you specify what you need. Using these attributes, you can run a reverse auction for available production capacity. Where the shoes are more or less generic like black pumps, you might want to overstock your store at all times with the generic popular model, and you auction your demand to suppliers on an ongoing basis.[17]

Oracle CEO Larry Ellison told us that General Motors intends to build reverse Internet-based procurement auctions into routine supply-chain management.

Business-to-business exchanges. After a century of state government regulation, on April 1, 1998, the California Power Exchange became the market maker for 80 percent of the state's power grid. Rather than setting fixed rates in government hearings, the industry's b-web negotiates prices continuously via the exchange's Web site. The market, not state utility commissions, now controls electricity prices.

Market participants include regulated (like Pacific Gas & Electric) and unregulated power companies, "green" and other independent power generators (e.g., Sunlaw Cogeneration Partners), municipal utilities (e.g., San Diego Gas & Electric), and third-party power marketers (e.g., Enron Power Marketing). In its first year of operation, the exchange processed $8 billion in transactions.

Electricity seems so bound up with the wires on which it flows. Deregulation turns it into a tradable commodity: If you can buy and sell electricity on an exchange, then you can buy and sell just about anything. The California Power Exchange exemplifies what will transform the economics of dozens more industries. We discuss the transformation of the power industry in chapter 6.

One industry ripe for exchange markets is chemicals, a $1.6 trillion global business. Chemicals are everywhere—including clothes, food, electronics, drugs, and fragrances. The crudest and most popular of chemicals—mostly petrochemicals—already sell through global exchanges. But the millions of other specialized compounds trade bilaterally between buyers and sellers. Yet thousands of these compounds have the characteristics of commodities mentioned earlier: They are in high demand, available in volume from a variety of producers, and relatively undifferentiated.

ChemConnect is the first new-generation global chemicals exchange. In its 1999 start-up phase, it offered only a few hundred product lots in seven primary categories such as plastics and polymers, fine and specialty chemicals, pharmaceuticals, and agrochemicals. Though small, the diverse and impressive list included exotica like 5,000 kilograms of valerian root from New York, 50 metric tons of calcium hypochlorite from Tianjin, and 150 kilograms of phenylpropionic acid from Warsaw. Each of these unique chemicals, and thousands of others, could turn into globally tradable, price-efficient commodities.

Unless you are in a pure knowledge business, you will likely trade many of your current production inputs—and outputs—in this way. Must businesses like Coca-Cola or Kellogg's always manage their outputs systemwide in a quasi-monopoly manner, as a straight-line Value Chain to the consumer? Maybe not.

Business-to-Consumer

Have you ever passed through a seedy retail district where neon-lit stores flaunt dubious, discounted goods too aggressively—and where the buying experience leaves you wondering who did what to whom? Many business-to-consumer Agoras on the Web come on just as strongly, like liquidation auctions Onsale and DealDeal. HaggleZone engages consumers in cute, rude, and engaging price negotiations with cartoon character avatars. Dealing with software that simulates a person, one can only assume that the programmer has set an inviolable bottom line for every item in the catalog. The site generates buys. Even on the Net, there is one born every minute.

Despite such drawbacks, business-to-consumer Agoras promise to increase both customer power and market liquidity. Priceline describes its approach as buyer-driven commerce, in which consumers "name their price" for air travel, hotel rooms, car purchases, groceries, and home mortgages, to name a few. For most of these goods, consumers must relinquish control over some features in exchange for the privilege of naming their price.

To buy an airline ticket, customers input the dates and destination of the proposed trip, state the amount they wish to pay, and provide credit card authorization. They agree to fly anytime between 6:00 A.M. and 10:00 P.M. on the airline that Priceline selects. The customers must wait one hour for an answer to their offers, although Priceline can actually match an offer almost immediately. Priceline founder and vice chairman Jay Walker explains that the delay is designed to "convince the customer that we are looking hard on his behalf." The company's software compares the customer's request against an inventory of discount fares from participating airlines. If it can find a flight for a price cheaper than the customer's offer, it then closes the deal. Priceline buys the ticket and resells it to the customer at the price that the customer requested; the difference between the two prices is Priceline's margin.

Walker, with perhaps excessive humility, describes a bottom-feeder role for his company: "[Let suppliers and other distribution channels] successfully generate and meet all the market demand they can. Priceline's role in the ecosystem is to salvage and recycle the excess capacity that the system creates and cannot easily dispose of on its own."[18] The company said that in a May–June 1999 comparison, its customers saved 21–44 percent over airline ticket consolidator prices and 18–52 percent over hotel reservation services[19] (the ranges were due to differences in air travel routes, the destination city, and the quality of the hotel rooms).

Priceline targets its value proposition to both consumers and suppliers: Consumers trade product certainty for discounts. Suppliers sell theoretically excess inventory without theoretically jeopardizing their brand. However, a by-product of the Priceline model is a sense of brand equivalency: "Give me your cheapest toothpaste—Crest or Colgate."

Priceline takes its structural capital seriously. Its business model is patented, and the company sued Microsoft in 1999 for infringement.

Business-to-consumer Agoras abound. Like eBay, many replace the newspaper classifieds, as well as human middlemen like employment agents (Monster.com is the biggest b-web employment agency), car salespeople (e.g., Autobytel), and, perhaps soon, real-estate agents. In late 1999, the National Association of Realtors operated the biggest real-estate b-web, Realtor.com. It insistently referred home buyers and sellers to locally based realtors, that is, real-estate agents belonging to the National Association of Realtors. The entrepreneur who, as a b-web context provider, figures out how to create and facilitate a consumer-to-consumer Agora for real estate may well crush Realtor.com and its competitors.

Also in late 1999, eBay still promoted its brand as a "person-to-person auction community." Nevertheless, a big chunk of eBay's inventory comes directly from business sellers. For example, Henry's is a leading camera store in Toronto. Its Web page that is devoted to surplus equipment escorts you directly to its current listing of goods on auction at eBay.

Clearly, business-to-consumer Agoras have growth potential. And no one has yet brought buy-side or exchange mechanisms to the consumer marketplace. Consider two scenarios:

- A buy-side auction enables consumers to accept competing bids from grocery retailers. In exchange for a commitment to spend $5,000 at the winning retailer, the consumer receives a 5 percent discount off a year's bill. The auction context-provider tracks his or her purchases with a loyalty card. The customer then receives the discount from the winning grocer as a lump-sum payment at the end of the year (just in time for the holidays)—if the person meets his or her commitment. The following year, a competing chain offers a better discount, plus frequent-flyer miles.

• Consumers participate directly in the California Power Exchange. The least adventurous have dishwashers with smart agents that figure out the most cost-effective time to run themselves every night. Consumers that are more aggressive generate their own power—solar, wind, or fuel cell—and sell their surplus into the grid. They trade energy futures and other such instruments.

KEY SUCCESS FACTORS

Identify ways to improve the price-discovery mechanism. Industrial-age auction participants must communicate one at a time in a linear fashion. The Net eliminates the constraints of time and space. eBay has shifted the price-discovery mechanism for its customers from local haggling to global auction. Priceline and OptiMark actually invented entirely new, digitally enabled mechanisms. In doing so, all three have dramatically increased liquidity for buyers and sellers.

Build critical mass quickly to generate value. Unlike other types of b-webs, the value of an Agora depends on its participants. Priming market activity and building relationship capital are cornerstones of Agora strategy; once achieved, critical mass yields network effects that produce value for all participants.

Continually engineer and adjust your Agora b-web to its participants and the business system in which they reside. Priceline, eBay, and OptiMark have accumulated great reserves of structural capital via their Agora b-web engineering capabilities.

Consider insider advantage as a design decision. Few Agoras are level playing fields; their rules favor insiders to varying degrees. Building and electronically codifying appropriate rules is a legal and social, not just economic, design challenge.

Treat software-encoded rules as explicit and flexible. Automation can implement and enforce complex rule sets. Tailor your rule customization to behavior, or to differentiate between classes of participants.

Use and preserve an audit trail of participant behavior. Tracking online behavior can serve many goals—from improving a service offering to building demographic profiles. Goals specific to Agoras include auditing users' compliance with rules, helping participants make choices (e.g., eBay's feedback profile system), and producing real-time snapshots of shifting market dynamics.

Prepare for digital intermediaries and agents. Today the OptiMark matching system acts as a trusted intermediary for matching trades. More sophisticated agents, like the dishwasher's minion that negotiates the best power price before turning itself on, will create new opportunities.

Pay attention to hygiene factors. Agoras have many hygiene factors: trust, privacy, regulatory issues, and taxation, to name a few.

LEADER'S GUIDE TO AGORAS

Definition: Liquidity, the ease of converting assets into cash, is the core value proposition of Agoras. Agoras achieve liquidity by matching buyers and sellers and by the facilitation of price discovery, whereby buyers and sellers cooperate and compete to arrive at a mutually acceptable exchange.

Significance: Economic theory suggests that auctions and exchanges are more price-efficient and rational than fixed-price systems because they can continually attune pricing to supply and demand.

Types: Agoras include the following forms.

• An open market (like Monster.com) is set up for one-to-one private negotiations—haggling—between buyer and seller. Open markets tend to work best for unique goods, each of which is of interest to a limited market.

• A sell-side auction (e.g., eBay) is a one-seller-to-many-buyers competition. Sell-side auctions tend to be for unique, distressed, surplus, or perishable goods. Here, the seller may specify the timing, the minimum bid, and a reserve price.

• Buy-side auctions (e.g., FreeMarkets) enable a buyer to receive bids from several sellers. They work best when the buyer's budget is high relative to the cost of bidding, and sellers engage in market competition.

- Exchanges (e.g., NASDAQ, California Power Exchange) are the most advanced and complex type of Agora, typically trading commodities, goods whose supply and demand are both high and in continuous flux. Exchanges work as a series of multiple auctions, through which many players simultaneously trade various goods in different volumes using fast-paced bid-and-ask mechanisms. Sellers and buyers frequently switch roles. The same items may be sold and resold day in and day out, with continually fluctuating spot markets that set the price of a commodity or security from one moment to the next.

Key transformation: Time- and space-bound Agora mechanisms with limited applications become transformed into global, malleable, and widely useful tools for transforming the economics of many different industries.

3aggregations

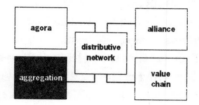

Aggregation b-webs, like Webvan and the Ariba Network, organize and choreograph the distribution of goods, services, and information. They intermediate transactions between producers and consumers, creating value for both and for their shareholders. An Aggregation's value proposition depends on six complementary variables: selection, organization, price, convenience, matching, and fulfillment.

Aggregation b-webs exist in business-to-business and business-to-consumer realms. Interestingly, many business-to-consumer digital Aggregations were not initially profitable, whereas those in business-to-business markets quickly emerged as genuine e-business success stories.

Aggregation b-webs that deliver greater value and producers who connect directly with end-customers threaten industrial-age Aggregations.

THE DIGITAL GROCER

What are the most attractive e-business consumer markets? Conventional wisdom suggests books, video games, or maybe compact discs. These high-margin goods are durable, standardized, easy to deliver, and simply cataloged for, promoted to, and sampled by consumers online.

Pure information goods, like securities and banking services, are even better since they can be fulfilled digitally.

But the most attractive consumer market for aggregated physical goods may very well be groceries. On the surface you might not think so. Groceries turn on paltry margins and can rot in transit. Their packaging, handling, and storage requirements vary wildly from one product category to another, and home delivery requires specialized and costly infrastructures. The Web can't—yet—deliver the sensory experiences that grocery shoppers enjoy, like the rich colors and feel of fresh produce or the appetizing smell of fresh-baked bread.

The numbers are compelling. Groceries dwarf the book market— $450 billion versus $30 billion in the United States. Consumers spend a tenth of weekly earnings, between $60 and $100 for the average household, on groceries. Even fanatics spend less on video games or CDs. The typical shopper visits a grocery store 2.2 times a week. No other kinds of goods are purchased with such regularity. Grocery shopping is the quintessential sticky application. E-mail may be addictive, but you don't need it to survive.

Research supports the potential for selling groceries online. According to Andersen Consulting, 15 million Americans are "shopping avoiders," who detest the supermarket experience, from traffic jams and lengthy queues to picking and packing goods.[1] All consumers are becoming time starved; they increasingly lack the two to three hours a week that shopping demands. The value proposition of online grocery shopping is convenience and time. Web-based ordering drastically reduces the time required to find, evaluate, and select goods. You can shop any time you like. Home delivery saves a trip to the store. Customers of Streamline, a grocery b-web in Boston, need not be home to receive their orders, because the company installs a temperature-controlled, secure delivery box in each customer's garage.

Forrester Research pegs the market potential for online grocery sales at $60 billion, about the same size as the U.S. computer chip industry. Moreover, the online grocery business could generate healthy profits. Harried, time-starved shoppers might even pay premium prices. Value-added, information-based services like home inventory management or nutritional counseling potentially offer new streams of revenue. All the participants in a grocery b-web stand to gain, from shoppers, who get more value and do less work, to producers, who get operating efficiency and more direct access to customers.

However, in late 1999, the jury was still out on fulfillment—the crux of the online grocery business model. Transforming an electronic grocery basket into a real one and delivering it quickly and efficiently demands operational sophistication unprecedented in any other industry. The goods themselves are problematic: Shipping eggs, bread, and ice cream together is no small feat. How to ensure that the eggs arrive unbroken, the bread unflattened, and the ice cream unthawed?

Product returns compound the home delivery problem. Even electronic order systems make mistakes, and the quality of goods will sometimes disappoint customers. Returns are a major dimension of the design and cost equation for online grocers.

A Tale of Two B-Webs: Peapod and Webvan

Peapod is the seasoned veteran of the virtual grocery business. Brothers Andrew and Thomas Parkinson, both former Procter & Gamble employees, founded the company in 1989. Peapod's original business model was simple and ingenious.

The Parkinsons financed the company on a shoestring and had neither the resources nor the inclination to operate stores or warehouses. They didn't consider themselves retailers. So they partnered with the local Jewel supermarket chain and dispatched Peapod employees to pick and pack orders (which came in by phone or fax) right off the shelves. Peapod vans delivered goods to the customer's door. The company focused on the context—processing orders, delivering them on time, collecting fees, and managing complaints. It left the rest to Jewel, its content provider, which gained incremental sales from the arrangement. Busy, affluent suburbanites, Peapod's target, buy lots of groceries but can't always make it to the store. Peapod quickly built relationship capital, in brand equity and customer loyalty, by leveraging Jewel's physical assets.

Peapod's speed to market came at a cost. Its own operation was inefficient, and its cost structure embedded Jewel's overheads. Even after charging customers a $16 service fee per order, Peapod failed to break even. Between 1989 and 1996, it reputedly lost $53 on every order. Still, the market rewarded its efforts in a 1997 IPO that raised $64 million.

Peapod built an Internet context for order taking and cut deals with supermarkets in several other U.S. cities, including Randall's in Houston and Edward Super Food Stores in New York. Ultimately, volume overwhelmed Peapod's fulfillment model, prompting redirection. In 1998, the company announced plans to build and operate distribution centers in its busiest markets. The distribution centers radically altered Peapod's balance sheet and its business model. The company now carried inventory and assumed the risk. It became a buying organization with real payables and greater working capital demands, like a typical supermarket.

Peapod's distribution centers eliminated stock crises and drove out some costs. But the company continued to lose money. Through three-quarters of 1999, it lost $20 million on $50 million in sales. In early 2000, Peapod stock traded at around $9½, well off the $16 IPO price.

Peapod's travails did not discourage big names from betting on consumer direct. Amazon.com paid $42.5 million for a stake in Seattle-based HomeGrocer. The Barksdale Group, a venture-capital firm launched by former Netscape boss Jim Barksdale, chose NetGrocer for its maiden investment. Across the continent, Boston-based Streamline raised $36 million in investments from Intel, SAP, GE Capital, and Nordstrom.

Webvan, founded by Louis Borders of Borders Books, was the most daring bet of all. In the summer of 1999, it secured $275 million in venture capital. In its subsequent IPO prospectus, Webvan predicted a loss of $300 million in 2002, yet it raised nearly $400 million. Selling into a single locality (San Francisco), the company's market capitalization peaked at $8 billion in late 1999, half that of traditional grocery giant Safeway.

Why the excitement over Webvan? Investors viewed it as the most robust of Web grocery business models. Webvan claimed that it would accomplish the following:

- *Solve the customer fulfillment problem.* Webvan's 80,000-square-foot (7,500-square-meter) distribution centers, at a cost of $25 million each, feature state-of-the-art automation, ergonomics, and information management. Miles of conveyer belts move goods to super-efficient human packers, who never travel more than 19½ feet (6 meters) in any direction. Sophisticated logistics software optimizes the entire supply chain, from purchase click to package delivery.

Webvan used significant financial capital to develop an efficient home delivery system, structural capital that it will deploy across a $1 billion national distribution network.

- *Improve profitability.* Typical supermarket margins are 1 percent. Webvan predicts that its operation, when at capacity, will generate 8 percent margins, even with low prices and free delivery of orders greater than $60. Low costs for real estate and labor; reduced shrinkage and spoilage; and improved buying power will make the difference. If Webvan cannot operate at or near full capacity—a distinct possibility if customers are slow to adopt the service—the model fails.

- *Find the best people.* Shortly before its IPO, Webvan hired Andersen Consulting's managing partner, George Shaheen, to become its CEO. Shaheen's e-commerce expertise and Borders's retail acumen are a potent combo. The company's board of directors includes CEOs Tim Koogle of Yahoo! and Christos Cotsakos of E*Trade, and prominent venture capitalists from Sequoia and Benchmark Capital.

- *Lock in customers.* The Webvan promise to customers—low prices; vast selection; free shipping; convenient, half-hour, customer-specified delivery windows—is tough for both online and offline competitors to match. Webvan predicts that customers will settle on a single, trusted supplier of household services, and that it will ultimately command a hefty share of their wallets.

With the customer capital generated in its core business—groceries and drugs—Webvan will be positioned to extend its offering well beyond traditional industry borders. The key is trust. If shoppers trust Webvan to deliver them fresh, safe food products—to squeeze tomatoes and smell fresh bread on their behalf—then this customer capital can be leveraged into just about any other market for goods and services.

How is the $500 billion supermarket industry responding to the e-business challenge? First, it consolidated. Over $50 billion in grocery deals happened in 1998–1999, as supermarkets and wholesalers extended their scale advantage over newcomers and innovators like Wal-Mart. Second, some established grocers, like Kroger, made online plays of their own.

But many of a supermarket's product-centered core assets, including its industry-specific knowledge, business processes, and management practices, do not apply to business on the Internet. Grocers' primary unit of analysis is the category: a group of related products like orange juice or canned beans. Supermarkets manage categories, more so than individual products, for profitability. Informed by aggregate and anonymous customer purchase information, managers design a portfolio of assortment, price, shelf placement, and promotional activity intended to yield the best return for the category. Much of this analysis draws on the four P's of marketing: product, promotion, placement, and price. Prudent category management might eliminate a particular kind of orange juice—extra extra pulp, for example—and lose a long-term, profitable customer who buys a large basket of assorted other goods.

Web grocers, on the other hand, are customer-centric. Streamline CEO Tim DeMello says his business has little to do with groceries at all: "We are not in the grocery business, we are not in a product business. We are in a customer lifestyles and relationship business." The customer is the central unit of analysis and the primary variable in the profitability equation. Individual customers drive product assortment, placement, pricing, and promotions. Traditional marketing management and the four P's as we used to know them become obsolete.

A basket of groceries from Webvan or Streamline provides service-enhanced customization. It might contain items auto-replenished by the grocer, who knows when the customer needs soap before he or she does. Streamline's products are secondary to its convenient shopping experience.

The remaining three P's, promotion, placement, and price, also change. Promotion evolves from unidirectional broadcast to two-way communication. No more unwanted flyers and junk mail; customers implicitly evoke promotional materials through their consumption habits and shopping behaviors. Placement turns to convenience. And rather than focus on price, vendors engage consumers in a mutual price-discovery process. In chapter 8 we present a digital economy framework to replace the four P's of marketing.

Customer-focused b-web context leaders add value for content providers (i.e., producers and suppliers) via better access to customers, customer information, and improved inventory management. Deep customer intimacy defines market segments with great precision. Highly targeted, interactive, cost-effective promotions can happen every day. Strategic cross-promotional activities lead to symbiotic relationships among b-web suppliers.

Why don't grocery producers cut out middlemen entirely? What stops Procter & Gamble (P&G) from building an e-commerce engine and selling Pampers directly to consumers? Shoppers have neither the time nor the inclination to search out and evaluate the millions of product alternatives offered by thousands of suppliers. They want a manageable and convenient selection that corresponds to their needs. Similarly, P&G excels at brand building and product innovation—not demand aggregation, transaction processing, or customer fulfillment. Both consumers and producers need intermediaries for such services.

WHAT DO AGGREGATIONS DO?

Aggregations benefit customers when they select and organize goods, set prices, and help customers match goods to their needs. Aggregations make purchases convenient for customers and fulfill transactions by delivering goods part or all of the way to where they are consumed. The Aggregation's core customer value proposition is an optimized combination of these six elements: selection, organization, price, convenience, matching, and fulfillment.

Content providers, the producers or suppliers of goods, also gain from participation in Aggregation b-webs. Aggregations segment and capture markets as they select goods, and grant producers convenient, efficient access to these segments. Content organization can powerfully influence customer purchase decisions. Aggregations set prices and manage fulfillment, reducing producer operating and transaction costs. Figure 3-1 shows the benefits enjoyed by participants in Aggregations like Webvan.

Aggregations add value to the exchange process, rather than to the goods themselves. A hammer purchased from The Home Depot, rather than the manufacturer, costs more because The Home Depot wraps value around the hammer. This value includes a variety of hammers (and nails) to choose from, expert assistance, convenient access, and The Home Depot's brand, which vouchsafes quality.

Furniture.com is another Aggregation in action. An Internet-only furniture retailer, Furniture.com serves the U.S. market. Its selection of

FIGURE 3-1 Webvan Value Map

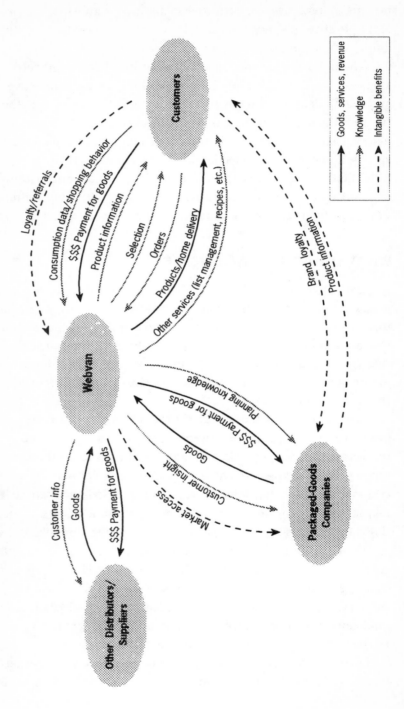

over 50,000 home furnishing items, from couches and chairs to lighting and art, is twice that of most large bricks-and-mortar retailers. Furniture.com combines slick Web-based ordering with sophisticated logistics management to beat traditional retail prices, while offering free delivery anywhere in the United States. Recognizing that coaxing shoppers into buying furniture sight unseen is a significant challenge, Furniture.com leverages new technologies to innovate customer services that enhance its matching function. RoomPlanner is an interactive tool built on Macromedia Flash software that lets shoppers create and furnish virtual replicas of their living spaces. Live design consultants are available twenty-four hours a day over the telephone or via Web chats. Furniture.com targets a prized demographic—affluent, Web-savvy thirty- to forty-year-olds shopping for medium- to high-end goods. The content providers of its b-web, which include 150 manufacturers, financial service and insurance providers, and a post-purchase maintenance service called FurnitureMedic, gain nationwide access to this valuable market segment. Furniture.com could transform today's $55 billion fragmented and inefficient furniture retail industry into a scale business and become its first power brand.

Chemdex distributes laboratory chemicals and supplies (which include everything from Bunsen burners to bled rats) to life science research institutions, a $1 billion global market. Before Chemdex, busy Ph.D.'s typically spent hours thumbing through dozens of independent supplier catalogs to locate items, managing multiple paper trails to place and track their orders. According to one Chemdex customer, "a $25 reagent might cost $50 with overheads tacked on."[2] Chemdex combines the catalogs of more than one hundred suppliers representing 120,000 products. Its Web content, augmented by information resources like the *Dictionary of Cell Biology* and GenBank, a database of gene sequences, is organized to maximize customer convenience. Intelligent search software helps purchasers quickly locate the products they need. Buyers can search multiple supplier catalogs by product name, category, vendor name, or key word, and purchase chemicals from many companies in a single order. Chemdex suppliers, many of which are tiny companies, get to post their catalogs for free and instantly gain access to the global market at a fraction of the cost of paper catalogs. Chemdex carries no inventory. Instead, FedEx and UPS ship orders straight from the manufacturer to the customer, providing tracking services through the Chemdex site.

PlasticsNet is a business-to-business portal for the plastics industry. The company aggregates sellers (suppliers of resins and other raw materials, equipment manufacturers), buyers (plastics producers and professionals), and a wealth of industry-specific information (material specifications, process training modules, career opportunities), creating a fertile context for value exchange. Buyers slash their search and evaluation costs, make more informed purchase decisions, and execute global sourcing strategies. As another benefit, buyers can create custom cross-vendor catalogs for frequently purchased items. Sellers plug into a low-cost sales channel with global reach. In late 1999, the site received 100,000 qualified hits from the plastics community every month. Like Chemdex, PlasticsNet facilitates transactions and consolidates orders on both the buy and the sell sides. More sophisticated supply-chain management services like demand forecasting leverage customer capital and diversify its revenue streams.

What is the growth potential for a b-web like PlasticsNet? Estimates suggest that 35 percent of the $370 billion plastics industry (in the United States alone) is economic friction created by inefficient distribution.[3] If PlasticsNet and its competitors eliminate just 10 percent of these costs, they will unlock $13 billion in value.

As these examples illustrate, Aggregations deal in three categories of goods: tangible, physical products like books, groceries, electronics, and cars; information goods such as news, entertainment, job postings, and industry directories; and services like e-mail and professional expertise. In other words, Aggregations can manage just about any good valued by any customer in any market. The sheer value of aggregated goods in the U.S. economy is more than $1 trillion.

Aggregations usually sell goods at predetermined prices, though arguably no price is permanently fixed. Retail shoppers can—and sometimes do—lobby successfully for price breaks. Business buyers negotiate when they buy in bulk or pay early. But by and large, fixed price has been a fixture of the industrial economy because physical products are easy to price. The formula is simple: Price equals marginal production and distribution costs plus a markup that covers overhead and provides a reasonable return to investors. Services too have production inputs and distribution costs and are priced roughly the same way. Information has always differed. The real costs of producing a newspaper article, for example, are sunk into the first copy. The marginal costs of printing and distribution greatly influence the newspaper's price. As Carl Shapiro and Hal Varian point out in their book *Information Rules,* the Internet changes the rules for information goods, because their marginal distribution costs tend toward zero.[4]

Despite its long tradition, fixed pricing is under assault. Not just for information, but for services and hard goods as well. Whether it is Coca-Cola tuning its prices on hot days (in real time, across a network of smart vending machines) or Wal-Mart setting prices to maximize the return on a basket of household goods (instead of its constituent items), fixed pricing is fated to become less common. We discussed dynamic pricing in chapter 2.

AGGREGATIONS: DEATH (AND LIFE) OF A SALESMAN

Aggregations are as old as commerce itself. They were last transformed during the Industrial Revolution. Then, as now, network technologies—railway, telegraph, and postal services—catalyzed the change. General merchants, town markets, and country storekeepers were swept aside by new (at the time) Aggregation business models like the department store (Macy's), the mail-order house (Sears, Roebuck and Company), the retail chain (Woolworth's), and the specialized wholesaler. Such industrial-age aggregators dominated distribution through the twentieth century.

Traditional Aggregations face a new set of strategic challenges. So do producers that depend on aggregators to distribute or market their goods. Regardless of your industry, you will face one of four scenarios:

Scenario one: Outsider Aggregation b-webs invade your industry, design new business models, build digital infrastructures, and offer customers unprecedented kinds of value.

Scenario two: Producers deal directly with customers.

Scenario three: Existing middlemen recognize the promises and perils of the digital economy and transform themselves into b-webs.

Scenario four (most likely): Scenarios one through three all happen.

In chapter 1 we labeled what happens in scenario four as *polymediation,* or the proliferation of value-adding intermediaries between buyers and sellers. Polymediation already occurs in lively consumer markets like entertainment and in more mundane business-to-business trade.

STRATEGIC POINTS OF LEVERAGE

Consider the $1.3 trillion global market for operating resources that companies consume, including goods like computers, office supplies, telecommunications equipment, and travel. (Direct inputs to production like General Motors's steel purchases or Microsoft's labor costs don't count.) Businesses of all sizes, in all industries, must have operating resources.

The Ariba Network aggregates suppliers and consumers of operating resources. Its customers include medium-sized companies of a few hundred employees, Fortune 500 giants Chevron and Dow, and consumer-direct computer manufacturer Dell. Dell is also a supplier on the network, as are Chemdex, retailers Staples and Barnes & Noble, and seventy-year-old maintenance-supply distributor Grainger (proof that traditional Aggregations can change their spots and adapt to the new economy).

Ariba quickly became one of the NASDAQ's hottest stocks. By January 2000, its share value had grown 800 percent since its June 1999 IPO, and most analysts continued to rate it a "moderate to strong buy" for a relatively new company in an obscure market—operating resource management (ORM).

Before Ariba came along, ORM wasn't much of a market. Most companies purchased operating resources from a patchwork of suppliers with whom they maintained loose, independent relationships. The buying process—from order initiation to fulfillment—was awash with paper. Cataloging and billing standards did not exist. Internal purchasing systems, typically enterprise resource planning (ERP) software running on client-server technology platforms, weren't designed for ORM. Anyone in a company could requisition a new office chair, but few could access or understand the complex ERP systems. Maverick buyers skirted lax corporate controls and paid premium prices to nonapproved suppliers, or simply bought things they weren't supposed to. Maverick buying alone added a third more costs to an already inefficient process.

In early 1996, Ariba's seven founders saw an opportunity for an entirely new business model. The potential was huge, since any company in any industry would benefit from ORM. The business process solution had to efficiently and effortlessly connect millions of end-customers (the employees within the corporations) to thousands of suppliers and facilitate millions of transactions. It demanded an open, scalable, ubiquitous network—perfect conditions for an Aggregation b-web.

Ariba began by focusing on a single element of customer value—convenience. In the words of Ariba cofounder Bobby Lent, Ariba was searching for the "strategic high ground."[5] A relatively uncomplicated piece of Ariba software, browser based and accessible over a corporate intranet, permitted individual employees to initiate purchase orders. The interface was clean, simple, and intuitive. Ariba calls it a *walk-up user interface*, an application whose use is self-apparent. Because it was convenient, employees used it and implicitly conformed to corporate purchasing controls and protocols. Ariba software, though not yet fully integrated with suppliers, saved its customers lots of money.

The company next moved to increasing selection. It had carefully chosen its first customers, who were not necessarily the largest purchasers of operating resources, but were respected names like Visa and AT&T. In 1997, Ariba approached the supply community with a compelling value proposition: Big, important companies use Ariba software; if you want access to them, you'd better adopt our standards. According to Bobby Lent, landing Cisco as a customer was a powerful draw for suppliers: "Here they had the godfathers of the Internet telling them to join." Many did. With more suppliers, selection grew. Racing to critical mass, Ariba leveraged its growing selection to sign up more customers.

Ariba's closing gambit was the Ariba Network, an open ORM marketplace on the Web. The Ariba Network delivers the remaining elements of its value proposition. Web-based transaction routing removes steps and costs from order fulfillment. Employees initiate purchase orders that are routed directly to suppliers electronically. Paper costs vanish. Cross-vendor searching and supplier rating services help buyers match goods to meet their needs. Efficiency drives down prices. Deep-focused, organized information makes the Ariba Network tick.

From 1997 to 1999, annual revenues grew to more than $40 million dollars. The network has over 20,000 suppliers and more than fifty customers who spend a combined $150 billion on operating resources.

Ariba approached business-model innovation by identifying and systematically applying strategic points of leverage to its target market. Aggregations should identify strategic leverage points by asking the following questions: How do internetworked technologies affect selection, organization, price, matching, convenience, and fulfillment, both independently and in relation to one another? Any element of the value proposition that can be delivered more efficiently, in greater quantities, or even just differently is a strategic point of leverage. Next ask, How do customers affect the value proposition, both as individual contributors and as members of a community? By finding new ways to combine the value elements and engage customers, new business models emerge.

Selection

Vast cross-vendor selection in business-to-business Aggregations like Ariba is a powerful customer draw. Selection has long been a point of leverage for business-to-consumer aggregators as well. In the 1920s, the self-serve supermarkets (Memphis-based Piggly Wiggly was the first) bulldozed the corner grocer with big stores and great selection. In the early 1980s, warehouse retailers like Price Club and Costco returned the favor; they blindsided supermarkets with their big-box no-frills format (less selection and bigger lots) and grabbed most of the industry's growth for a decade.[6] Category killers like Toys "R" Us and Staples combined narrow product focus with substantial depth and dominated retail in the 1990s. Physical retailers could always trump competitors with greater selection, provided they could cope with greater investments in inventory, real estate, shelf space, and so on.

Digital Aggregations must rethink selection. For one, shoppers can use the Internet to perform broad, thorough, and cost-effective cross-vendor searches to generate selection on their own. Intelligent agents (see sidebar) make consumers more self-sufficient. Customers no longer value aggregators for selection alone.

Because the Internet facilitates the separation of selection from physical inventory, online retailers can start out with a super selection of goods. Of the 1 million titles Amazon.com offered on its first day of operation in 1995, it stocked but a handful. Five years later, the title selection had grown to 4.5 million. The company now carries lots of warehouse inventory, but still only stocks a fraction of the selection it offers. Amazon.com's "sell all, carry few" strategy demands complex b-web orchestration and integration. The site seamlessly presents selection and availability data on books from multiple content providers, including distributors like Ingram Book Group and Baker & Taylor, and individual publishers like McGraw-Hill and IDG Books.

Selection provides new competitive opportunities when it crosses traditional product, industry, and geographic boundaries. Customer needs—not traditional market categories—should dictate its scope. Groceries anchor Streamline's selection, but dry cleaning, bottled-water services, home video rentals—products and services that complement busy suburban lifestyles—help to differentiate it. Streamline would do well to add banking, car-pooling, or diaper services to the mix. Amazon.com built its selection masterfully, moving quickly into CDs, videos, DVDs (digital video discs), toys, software, and electronics after gaining its stranglehold on books. The company's auctions and Z-Shops (a diverse collection of merchants who rent space and pay transaction fees) elevate its selection to more than 19 million items.

ORGANIZATION

Ariba's selection covers everything from embroidered hats to Ethernet cable. It organizes selection first around a business function (e.g., ORM) and second around customers. Buyers in turn organize content by frequency of purchase and vendor preference. Generally, the organization in business-to-business Aggregations makes buying convenient and efficient.

In retail, content organization has typically served two masters—buyers and sellers. Aggregations arrange goods predictably and intuitively so that buyers can easily find what they need. But they also design the organization of goods to influence buyer decisions. Sellers pay for spots on eye-level shelves or high-exposure end displays. Physical supermarket layouts maximize shopping time, not convenience. To get from produce to dairy, you have to cross the entire store.

Digital Aggregations can't exploit space as easily. An online grocer can't force customers to view pages of steaks before letting them buy vegetables. Similarly, if Charles Schwab consistently used navigational tricks to promote its own branded mutual funds over those of its competitors, customers would question its objectivity.

Some Aggregations grant customers explicit control over organization. Excite, a consumer portal, invites users to create personal portals where they choose content layouts and pick the color of fonts and headers. People who invest time to customize an Excite page are more likely to return. Western Governor's University lets students organize their

AGENTS

Software agents, especially those deemed intelligent, may turn the entire Web into a virtual megamall. Although agents are a boon for customers, they could render Aggregations obsolete.

That's because software agents can easily replicate many of the Aggregation's basic functions. Simple agents like Jango and Bargain Finder create selection by searching and evaluating goods across vendors. Customers choose criteria like price, manufacturer, and brand. (It is worth noting that the agents of 1999 typically searched at the retail/wholesale level, not the producer level. Rather than disintermediate the channels, they polymediated them.)

The next generation of more sophisticated agents will satisfy requests such as, "My daughter graduates high school today and I have no idea what kids like these days." In this case, the agent helps the customer both refine the request and find suitable goods. This kind of service could be considered a 911 service for gifts. You can, for example, ask it to find you an unusual gift for a co-worker for under $20 dollars. (Note: We tried, and it suggested a juniper bonsai for $34.) These agents compete with the Aggregation's matching function.

Agents could also force Aggregations to negotiate price. Imagine agents fomenting bidding wars among vendors as they prowl the Web hunting for the best offer. To counter, vendors might use agents of their own.

Tomorrow's agents will create ultrasavvy shoppers with even more control over the value mix. Agents will sort out complex trade-offs between price, quality, brand, delivery, and payment options in order to maximize customer value. This is precisely what Aggregations do.

education by choosing courses from multiple educational institutions. Other Aggregations automatically organize content based on a customer's past visits. MP3.com's "My Favorites" box compiles a user's past music choices; with one click the selections play again as a continuous list.

Of all the elements of the Aggregation's value proposition, organization has the greatest promise for innovation. A bricks-and-mortar retailer can play around with the static orientation of goods in three dimensions; a publisher is confined to just two. The organization of digital content can be multidimensional, dynamic, and interactive. Time and the responsive reactions of online content replace the third dimension of physical space.

PlanetRx, an online drugstore, organizes content around multiple attributes, like traditional departments or brands. Its "eCenters" classify goods according to demographics (baby care, elderly care) or afflictions (Alzheimer's disease, breast cancer), and track a customer's shopping path to understand purchase motivations and improve service.

Digitally organized content can have unlimited depth. Behind every item on the shelf in a physical retail store lurks another just like it or an empty shelf. Digital shelf space goes on forever. Imagine placing a *Terminator 2* DVD in your electronic shopping basket and immediately seeing all *Terminator*-related content: video games, action figures, other Arnold Schwarzenegger films, links to fan sites, and more. Click the "Arnold" icon, and the content reorganizes to show you video clips of *Pumping Iron* (a 1970s documentary film on bodybuilding), an invitation to join the Republican Party, and a complimentary electronic issue of *Cigar Magazine*.

Matching

Separation of selection from physical inventory can disrupt buyer behavior. Clothing shoppers like to touch and try on garments. Cosmetics shoppers want to test colors against their natural skin tones. Here, Web retailers are at a disadvantage compared with their physical counterparts.

Some Aggregations have created innovative second-generation digital solutions. Lands' End Web shoppers can build and dress personalized three-dimensional models based on body type, hair color and style, and skin tone. Swedish clothing boutique Boo.com offers an even more elaborate virtual shopping experience, where shoppers can spin virtual models and interact with sales avatars. Such features may work better as marketing gimmicks than as matching tools. The best services are simple. Furniture.com, for example, delivers real fabric swatches in forty-eight hours.

Customers can taste bits of digital content for free. Most online CD retailers post audio samples. *The Wall Street Journal Interactive* gives away archived headlines and bylines.

Business-to-business buying is a higher-stakes game that runs on information. Portals such as PlasticsNet aggregate content from supply catalogs, technical reference guides, and the brains of salespeople, enabling business-to-business buyers to make better purchase decisions in a fraction of the time.

Matching can be a viable business unto itself. Unlike a traditional real-estate agent, who benefits most when you purchase one of his or her listed properties, HomeAdvisor helps you find the right home from among all available, by aggregating a rich assortment of information to support the buying process. HomeAdvisor collects referral fees from its partner mortgage lenders when it brokers a good match.

Price

The world will beat a path to your door for a better mousetrap—or a cheaper one. In the short term, Aggregation b-webs can leverage reduced transaction costs to slash prices or to cover the cost of added services like free home delivery. Customers will flock to the Web, since everybody loves a good deal. In the long term, these cost advantages will erode, and Aggregation b-webs will compete by differentiating their offerings and knowing their customers intimately.

In a world where auctions and other dynamic-pricing business models are spreading fast, Aggregations will bend the rules of fixed price to compete. This used to be hard to do, since all buyers shared price knowledge. But as the Web evolves from a network of public access points to a collection of personal shopping portals, everything becomes customizable—including price. For example, Aggregations can accomplish the following:

Reward customer loyalty. Typical businesses have little incentive to reward customer loyalty. Since loyalty reflects the value that customers place on products or services, you can charge your best customers premium prices, suggest Don Peppers and Martha Rogers.[7] Many companies already do: Introductory offers for magazine subscriptions reward new customers, not loyal ones. Peppers and Rogers argue that with customization, sellers can actually increase margins for their best customers over time. Maybe, but customers spurn such practices in the offline world. Customers in ultratransparent b-webs may not stand for such discrimination either.

What about the opposite—rewarding your best customers with lower prices? Loyal customers are already the most profitable. They buy more, and their predictable demand patterns and low servicing costs lower operating expenses. Loyal customers refer new ones and, when plugged into commerce communities, become powerful marketing agents. Aggregations could adjust prices to reflect the value that individual customers generate. An Internet grocer could issue year-end rebates to high-volume shoppers with low fulfillment costs. Lowering prices for loyal customers reinforces digital customer capital.

Bundle, bundle, and bundle. Discounts for volume purchases (buy two suits, get a third for half price) or purchases of complementary goods (buy a case of wine, and the glasses are free) are common, but not very interesting. On the Web, where traditional industry borders are dissolving and technology makes the improbable probable, we can imagine entirely new ways to combine and price goods. For example, the price of a basket of groceries could change in real time according to the number of like-branded products it contained. Consumers would build their shopping baskets like jigsaw puzzles, piecing together individual items that together fetched the best overall price. Or, grocery b-webs, in concert with financial-services content partners, could contribute a penny to a customer's education savings fund with each purchase of a box of Pampers.

Think small. Capture the collective wealth crammed into penny jars across North America, and you'll be rich. People rarely turn this copper into gold because the transaction costs (rolling the coins and lugging them to the bank) exceed the value of the transaction. Sellers have the same problem when trying to collect small payments on the Web. Micropayment systems, capable of clearing tiny transactions at negligible costs, crashed and burned in the early days of the Web. But the problem will be solved, and a panoply of new pricing models unleashed. Global Sources aggregates product information (from silicon chips to rubber flip-flops) from thousands of suppliers. The value of a single product spec sheet to any customer is minuscule. Without micropayments, Global Sources couldn't think of charging for individual records. With micropayments, Global Sources has an alternative to its advertising-driven business model.

Convenience

The epitome of convenience is doing nothing at all—having your needs met without exertion or effort. More convenient still would be having your needs met before you're even aware that you need anything.

The Web changes enduring notions of convenience like location and store hours. People do business on every corner of cyberspace at any time, day or night. From initiation to fulfillment, a convenient e-commerce experience conforms to customer needs, expectations, and behaviors. And to borrow from Bill Gates, it demands the integration of the Web into people's lifestyles, not the other way around.

Streamline's "Don't Run Out" service offers a glimpse into the future of convenience. Users specify their must-have items, like razors and laundry detergent, and Streamline replenishes them automatically. Today, customers set the replenishment frequency in advance, but tomorrow they won't have to. The grocer will learn their consumption patterns and never let them run out.

Fulfillment

Amazon.com's fulfillment model has evolved since it was just a bookseller. Then, fulfillment was simple and easily off-loaded to b-web partners. Amazon.com forwarded orders to Ingram, where they were packaged and handed over to UPS for home delivery. Amazon.com paid Ingram a premium for drop-shipping and charged customers a separate delivery fee. As its book sales grew, the online bookseller began carrying a limited inventory of popular titles. Filling orders from stock yielded higher margins and lessened the risk of stock outs, which threatened customer relationships. When the company moved into music, movies, software, electronics, and toys, it continued with this model, forging partnerships with content providers (distributors, wholesalers, and manufacturers) who were willing to drop-ship to customers and stocking selected high-turning inventory itself.

In 1999, Amazon.com built seven large-scale distribution centers across the United States (to the chagrin of some analysts and shareholders who viewed Amazon.com's leanness as a source of agility and profits). But the growing complexity of its business left the company with no alternative. A customer might order items from ten different suppliers at once for next-day delivery. More important, Amazon.com's prospects for long-term profitability depended on increased margins and growing per-customer share through cross-selling.

Like Webvan, Amazon.com focused on fulfillment as a source of advantage:

Higher margins. Amazon.com will remove many distributors from the selling ladder and deal directly with producers. Rather than pay distributor markups plus drop-shipping premiums, the company will buy in volume, at reduced prices, and collect shipping costs from customers.

Sophisticated demand management. Amazon.com uses best-of-breed applications from distribution software supplier i2 to mine its customer databases and predict demand. This information helps determine the items to profitably stock in inventory.

Order stratification. Amazon.com employs an "A, B, C" order stratification system that allocates fulfillment responsibilities to the appropriate content provider. "A" items are bestsellers to be filled from Amazon.com's inventory. Distributors ship less popular "B" items just in time. "C" items are typically drop-shipped by distributors like Ingram.

Efficiency. The entire system is designed to maximize customer satisfaction through on-time delivery while minimizing costs.

ENGAGE CUSTOMERS TO CREATE VALUE

So far we've focused on the value that Aggregations deliver to customers. Successful b-webs engage customers in value creation as well.

Customers don't always know how much they contribute. Procter & Gamble estimates that customer contributions represent 13 percent of the grocery industry's cost structure. Assuming gross margins of 20 percent and total U.S. sales of around $450 billion, that works out to $10 billion per year.

Customers generate valuable information as they shop. In a traditional retail context, the information trail that shoppers leave is unrecoverable. What *didn't* they buy, and why? What evaluation criteria did they use? Which of their needs went unmet or unexpressed? Which in-store promotions did they fail to notice? How might they evaluate the overall shopping experience? Supermarket operators scrape together a partial story at the checkout counter and wisely use the information to manage inventory, tinker with product selection, and tweak promotional strategies. But traditional retailers miss the opportunity to create higher orders of value for the customer.

Interestingly, the corner grocer of the early twentieth century more closely resembles today's b-webs than do supermarkets. Corner grocers knew their patron's names, preferences, consumption rates, and buying habits. They greeted familiar faces at the front door and tailored the shopping experience to individual tastes. From the busy mother fetching a prearranged order to the tireless penny-pincher looking for the best deal, the corner grocer tailored the experience to each and all.

Digital Aggregations offer the same kind of customer intimacy by enabling customers to substitute some or all of their traditional inputs—time, labor, and money—with information. Customers do less work; their information does more. Customers provide crucial inputs to nearly all the Aggregation's value-added services.

Streamline initiates its customer relationships with a home inventory to glean data on commonly consumed products, preferred brands, and base levels of stock. After Streamline posts the information online, it immediately becomes networked customer capital that its entire b-web leverages to create value. Customers use it as a dynamic shopping list. Streamline uses it to optimize its buying, inventory, and fulfillment activities—it knows what the new customers will purchase before they ever set foot in its store. Suppliers like P&G use the information to design targeted promotional campaigns.

CUSTOMER RELATIONSHIP MANAGEMENT

Successful Aggregation b-webs capture and create value from customer relationships. The winners will deploy customer relationship management (CRM) applications to integrate customers into their b-webs. Dominating a burgeoning CRM industry in late 1999 were a handful of vendors, including enterprise application veteran Siebel Systems and Net-focused start-ups BroadVision and E.piphany.

CRM does two things. First, it allows businesses to discover who their customers are. The software captures data from multiple sources: customer behaviors (click-and-search patterns), direct inquiries (profile data, surveys), and transactions (preferences, purchase frequency). The data is integrated and shared among customer-facing business functions like marketing, sales, and customer service. The groups are thus armed with fundamental information, such as who their customers are, how they behave, and what they want.

Second, CRM enables businesses to respond quickly, coherently, and appropriately to unique customer circumstances. For example, CRM analysis could trigger a timely promotional discount and convert a window shopper into a buyer. Or, it could signal the need for a customer-service intervention, like a phone call, to salvage a relationship. Merchandizing strategies, like up-selling higher-quality, higher-margin goods, can be executed with pinpoint accuracy. With CRM, Aggregations personalize the customer experience, from first impression through the entire relationship cycle.

CRM lets businesses get beyond professing one-to-one customer service to actually delivering it. In the process, companies reduce customer acquisition and servicing costs and increase customer satisfaction and profitability.

Many firms opt for packaged CRM applications over custom-built proprietary systems. In addition to being cheaper to acquire and implement, packaged CRM enables these firms to get up and running in a fraction of the time. Other firms, including Cisco, Dell, and Amazon.com, invest in homegrown CRM as a source of competitive advantage. Web-based CRM is a b-web-enabling technology, allowing context providers to network customer capital and share it with partners.

The Community Effect

Information captured from individual customers creates value that increases exponentially when shared across entire buying communities. A great failure of industrial-age aggregators has been their inability to capture value from community. (Online community is an Alliance-type dimension of the b-web mix, as we discuss in chapter 5.)

In Aggregation b-webs, customer communities become vital digital capital. Members of E*Trade's community, some 200,000 strong, swap information on hot (or not) stocks or industries to watch, which helps them make better trading decisions. Community drives individual investors to purchase mutual funds from content providers like Scudder and J. P. Morgan or research reports from InvesTools. E*Trade monitors community discussions to better understand its customers' trading styles and behaviors and to improve its value proposition accordingly.

Online travel site Expedia offers forums in which travelers can get the scoop on places they have never been. The forums, which cover topics like family travel and amusement parks, benefit Expedia's content providers, like major airlines and hotels, because they segment the user base.

Digital customer capital of community, mixed with the structural capital of software, creates yet more value. Amazon.com's collaborative filtering software recommends books, music, and videos based on the purchases of other like-minded shoppers. MediConsult mines its user communities for useful advice generated in discussions and forums. Business-to-business Web communities are logical extensions of professional and industry associations that have flourished since the industrial age.

KEY SUCCESS FACTORS

Design value propositions that let customers conduct business "their way." Customer processes, not your processes, should guide you. Understand how customers purchase and use the goods that you sell, and optimize your value proposition around those preferences and behaviors.

Treat everyone as an information Aggregation. Information drives all business models, whatever the core good: physical products, services, or information. Aggregators of physical products or services manage information *about* their products as a separate, online good to improve customer services (selection, organization, matching) and create efficiencies that drive prices down.

Organize content to enhance customer experience and control. Organization changes the situation from static and three-dimensional to dynamic and multidimensional. Content organization is infinitely customizable, based on explicit customer preferences and implicit shopping behaviors.

Extract value from customer communities. Networked customer communities become self-serving, which means that they create content and solve their own customer-service problems. Communities instill customer loyalty in Aggregations.

Face the fulfillment challenge. If you sell physical goods on the Web, you still have to get the goods to customers via conventional Distributive Networks, like the mail. The magnitude of the challenge varies with the size of the assortment and the complexity of the good. The make-versus-buy question is central and can lead to strategic advantage.

LEADER'S GUIDE TO AGGREGATIONS

Definition: Aggregations intermediate between producers and customers, enabling the flow of goods and services, and creating value for both. Their value proposition includes multiple elements—selection, organization, matching, price, convenience, and fulfillment. Context providers in Aggregations define and execute an optimal combination of these elements for any given market opportunity.

Significance: Aggregations are everywhere—in business-to-consumer and business-to-business markets for products, services, and information—and they aren't going away. Most industries will reach a steady state of polymediation, in which multiple Aggregations, each with a unique value proposition, exist between producers and suppliers.

Types: Aggregations can take many forms, including the following:

- *Superaggregations* create super selection across traditional product categories, in search of scale efficiencies and large returns on investments in customer relationship capital. They typically make money the old-fashioned way—through product margins. Examples include Amazon.com and Checkout.com.

- *E-sources,* like E*Trade and Travelocity, aggregate information related to complex or risky purchase decisions. They empower customers by granting them access to resources traditionally only available to specialized service providers. E-sources earn revenues from transactions.

- *E-brokers,* like Chemdex and Milpro.com, consolidate fragmented markets. For suppliers, e-brokers aggregate demand. For customers, they aggregate supply, reducing search and evaluation costs and usually price. E-brokers typically charge commissions to suppliers in exchange for the cost efficiencies they facilitate.

- *Integrator b-webs* like Streamline and HomeAdvisor rationalize previously disjointed purchasing, business, and consumer processes. Some, like Streamline, charge customers for simplification. Others, like HomeAdvisor, charge their content providers finders' fees.

- *Industry hubs,* such as the Ariba Network and PlasticsNet, aggregate industry information and services, and broker business-to-business transactions. These hubs are becoming important links in efficient Internet-enabled Value Chains. Industry hubs either charge sellers for access to well-defined market segments or take a cut on the transactions they facilitate.

- *Consumer portals* and hubs, like Yahoo! and Excite, attract vast numbers of customers with free aggregated content and services. As customers act on their preferences, they create sharply defined market segments. Consumer portals generate revenue by charging sellers of products and services for these segments, through advertising, page placements, and links.

Key transformation: The Internet facilitates the separation of buying processes from fulfillment processes, enabling new business models and propelling existing ones to greater efficiencies.

4 value chains

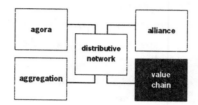

A new logic of value creation now drives the production of goods and services. Demand-driven Value Chains are replacing old make-and-sell, push models, as producers build b-webs that link and respond directly to customers. Value-Chain innovators increasingly delegate physical production and other non-core functions to b-web partners around the world, focusing instead on value-added design process and relationship management. The new value proposition is service-enhanced customization. A new generation of applications will ultimately link a global web of b-webs. The result? Innovation, quality, time to market, and return on invested capital.

CISCO: THE QUINTESSENTIAL B-WEB LEADER

In 1998, several global manufacturers—Bay Networks, Cisco Systems, Ericsson, Fujitsu, Lucent, Motorola, Nortel, and 3Com—were competing for the right to sell telecom equipment to Italian companies. The government stipulated that the winning bidder must establish a manufacturing facility in Italy. For most contenders, this requirement posed a problem.

Why build a plant in Italy? How would it fit into their global game plan? Would the value of the contract offset the investment risks? While its competitors grappled with these questions, Cisco cut a deal with a local manufacturer. Within weeks, Cisco had its name on a plant in Italy. It was one of the first foreign companies to win government approval. For Cisco, signing up a partner rather than spending millions to build a plant of its own was an obvious decision. But none of its competitors did the same thing. Are Cisco managers smarter than their counterparts in other companies? No. Their webs are wired differently.

Cisco's leadership model crystallized in response to a crisis. When its simple, box-oriented router business encountered new competition during the early 1990s, the company augmented its value proposition to include leading-edge, comprehensive network solutions. When Cisco realized it wasn't innovating fast enough, it began forming partnerships with other technology companies and embarked on an aggressive acquisitions campaign (forty companies in five years, topped by a 1999 deal for Cerent in exchange for $6.9 billion in stock). When the opportunity arose to use the Net as a sales, support, and partnering infrastructure, Cisco quickly established what became the world's busiest commerce Web site. By September 1999 (these numbers rise every month), 78 percent of Cisco's orders—$30 million per day—came via the Cisco Connection Online Web site. And the site routed 80 percent of customer-service inquiries, resulting in claimed annual savings of $75 million. In January 2000, Cisco's market valuation exceeded $360 billion. Its 1998 revenues per employee were $689,000, compared with $271,000 for Lucent and $234,000 for Nortel, its biggest competitors. No wonder Cisco has become a model that its own customers want to copy.

What is the company's secret of success? Is it great products? Its notorious acquisition strategy? Web commerce? Maybe it's the company's near fanatical agnosticism about technology, a willingness to go wherever its customers and the logic of innovation might take it. Or perhaps it's salesmanship, demonstrated by CEO John Chambers. Of course, it's all of the above.

But what makes this success possible? The answer is Cisco's revolutionary Value-Chain b-web business model—how the company orchestrates the value contributions of its customers, distribution partners, suppliers, and employees. The structural, relationship, and customer capital pools inside Cisco's Value-Chain b-web are the foundation of its competitive advantage.

If Ford and "Fordism" were the reference model for Value Chains of the industrial age, then Cisco—rather, "Ciscoism"—is the model for Value-Chain b-webs of the digital economy.

VALUE CHAINS DEFINED

Value Chains design, produce, and deliver products or services to meet a specific set of customer needs. As the spinners of wealth in any economy, Value Chains first identify and define needs, then design and build solutions. Through a sequence of steps, Value Chains transform raw materials—atoms in the physical world and bits in the electronic world—into finished goods and services. They deliver the goods to points of distribution or directly to end-customers and often provide documentation, service, and support. Value is added each step of the way, from the extraction of raw materials through to customer fulfillment.

In a Value-Chain b-web, the context provider—like Cisco—leads the process (figure 4-1). It defines the goals and coordinates the integration of value contributions from content providers, including third-party designers and technologists, parts suppliers, assemblers, distributors, resellers, solution integrators, and other partners. Typically, the context provider also plays the role of a content provider (Cisco produces software content, for example). Most important, the context provider controls the design of the product and choreographs the key steps in value integration.

Two Kinds of Value Chain

Value Chains usually bring to mind routine mass production. Industrial-age routine production is "product-centric," focused on making, moving, and marketing physical goods. Activities tend to be fixed, and the goods are uniform—mass customized at best. Improvement initiatives traditionally focus on process efficiency and cost.

The make-and-sell logic of physical capital drove the old production model. Marketing strove to quantify and predict consumer demand, but mostly, customer integration (relationship capital) was flimsy. Goods were designed for mass markets and production efficiency.

Inventory is the necessary evil of routine production—the buffer between a steady stream of producer output and the idiosyncrasies of

FIGURE 4-1 Cisco Value Map

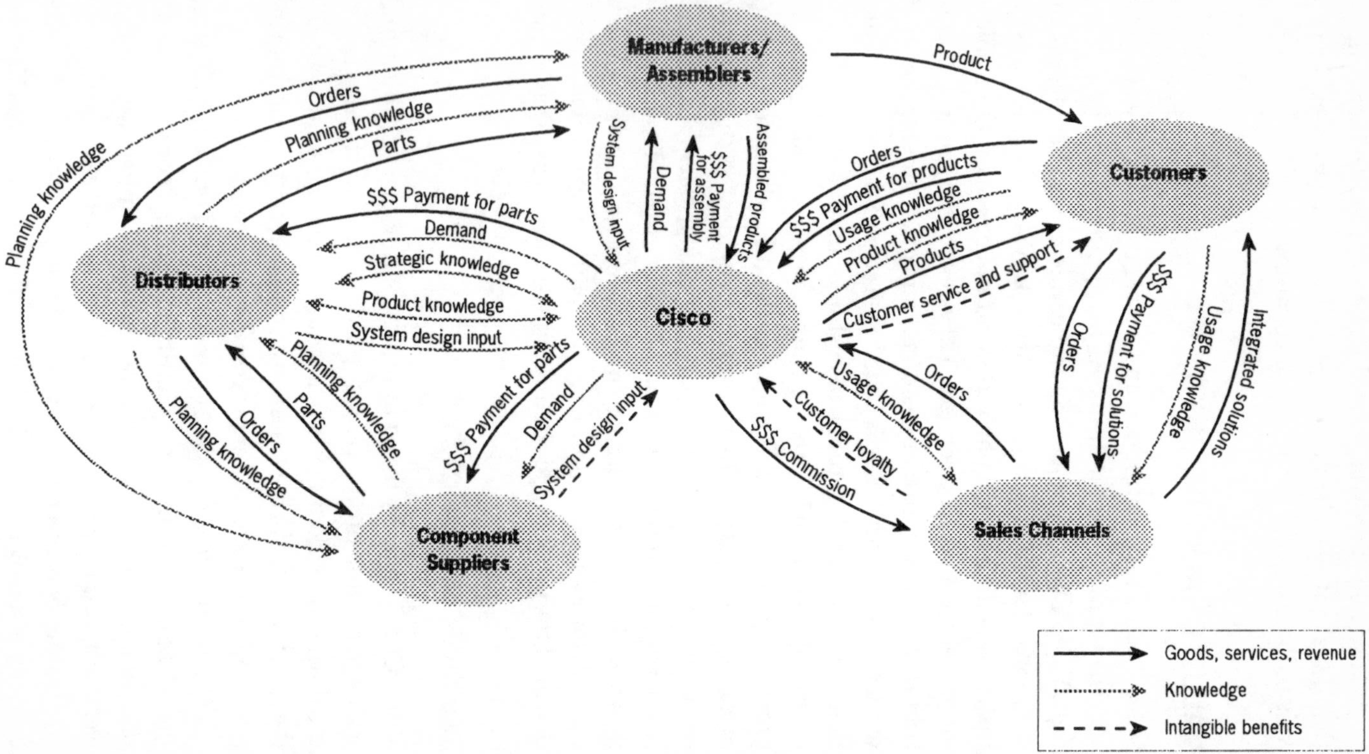

Legend:
- Goods, services, revenue
- Knowledge
- Intangible benefits

customer demand. The Fords and GMs of the 1990s automated linkages to their closest suppliers, only to displace inventory management problems to their suppliers' suppliers. Make-to-stock and continuous-replenishment production models both support a make-and-sell approach. Demand forecasts drive make-to-stock models, whereas with continuous replenishment, producers receive orders that replace sales.

A second type of Value Chain works quite differently. We call it shop production, rather than routine production. Typical "shops" include professional services (e.g., health care, legal, consulting), construction, and industrial research and development.[1] Shops create custom solutions in response to unique demands, such as transforming an ill patient into a healthy one; converting zoning approvals, blueprints, and construction materials into a building; and turning a vision into a product design.

Shop differs from routine production in three ways. First, shop activities are not routine, but styled and scaled to the customer or project. Each customer or project involves a unique set of value-creating activities: Every patient, construction project, research and development initiative, and so forth, is different.

Second, rather than follow the make-and-sell logic of a traditional routine producer, shops are driven entirely by demand. In other words, the end-customer initiates the value-creating cycle. Only after selling a good does a shop make it. In a legal office, a client solicits advice on a problem, which the counsel then addresses. In a medical practice, there is no "production" without a sick patient seeking treatment.

Third, a shop's customer usually participates in the design, and sometimes the delivery, of the solution. The client for a construction project provides necessary input to the design. A patient contributes to his or her wellness by following a treatment regime and providing feedback.

Content providers in shops tend to be specialized and distributed. Efficiency and effectiveness depend on high coordination across teams of experts. Project management is a critical competency, especially since projects are iterative, involving several rounds of input and output, review, and redesign. Management of resources—knowledge, in particular—is crucial. Management consulting firms, who are classic shop producers, were among the first to use information technology to capture and deliver knowledge to the point of need, turning human capital into structural capital.

Routine and shop production were often mutually exclusive in the industrial age. Now, Levi's custom-designs its "Original Spin" blue jeans on demand, using three-dimensional body-scan technology. U.S. health management organizations try—and sometimes succeed—in delivering top-rate personal care while imposing factory-like efficiencies.

One way to think about Dell's build-to-order business model is as a revolutionary hybrid of routine and shop production. Customers order directly from the producer, bypassing channels and avoiding guessing games. If there are no orders, then Dell won't make anything. As in a shop setting, the consumer configures the purchase during the ordering process. A buyer can customize twenty different features of a personal computer.

Cisco, another routine/shop hybrid, deals in even greater complexity than Dell does. As described earlier, everything that Cisco provides—hardware, software, and services—must be assembled and configured to order. At the same time, many of its components are mass-produced.

THE CRISIS OF INDUSTRIAL-AGE VALUE CHAINS

Industrial-age business-model design was originally about vertical integration, that is, linking the disparate elements of the Value Chain through ownership. For Ford, General Electric, Standard Oil, and other giants, forward and backward vertical integration was a response to the high transaction costs of creating and maintaining linkages outside the firm.

Vertical integration meant unity and coherence. Command-control management cemented relationships and focused processes across the internal supply chain. And it seemed cheaper to "make" a product or service than to "buy."

But for all its benefits, vertical integration had severe limitations:

- True vertical integration was only possible for the big. Even there, wholly owned supply subsidiaries could not achieve the economies of scale needed to reap the benefits of "insourcing."

- Vertical integration resulted in big, discombobulated firms that were inflexible and difficult to manage. Conditions that justified making rather than buying were rarely static, and corporations could not readily act on innovation and changes in the competitive marketplace.

• Absolute self-sufficiency was risky. If an upstream subsidiary could not deliver the goods, then the firm could not always rely on an independent supplier to bail out the enterprise.

• A vertical business might have been a jack-of-all-trades, but it was master of none. The Singer Sewing Machine Company, like Ford and Hearst, even managed and logged its own timber forests. Such strategies often meant low quality, slow innovation, and major gaffes. Doing everything poorly is not a competitive strategy.

• Vertical integration plus command-control management all but destroyed the innovation and creativity of the firm's human capital. In the digital economy, this capital is at a premium.

As we explained in chapter 1, Japanese management techniques influenced attempts to improve Value-Chain performance. The strategy theorist Michael Porter points out that industrial-age Japanese businesses exploited the potential of Value-Chain linkages inside and outside the enterprise far better than did their North American competitors.[2]

From MRP (materials requirements planning) and JIT (just-in-time delivery) to TQM (total quality management), lean production, and outsourcing, each initiative sought to reduce costs and tighten the supply chain. Japanese *keiretsu* pioneered interindustry collaboration, whereas JIT minimized lead times and practically eliminated inventory costs. But such improvements netted disappointing productivity gains, since information systems and business culture remained inside the firm.

In the dying years of the industrial age, Value Chains were still inefficient, incoherent, and supply-driven—and the customer remained outside the loop. Having learned quality management from the Japanese, wrestled with electronic data interchange (EDI), flirted with the virtual corporation, and reengineered themselves to distraction, North American producers (whether they knew it or not) were ready for something new. Enter the Internet.

TRANSFORMING VALUE CHAINS

Porter suggests that to understand Value Chains, we should view them as a series of linked value-creating activities. *Linkages* refer to the flow of goods and information between activities both inside and outside the firm. Linkages, Porter says, affect "the way one value activity is performed and the cost of performance of another."[3]

Returning to our theme of transaction costs, linkages are transaction mechanisms; the better your linkages, the lower your transaction costs, and the more efficient and effective (and profitable) is your b-web. Industrial-age Value Chains were hampered by clunky and expensive hub-and-spoke linkages—at best EDI and proprietary client-server computing. Pervasive, elegant, and cheap Internet technologies now enable true end-to-end integration, fusing enterprises with one another and bringing the customer inside the Value Chain. In contrast to the static hub-and-spoke models of the previous era, digital applications engender a fluid and interconnected environment of plug-and-play Value Chains.

Cisco calls its b-web the single-enterprise system. Through networked applications, the company connects chip manufacturers, component distributors, contract manufacturers, logistics companies, employees, systems integrators, and customers. These b-web participants can perform like one firm because they all draw upon the same Internet-based well of information. Paul Esling, a former manager at parts distributor Avnet, told us, "For all practical purposes, we *are* Cisco."

Cisco's core products—networking devices and software—are more or less mass-produced. Though known as a manufacturer, Cisco itself owns just two of the thirty-eight plants that assemble its products. It delegates nearly all the complicated manufacturing, assembly, product configuration, and distribution activities to partners. Its mind-set is shared responsibility for customer satisfaction—not control or micromanagement.

Such delegation is by no means simple. Every major customer order requires extensive customization. Each installation—whether at a large corporation, a small or medium business, a telecom service provider, or even a home consumer (an emerging Cisco market)—has unique requirements. Cisco and its resellers must specify or spec out those needs, design the solution, and then configure, deliver, and install a custom hardware/software package.

Rather than expand its own service organization or buy a services company as Lucent has done, Cisco in 1999 invested $1 billion in global professional services company KPMG in exchange for an equity position and a commitment to deploy four thousand Cisco-competent techni-cians. Despite this investment, Cisco continues to work closely with other third-party services companies—including KPMG competitors like EDS and IBM. Figure 4-2 depicts the linking applications in Cisco's value network, in which a combination of the Internet, EDI, and resource management tools draws together customers, suppliers, and value-added resellers (VARs).

In a Web-enabled environment, new and improved linkages help make value integration faster, better, and cheaper. Information (struc-tural capital) flows through the entire Value Chain in real time, processes become more efficient, transaction costs decline, and relationships become flexible.

FIGURE 4-2   Cisco's Enabling Applications

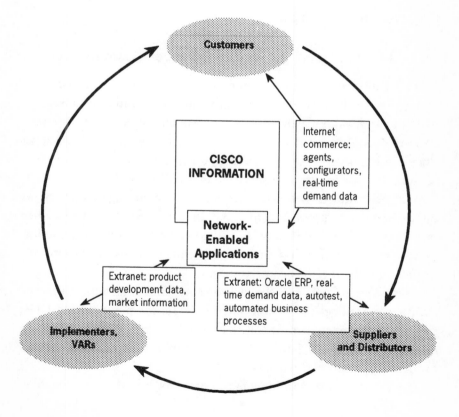

Clearly, companies no longer do it all internally. But doing it within a complex and ever-changing b-web is no mean feat. In the next section, we discuss the points of leverage in a Value-Chain b-web, addressing four questions:

1. What is the essence of the value proposition that we offer to our end-customers?

2. What are the most effective, value-adding contributions that we can make and that also reinforce our leadership position?

3. How do we design our b-web as a customer-fulfillment network, in which all participants have the knowledge and the motivation to focus on end-customers?

4. How do we work with suppliers to develop win-win partnerships and improve efficiency and quality?

POINTS OF LEVERAGE

From Mass Production to Service-Enhanced Customization

What is the essence of the value proposition that we offer to our end-customers? In the digital economy, where innovation and cost savings go hand in hand, Value-Chain leaders compete on both cost *and* differentiation, transforming the value proposition across multiple dimensions. They must become solution-oriented, turning the risk of commoditization into opportunities for service-enhanced customization.

Certain products *require* customization. Networking equipment, as discussed, must be precisely configured. Industrial equipment and office buildings are designed to spec. But as we move from mass production to mass customization and on to service-enhanced customization, off-the-shelf products also become targets.

Many Value-Chain b-webs include configuration tools in their e-commerce applications. These include K-Tel for personalized CDs, Chipshot.com for custom-fit golf clubs, Levi's custom jeans, and Barbie's design-your-own doll. Ford wants its consumers to design custom cars for delivery in two to three days.

You can customize a product in infinite ways, but where do you draw the line? Ford discovered that most sales were based on a fraction of the several million design combinations for a given model of car. In fact, for customization to work, you may need to limit choice. Teri Takai, director of Business Integration at Ford, explains:

> We have struggled with the complexity of our products. In the past, we didn't have a handle on the specific options that our consumers wanted. We blanketed that gap in knowledge with lots of product. That complexity drives through development, all the way through the supply chain. As we get better at predicting consumer needs, we can simplify our product offerings—and enable more efficiency in the supply chain. We need that kind of knowledge to leverage an e-business strategy à la Dell or Cisco.[4]

Codesigning products with customers is the ultimate in customization and is much more challenging than offering a menu of options. As customers become deeply integrated into the supply chain, their input can start at the design phase.

For shop production, collaboration is the norm: Customers work closely with the lead producer to design the good or service. Rather than playing a drawn-out Ping-Pong game of revisions, digitally enabled shop b-webs codesign projects in real time. Bidcom provides an online collaboration and project management service that initially targeted the $3.2 trillion global construction industry. Clients plug directly into the architect's or contractor's work environment; see drawings, photos, and videos of the project; and make sure it unfolds to their specifications, without the need for daily site visits.

In routine production, codesign is more of a challenge. Beta testing, now quite sophisticated for testing software, is a form of codesign. However, it is not individual customization. A more robust scenario for routine production may entail market testing of virtual prototypes throughout the design process. For example, an automobile prototype might be delivered to a buyer as a virtual-reality application. The customer experiences and adjusts the car in all its dimensions—from what it looks like to how it handles the road.

Car companies are racing to redefine their value propositions. Rather than just selling cars, they are shifting to selling personal transportation solutions. They will bundle insurance, lifetime maintenance, and even more. Instead of selling you a car, the company makes the right vehicle available when you need it, for a package price: a little runabout for daily commuting, a sport utility vehicle for ski outings, a truck for large loads. This model builds on rental and leasing, but is also akin to the free bicycles in the streets of Amsterdam during the 1960s—in this case, though, for a fee.

Examples of service-enhanced customization abound in many industries. Computer manufacturers sell communications in partnership with Internet service providers, and utilities become energy management companies.

As previously "dumb" products are embedded with computer chips, "smart" features differentiate product offerings and further blur the line between products and services. Car companies will offer custom digital information, entertainment, and security services, not just antilock brakes or double-sided sliding doors. The convergence of wireless communications, global positioning systems, and onboard computing opens the potential for services like roadside assistance, stolen vehicle tracking, "concierge" functions (restaurant and hotel reservations), and mobile shopping. Current systems include Ford's Vehicle Emergency Messaging System, GM's OnStar, Nissan's Infiniti Communicator, Jaguar's Assist, BMW's Mayday Phone, and Mercedes-Benz's Tele-aid. Cars are becoming personal information networks on wheels.

Other smart products include interactive toys, which create new markets for ancillary goods and become ancillary goods themselves. Microsoft Actimates dolls speak, sing, play games, and interact with special television and computer programs.

Focus on the Essence of Customer Value and Let Partners Do the Rest

What are the most effective, value-adding contributions that we can make and that also reinforce our leadership position? Executive vice president Don Listwin describes Cisco's value proposition in digital capital terms: "advice and the intellectual property around it." With this in mind, Cisco has strategically focused its own contributions to the b-web.

First, Cisco is ultra-aggressive about controlling the core technology and software designs that constitute the genetic coding of its solutions: the structural capital upon which its added value depends. Cisco stops at nothing to create, hire, or acquire leading-edge technical and design competencies—mostly software, but some hardware—to reinforce its position as a world leader. However, our point is how *narrowly* Cisco has defined its own content contribution to the value equation. Cisco senior vice president, Small/Medium Business Line of Business, Charles Giancarlo says, "We really don't have a not-invented-here syndrome. If there's technology outside Cisco that works well, then we acquire it. And if we feel that we don't need it internally, then we'll partner with that organization to help get it to our customers."[5]

Second, Cisco cultivates its relationship capital assets: brand, marketing, configuration services, support, and customer relationship management. It controls this customer dimension through a combination of human and mostly Web-enabled interactions.

Third, Cisco choreographs the knowledge infrastructure, processes, and culture of its entire Value-Chain b-web in the innovation, integration, and cost-efficient delivery of value. This third dimension involves cultivating supply-side relationship and structural capital.

Cisco's customers value its ability to design, deliver, and manage innovative network technologies, not whether it has manufacturing prowess or transportation expertise. To the customer, it makes no difference whether Cisco, Solectron, or Celestica assembles its routers, or whether they arrive on a Cisco, FedEx, or UPS truck. Cisco's partners have no fear that it will suddenly start building factories or enter the distribution business. Not only would such actions divert Cisco's focus from core activities, these actions would lower the company's return on labor, capital, and other investments. Listwin describes this philosophy as "using other people's capital":

> One of our customers, US West, has a new high-speed Internet service for consumers, called ADSL, for which it needs to install and uniquely configure an access device in each of its customers' homes.
>
> Before, US West would order and deliver the device to the customer's home. US West would then send someone to configure it. Or, the device would go to a US West location, where US West would open the box, configure and repack the device, and send it to the end-customer. US West studies show that it costs $125 every time they touch a box. That's twelve months of the profit associated with the service.

Now, when US West places an order for Internet access devices through Cisco, our Web-based order form includes delivery to the end-consumer, and the configuration of each device. The order enters our system and is transmitted to Celestica, the contract manufacturer in Florida who physically builds the box. Celestica does the required configuration, sticks on the waybill, and ships it directly to the customer via UPS.

The knowledge about the end product—the UPS delivery information, the customer configuration, and the US West end of it—is all managed through the Internet. The box goes directly from point A to point B. Our return on invested capital is enormous because, at the end of the day, we take electronic cash for the execution of our intellectual property—by other people. And the higher your return on invested capital, the higher your price earnings ratio in the stock market.[6]

While Cisco and Dell accumulate massive reserves of digital capital, companies in more traditional industries like the automotive industry wrestle with the issues of a physical capital legacy: to build versus to outsource, to modularize or not, customization lead times, inventory glitches, marginal differentiation, franchise headaches, and the like. They try, simultaneously, to be world leaders, peer partners, competitors, and outsourcers in widely disparate functions throughout the Value Chain of design, manufacturing, assembly, information technology, distribution, direct sales, service, financing—the list goes on. Jack-of-all-trades, indeed!

The car industry slowly began shifting its final assembly upstream in the late 1990s. In 1998, tier-one automotive supplier Magna International bought a controlling stake in Steyr-Daimler-Puch, Austria's biggest car assembler. This acquisition led to Magna's direct participation in the final assembly of automobiles for DaimlerChrysler. According to Magna International president and CEO Don Walker, "If a customer asks us to develop and assemble a car, we have the capability. The natural evolution of the industry dictates that one day we will do that."[7]

Some analysts speculate that automotive suppliers will eventually control the Value Chain. We believe, however, that if branded car companies succeed in transforming themselves into design-oriented b-web context leaders delivering information and service-enhanced personal transportation (as discussed earlier), then they will drive the value proposition down a more interesting path. The path will be toward customer experience and service, instead of mere physical vehicles.

Bring the B-Web into the Customer and the Customer into the B-Web

How do we design our b-web as a customer-fulfillment network, in which all participants have the knowledge and the motivation to focus on end-customers? The Cisco Connection Online (CCO) Web site engages customers in creating their own value. It generates customer capital through bulletin boards, network equipment selection and configuration tools, and online ordering, tracking, and service. These customer-support functions are nearly as important as the company's product sales. Cisco estimates that it saves $250 million per year by having customers download software upgrades from the Web, and it saves several times this amount by posting all its support and marketing documents. Before CCO, incorrectly configured orders topped 20 percent and were a major drain on the company's profits. The site also imposes switching costs; as customers engage with CCO, they become reluctant to invest time in a competitor's site—and Cisco's customer capital grows.

Some of Cisco's biggest customers don't use CCO, since it doesn't connect seamlessly to their back-end or EDI systems. These firms, typically telecom equipment distributors or network operators, lack the time to visit dozens of supplier Web sites to enter the hundreds of orders per week that they need to fill. Cisco built a system called ICS (Integrated Commerce Solution) for these companies. A Cisco server behind the customer's firewall has a set of program interfaces that link to the customer's purchasing systems. According to Todd Elizalde, Cisco's director of e-commerce, after a $50,000 investment to set up ICS, customers achieve payback in three months.

Dell's Web-based customer-integration initiatives began with its Premier Pages, which customize options, pricing, and policies for each customer. According to Michael Dell, they are "a place to share information, to run contracts globally, special pricing, nondisclosure information about future product plans, commerce, and support. Our Premier Pages represent 70 percent of the $18 million a day that we do online."[8]

In late 1999 (and 30,000 Premier Pages later), Dell extended the concept even deeper, to "direct commerce integration" into the internal resource management application systems of major customers. The pay-offs include fewer errors and faster order processing. Dell explains, "Orders go directly to our manufacturing facility without a human ever seeing them or touching them. Customers have told us that they save money in their procurement and requisition process with a system like this. And, of course, it's cost reduction for us as well."[9]

The clincher of customer integration, however, is how it shifts the orientation of the entire Value Chain toward customer value. Customers simply drive the whole system, providing precise demand signals along with detailed information about their preferences—customer capital at its best.

Direct customer integration is easy for a Cisco or a Dell, compared with those in other industries like consumer-packaged goods, fast food, or consumer electronics. Many businesses are typically two, sometimes three, steps removed from the end-customer. As Ford's Takai told us,

> *Our ability to collect information on consumer trends is actually more limited than people might think because a great deal of the customer information is with our franchise network of dealers. We do things like focus groups, but we realize that is a very limited view of what people want in our product.*

Bypassing or eliminating intermediary channels is not always easy. Many companies are bound by contracts and laws or still depend highly on dealers and franchisees. North American car manufacturers agonize over their dealer networks, which covet the customer relationship. In response to the threat of disintermediation, franchisees have sought and sometimes obtained state legislation to strengthen their channel monopolies.

Gaining direct access to customers is only part of the challenge. Many consumers who have tried doing Internet business with "direct" converts attest that the experience was less than satisfactory. This isn't a simple matter of entrenched intermediaries or the limits of technology. Companies that lack the relationship capital of direct customer access and the structural capital of customer-service processes can't just fabricate these assets overnight.

Michael Dell describes the difference between selling direct and through third-party channels:

Our competitors' environment taught them that the reseller *was the customer. Every part of their organizational mechanism was trained in a radically different discipline from the one we practice. That's a difficult change to make. It's like going from hockey to basketball. They're both sports. People run around the court chasing fast-moving objects. But they're very different games. You're taking an entire team and having them switch sports.*

Dell attributes the success of his company to its ability to understand and respond to the customer:

We have an intimacy with the customer that allows us to customize the product to meet their specific requirements. If we didn't understand their requirements, if we didn't have the skills to interpret them, and if we hadn't built systems that allow us to customize our product based on them, then we wouldn't be where we are today.

Dell excels at the game, but the company does have an advantage. It started out in direct sales. It never had to make the transition, and its offering is well suited to this sales model. Direct sales make sense for some other industries—like automotive—but less so for thousands of other consumer goods, from toothpaste to thumbtacks.

From "Just-in-Time" to "Not-at-All"

How do we work with suppliers to develop win-win partnerships and improve efficiency and quality? Effectively integrating suppliers into your Value-Chain b-web generates a level of knowledge sharing—structural capital—that can send efficiency into the stratosphere. With increased visibility and velocity of information, suppliers gain an immediate and undistorted view of demand, leading to pinpoint responsiveness. Web-enabled dynamic matching of demand and supply reduces the variability of information and, consequently, of inventory. Inventory turns are rising quickly: For leading build-to-order Value Chains, near-zero inventory is a meaningful objective. Describing how Celestica and other b-web participants enable Cisco's zero-inventory game plan, Don Listwin comments, only partly facetiously, "The model is to go from just-in-time to not-at-all."[10]

In Dell's build-to-order model, perfect information and tight linkages match supply with demand in real time. If there's no order, no computer gets built. Of course, orders flow continuously. Following the customer Premier Page principle, suppliers receive daily orders, sometimes hourly via custom supplier Web pages. In 1999, Dell operated with 6 days of inventory—compared with a 60–80 day average for the industry. Its inventory turn rate was 58–60 times per year, compared with 13.5 for Compaq and 9.8 for IBM's PC business.[11] Michael Dell comments:

> *That has allowed us to have a return on capital—260 percent last quarter—that's a little higher than the average company out there. At six days, we're pretty darn efficient. We might be able to go a bit lower, but you can't go from six to minus six days. The key is to link the information from the customer back to the supplier, so that they're feeding our production lines as we get demand.*[12]

For suppliers, such efficiencies require adjustment. Many are not accustomed to fulfilling small orders on a daily—let alone hourly—basis. However, they learn to manage a new type of consistent order flow. They end up selling more goods with fewer backlogs of obsolete inventory.

Like Dell, Cisco feeds clear demand signals to suppliers. Before it integrated suppliers via common information systems, each of Cisco's partners was building its own unique supply-and-demand forecasts based on duplicate information flowing from multiple points in the supply chain. To help minimize supplier inventory buffers, Cisco built a dynamic replenishment system. Market demand signals flow directly through Cisco's integrated enterprise resource planning (ERP) system to contract manufacturers, distributors, and parts producers in real time. In mid-1999, Cisco's inventory turns averaged ten times per year, compared with major competitors' four. In some commodity-like product lines, direct fulfillment by contract manufacturers had pushed inventory turns into the 25–35 range.

In addition to efficiency gains, the linking of suppliers to a common information system aligns and motivates partnership. Industrial-age car manufacturer relationships with suppliers were notoriously inflexible and often adversarial. Squeezed to the max, suppliers had only their lowest possible price to offer, with little or no value added. In high-performing b-webs, the lead producer works closely with the suppliers, codeveloping products through deals that benefit both sides. This trend began in the North Amercian auto industry with Chrysler, whose first-tier suppliers, once integrated into the extended enterprise, began to share responsibilities for design, quality, and process coordination.

For leading Value-Chain b-webs, such collaboration becomes pervasive standard practice. Dell's engineering and procurement teams share information—designs, schedules, product information, etc.—with suppliers. Michael Dell explains:

> *Through Web pages, we feed real-time data from our tech support and manufacturing lines directly to suppliers. If Celestica supplies printed circuit board number twenty-seven, and it's having a field fall-out rate that's 20 percent higher then their goal, they don't have to wait for the quarterly supplier meeting to find that out. They get that feedback minute by minute. We have links to a lot of our suppliers' manufacturing lines so that we can see their yields. This way, we can treat them like they're part of Dell. Right now we're building these sorts of links for our top twenty or so suppliers. After that, we'll do it for a much larger number.*

Though notorious for commanding its suppliers, Cisco does not always force its practices on them. If a supplier has a solution that works to the b-web's advantage, then Cisco adopts it.

Cisco also manages financial transactions among suppliers, particularly contract manufacturers like Celestica and Solectron and distributors like Avnet. One key to Cisco's single-enterprise strategy is transparency of relevant, nonproprietary financial information. The company's information transparency is so complete that Listwin assured us that by mid-2000, it would be able to close its books every twenty-four hours, to the satisfaction of its auditor, PricewaterhouseCoopers. With real-time access to all information, Cisco can engineer relationships that squeeze costs without damaging its partners. By structuring relationships in this way, Cisco has (1) removed incentives for short-term profit-taking from distributor–manufacturer relationships or the compounding of profits as goods move up the supply chain, (2) freed its supply partners' personnel from repetitive tasks so that they can focus on planning and optimization, and (3) oiled the whole supply chain so that everyone benefits from faster cash flows and inventory turns.

Vertical integration meant dependence on internal suppliers,

whereas "virtual" corporation hub-and-spoke models locked participants into relationships through proprietary communication links. In
Value-Chain b-webs, context providers can switch suppliers more easily when they need to.

Exemplary producers take advantage of this choice by developing
fewer longer-term supplier relationships. Twenty suppliers provide 85
percent of Dell's materials. Says Dell: "When we find great suppliers
that we can develop, we give them as much business as we possibly can
because we want them to be better partners for us. We'd rather have
one great partner than five little ones." B-web producers can afford to
invest in deep partnerships with their suppliers while minimizing
dependencies.

Suppliers share some of their knowledge with a producer's competitors. This might seem dangerous, but when direct competitors share a
supply base, such risks can also result in shared benefits. Paul Esling
presents an example:

> *Suppose 3Com, Nortel and Cisco were all bidding on a large piece of*
> *business, and they all showed a spike in their demand forecasts on the*
> *assumption they would all win the business. If we as a distributor*
> *accepted all these forecasts at face value, our numbers would be off. But*
> *we know only one of them will get the sale. So we factor that informa-*
> *tion into the data we're giving to integrated circuit manufacturers.*[13]

Such unofficial knowledge-sharing helps lower inventory costs for
everyone.

Strategy, rather than short-term parochial concerns, will increasingly
drive supplier relationships. Everyone—including and especially customers—will benefit.

VALUE-CHAIN TECHNOLOGY: DIGITAL SPINNING WHEEL

Baer Tierkel, executive vice president of worldwide marketing at PeopleSoft,
made some sharp comments on the state of enterprise resource planning
(ERP) applications, on which high-performance Value Chains depend:

> *Cisco and Dell have an incredible number of arrows in their back and*
> *have lost a lot of blood. They paved the trail. But the current generation*

of ERP applications from the Oracles, SAPs, and PeopleSofts of the world don't yet provide an approach to doing business that reflects what Cisco and Dell have been doing.

ERP software was intended to integrate an organization by aligning back-end processes like accounting, order processing, and human resource management, and to link in other activities like manufacturing. By the late 1990s, ERP had become the foundation of many businesses. However, in addition to being hugely expensive and time-consuming to implement, ERP does not support the b-web inter-enterprise approach to doing business.

Although ERP systems helped dissolve silos of information and functionality inside a company, they do not typically communicate with systems in other companies. Of the thousands of in-house ERP implementations, few communicate effectively with one another. So what do you do?

If you've read this far, then you probably think that you need to emulate the best of Cisco and Dell's accomplishments. On the other hand, you might not be too keen on building your Value-Chain software from scratch, as Dell has done, or even on enduring the arduous task of adapting pre-Web resource-management software, as Cisco has done.

Michael Dell says that his investment has provided a competitive advantage: "If you believe you don't add any value in your business in a particular area, it probably makes sense to use external software. But if you do add value, implementing a standard off-the-shelf system like ERP will eliminate the advantage that you might have had."

Let's say that you agree in theory with Dell—but remain more inclined to buy your b-web software off the shelf. Here are the facts about software kits for Value-Chain b-webs as we see them. The good news is that some of the best entrepreneurs and creative minds in the industry are tackling this opportunity.

First, this area is a moving target, and no one knows what or who will dominate. Established players like PeopleSoft, Oracle, and SAP; innovators like i2; and start-ups like Descartes Systems (a maker of logistics software) are tackling two core issues: First, what are the unique requirements for software-enabling Value Chain b-webs? And second, what business models are emerging for software-supported b-web activities and processes?

On the first question, systems providers are thinking about how you might want to interact with a b-web partner. Buying and selling goods and services, tracking fulfillment, and so on—those are obvious. But other activities include customer relationship management, collaboration in design, financial management, contractor health and benefits administration, environmental monitoring, knowledge management, advertising and public relations, documentation management, product and services support, marketing research, logistics management—the list goes on.

Consider the explosion in variability of information in the supply chain. Every customer and every business user has unique user needs, with information entering from an ever-changing variety of sources. The Holy Grail of variability management is to deliver all this information customized to the roles and needs of the individual users.

Art Mesher, executive vice president of strategy at Descartes Systems describes a scenario:

> A production scheduler wants to know—by 8:00 A.M.—everything that's not coming in that day that was scheduled and for which they don't have safety stock. That's what's going to affect his line going down. On the other hand, the warehouse people want to know everything that is coming in, because they have to plan their labor. In the past, the warehouse person and the production person would see the same massive database in the same formats. The truth is, they had lots of data, but very little information. Now, we can profile individuals for what they should and shouldn't see; we can trigger and push data to each desktop in unique formats. In other words, we can tailor data and processes to the individual. We can even treat each individual consumer as a quasi-channel.[14]

Baer Tierkel, senior vice president of strategy at PeopleSoft, addresses the broader picture:

> What's coming is ERP software systems that support inter-enterprise business processes. The next step is to create the virtual organization where business processes span from manufacturer through supply chain out through distribution and to the consumer. We will see ERP software and services that help participants subscribe to various b-webs. In one

scenario, service providers will provide a collection of trading partners, whose prices and services have already been negotiated and whose distribution is already greased. In another, you will plug in your own partners because you have a unique network. Typically you will do both: you will have personalized access to a collection of b-webs to meet a variety of needs.[15]

Several application and service delivery models have already appeared in response to such opportunities:

- Industry hubs (see chapter 3) like eSteel, GE TPN, and the Ariba Network automate business processes, like procurement or logistics, across one or more industries. Ariba Network customers use the company's buy-side procurement application and its affiliated suppliers of goods and services. Rather than create individual connections between each buyer using the software and overlapping groups of suppliers, all buyers subscribe to an aggregated supply base in one place. All the goods in all the catalogs of participating vendors are indexed on the site.

- More powerful than mere trading hubs, hosted applications available on demand—or "apps on tap"—are taking off. Bidcom, which we introduced earlier in this chapter, provides applications for the often-overlooked building industry, which represents 10 percent of the gross national product in most industrial countries. Bidcom's Web-based project management system, inSite, is the biggest construction-industry technology innovation since the release of the computer design tool AutoCAD. The inSite system integrates the full suite of design and construction business processes, enabling collaboration between all project participants from clients, architects, and engineers to subcontractors and suppliers in a shared environment. Construction companies can manage an entire project online, from RFPs to change-order approvals.

- Software suppliers are devising entirely new models of application design, which merge business process integration, customer relationship management, and the building and mobilization of b-webs and networks thereof.

These moves mark just the beginning. Ultimately, wide support for standards like XML (see sidebar) will likely make these solutions interoperable. As a savvy businessperson, you should determine how the availability of these enablers of b-web business models will change the competitive stakes in your industry. And place your bets accordingly.

KEY SUCCESS FACTORS

Provide service-enhanced custom solutions. The value proposition is shifting from products to the services that make a product useful. Dell's computers gain value because they come connected to support services. Identify the use-value that surrounds your products or services, and develop fully integrated solutions.

STANDARDS FOR A GLOBAL WEB OF B-WEBS

In the next few years, tens of thousands of trading communities will arise, built around specific applications (like the Ariba Network), industries (like Bidcom), and individual enterprises (like Cisco, Dell, and Ford). The challenge is to turn this state of potential digital anarchy into a virtual world where everyone can communicate. As noted by Jay Marty Tenenbaum, chief scientist at CommerceOne, "these communities will be built around an enterprise, or vertically, or horizontally, or regionally. They all have to come together to form a global web of interoperable markets, trading communities, and commerce portals. Collectively, they will create the world's largest, most valuable marketplace."[16]

Most standards efforts remain limited to the individual b-webs adhering to them. In other words, each of thousands of trading communities will have its own collection of standards. Buyers in one electronic procurement community can't always or easily trade with suppliers connected to another community.

Rather than try to create a single data standard for everyone, XML (extensible markup language) has potential as a universal "translator" based on a common dictionary of definitions. With XML "tags," users define the function of each piece of data in a document. In the same way that HTML (hypertext markup language) tags define the layout characteristics of Web page information (font type, size, spacing, etc.), XML data is tagged as price, date, time, or quantity.

Connect with every customer. B-webs gain advantage through *knowing* and *responding* to customer needs better and faster than competing b-webs. Switch from being a product-centered producer to a customer-centered one. Bring your customers into the b-web and the b-web into the customers.

Focus on what counts. Identify and stick to those activities that add the most value for your customers and bring you the greatest return on investment. Develop the b-web value network to support the creation and delivery of your offering.

Develop expertise in relationship management. The more you bring end-customers and partners into your Value-Chain b-web, the more energy you must put into these relationships. As *The Economist* points out, "the diplomatic art of managing ad hoc partnerships and alliances will become a key executive skill."[18]

XML-tagged information can be exchanged among dissimilar applications. For example, a product description in Dell's direct commerce software can be recognized as such by a customer's internal procurement system.

Although XML enables interoperability among trading communities, businesses must agree on content design and interpretation. There will still be competing dictionaries, or "libraries," of XML business documents such as purchase orders, invoices, and the components that make up those specific documents like dates, addresses, part numbers, and so on.

Achieving plug-and-play operability is not just a matter of data formats. It also means aligning business processes among participants across Value-Chain b-webs. How do you achieve this, not just among committed trading partners, but across an entire industry—or even multiple industries?

RosettaNet is a leading example of an industry-wide Value-Chain process standards initiative. Launched in 1998, RosettaNet develops business process interoperability standards for computer distributors and manufacturers, software developers, resellers, shippers, and end-customers. Members agree on a shared set of processes, both high level (e.g., what constitutes a return) and low level (e.g., part numbers). "Instead of businesspeople arguing over an XML tag," says RosettaNet CEO Fade Chehade, "they're saying, 'that's how I'd like to introduce a product to my business partner.'"[17]

Share knowledge with b-web participants to maximize trust and effectiveness. The goal is zero, or near-zero, inventory—for everybody.

Implement standards-based next-generation Web architectures and applications. Enable end-to-end integration through Web-enabled enterprise applications that distribute information quickly and efficiently—and that are customized to the needs of each individual user.

LEADER'S GUIDE TO VALUE CHAINS

Definition: The value proposition of a Value Chain is the design and delivery of an integrated product or service that meets a specific set of customer needs. In a Value-Chain b-web, the context leader defines the goals and coordinates the value contributions of the various participants, controlling the design of the product and choreographing the key steps.

Significance: Value-Chain b-webs are the spinners of wealth in any economy. They first identify and define needs, then design solutions to these needs. Through a sequence of steps, Value-Chain b-web participants marshal, then transform raw materials into finished goods and services. The participants deliver the goods to points of distribution or directly to end-customers and often provide documentation, service, and support. Value is added each step of the way, from the extraction of raw materials to customer fulfillment.

Types: Value Chains usually bring to mind manufacturing and routine production. But there is actually a second type of Value Chain that works quite differently. In shop production, participants create custom solutions in response to unique demands.

Key transformation: Value Chains transform command-control, hub-and-spoke, build-to-inventory management to efficient, interlinked b-webs that function as customer fulfillment networks.

5 alliances

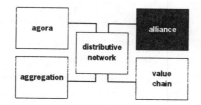

The [open-source] world behaves in many respects like a free market or an ecology, a collection of selfish agents attempting to maximize utility which in the process produces a self-correcting spontaneous order more elaborate and efficient than any amount of central planning could have achieved.

Given a large enough beta-tester and co-developer base, almost every problem will be characterized quickly and the fix obvious to someone.

—ERIC RAYMOND, *The Cathedral and the Bazaar*

THE OPEN-SOURCE PHENOMENON

Early in 1991, a twenty-two-year-old Finnish university student named Linus Torvalds confronted a dilemma. He wanted but couldn't afford market versions of Unix, a powerful and flexible operating system costing $5,000 for the software and another $10,000 for a specialized workstation. So he decided to build a Unix clone for a PC. He designed a simple kernel (the core of the operating system).

On October 2, 1991, Torvalds posted the first working version—Linux .02—on Usenet, the Internet's global information-sharing resource at the time. He dared others to try this "program for hackers by a hacker." Later, he patented it under the Free Software Foundation's general public license. This license made Linux free and available to all and required anyone who passed it along to include the source code (the source code of a computer program is like a musical score that programmers can readily modify).

Shortly thereafter, Torvalds received e-mail from five people who were running Linux on their PCs. Soon, a hundred e-mails arrived. "After that," said Torvalds, "I stopped being surprised."[1]

An initial hundred or so programmers seized on the idea, each testing the code, commenting back, and proposing changes. Torvalds incorporated what worked, dispatching new versions of the kernel at a rapid-fire pace—sometimes daily. Usage mushroomed. People added features as needed. For example, the first person who connected Linux to a Hewlett-Packard DeskJet 100 printer wrote the printer driver himself, then shared it via the Internet. During the course of the decade, programmers everywhere offered up tens of thousands of improvements to the system.

By 2000, Linux, complex to set up and manage but free for the asking, powered an estimated 20 million servers around the world. Microsoft acknowledged it as a challenge to Windows, its core product. A stable, reliable, highly functional product, Linux powered Web sites, e-mail services, and useful real-world applications. Top technology companies like Dell, Hewlett-Packard, Intel, and IBM lined up to endorse it. Stock prices of Linux software companies like Red Hat, Corel, and Cobalt Networks took off. The product had shifted from a hacker's dream to commercially viable technology, with lots of money to be made.

Like any general-purpose operating system, Linux is complicated. Designers of complex products—and certainly of most computer software—usually manage the design process very tightly, and within a single company. But Linux is different. Its development team includes countless part-time programmers around the world: academics, freelancers, and employees at thousands of companies. They contribute bits of code on a voluntary and unpaid basis, or their employers subsidize their efforts. The Linux community includes a loose collection of committees (Linux's context provider) that makes consensus decisions about what to include in the official version of the product. Users can download Linux over the Net at no charge, or they can buy an unlimited-use copy on a CD-ROM for about $50 from distributors like Red Hat.

The open-source design paradigm behind the creation of Linux illustrates how the Internet enables Alliance b-webs, wherein many contributors, all acting independently in their own self-interest, create a highly integrated "good" that provides value to themselves and to others. Humanity's highest achievements—including language and science—resulted from open, collaborative Alliance-type models of innovation and value creation. But moneymaking Alliance business models have been rare. Now, the Internet enables managers to consider Alliances as a new kind of strategy opportunity.

THE POWER OF ALLIANCES

If a Value Chain is like a marching band, an Alliance is like a jazz ensemble. A Value Chain's context leader, like a conductor, chooses the music and directs the performance. A context leader of an Alliance sets the direction, but each player contributes independently to a total value experience. An orchestra player simply follows the score; a jazz musician improvises within the group's musical style.

As discussed in chapter 1, an Alliance is the most virtual of b-webs, achieving high value integration through self-organization, and without hierarchical management. The value proposition of an Alliance b-web is collaboration for a common good. Participants form a creative community that designs or makes useful things, creates and shares knowledge, or simply has fun together.

Open-source teams, which have designed hundreds of other software tools, illustrate how Alliance b-webs work. The value proposition of an open-source team is a software tool, designed through creative collaboration within a community of individuals and business entities. The design architecture is modular; each contributor can work on a manageable chunk that plugs into the overall product. Contributors do not receive payment for their contributions, but they can freely share the outcome of the Alliance's work. Thus, each has reasons to contribute his or her best, with good expectation of realizing downstream benefits.

Other, less cozy approaches to Alliance-based innovation have achieved successes. For over twenty years, Microsoft succeeded in lashing

together an enormous, trillion-dollar Alliance b-web. Instead of free sharing, this b-web is based on for-sale software. Instead of open, inclusive
development, Microsoft keeps the core standard—Windows—under tight
control. Competitors and customers chafe and accuse Microsoft of self-
dealing and predatory practices. But, despite all this, the so-called Wintel
Alliance (led by Microsoft Windows and Intel) has produced untold value.
As Bill Gates points out, "Anyone can develop application software that
runs on the Windows platform, without having to notify or get permission from Microsoft. In fact today there are tens of thousands of commercially available software packages for the platform, including thousands of
offerings that compete with most Microsoft applications."[2] However, the
foundations of the Microsoft b-web have weakened due to the company's
sustained inattention to cultivating and conserving its relationship capital.

An Alliance's context leader, whether a person (Linus Torvalds for
Linux) or a company (Microsoft for Windows, Sun for Java), initiates the
work and sets the direction. As the first among equals, the leader embod-
ies the vision. Torvalds facilitates key decisions and b-web governance.
Various participants contribute to consensus decisions. The process self-
organizes and self-corrects—the best ideas win. Anyone can contribute,
from hard-core engineering teams at global corporations to individual
e-lancers in their home offices. Lively controversy and debate even apply
to issues of governance and participation (figure 5-1).

The Internet makes all this possible. Without the Net, Torvalds simply would not have found his expanding community of collaborators
or achieved high momentum of collaborative design and testing.

The Linux Alliance is a design collaborative, one of many Alliance
b-web variants. Alliances are rich, creative, exciting phenomena. They
include support groups, cybersex chats, gardening and investment communities, research initiatives, games, and innovation/competition collaboratives like the Windows and open-source development industries.
The scientific method, a manifesto for an independent meritocracy, artic-
ulates the best of Alliance values. In a different vein, when millions collectively mourn the loss of a beloved public figure—or join a riot—
they evince Alliance modes of organization.

Online communities have received a bit of a bad rap. Howard Rheingold, in his landmark book, *Virtual Communities,* described the potential
of communities as a choice between humanism and commercial fakery.[3]

FIGURE 5-1 Linux Value Map

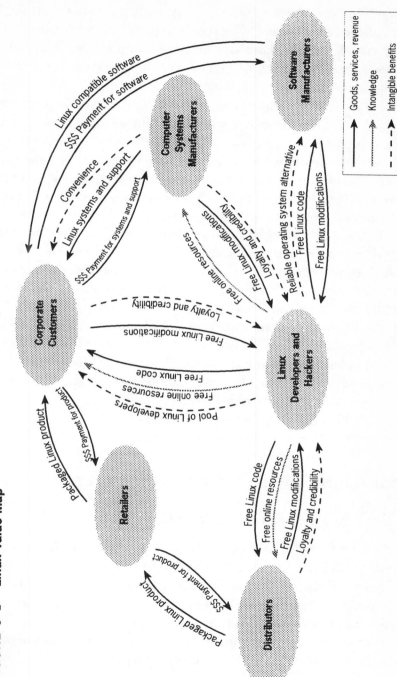

John Hagel and Arthur Armstrong, in *Net Gain,* redefined community as a marketing lever—a way to get surfers to come to your Web site so that you can sell to them.[4] Each view reflects a reality. But our focus differs: the self-organizing power of online communities and other Alliances as business models for creating value.

No one can force anyone to be part of an Alliance. Contributions are voluntary. You can leave any time. It is difficult, sometimes impossible, to legally penalize anyone for breaking the rules—though social or marketplace penalties often work very well. The open, free, consensus-based processes at the heart of the Linux Alliance explain its power and success—and its ability to construct a viable competitive threat to Microsoft's proprietary leadership model.

In the industrial-age economy, Alliances were important but marginal, because barriers of time and space slowed them to a crawl. Alliances now appear everywhere. Millions flow daily into online communities, producing an unimaginable diversity of shared experiences from the divine to the depraved.

Alliances do not jibe with the way we have been trained to think about productive work, because value tends to emerge from an Alliance b-web in less-than-predictable ways. Also, most Alliances function as economies of sharing (which we describe later as gift economies), wherein participants contribute help, information, work, or some other good without expecting an immediate return.

Let's take a closer look at how Alliances create value.

CAPTURING VALUE FROM ALLIANCE B-WEBS

Alliances: Where Network Effects Live

Alliance b-webs display increasing returns and network effects. As Carl Shapiro and Hal Varian say, "the value of connecting to a network depends on the number of other people already connected to it."[5] Alliance b-webs are networks of people and organizations, each contributing value in ways that enhance their own self-interest. Metcalfe's law (more a rule of thumb than a law) says that the value of a network increases exponentially with the number of users.[6]

... if the value of a network to a single user is $1 for each other user on the network, then a network of size 10 has a total value of roughly $100. In contrast, a network size of 100 has a total value of roughly $10,000. A tenfold increase in the size of the network leads to a hundred-fold increase in its value.[7]

Network effects drive demand-side economies of scale: The bigger the network of users, the greater its value to the users themselves. As railways spread across the United States in the nineteenth century, touching ever more towns and cities, their value increased exponentially, enabling new "network" business models like the Sears retail catalog. The first person who owned a fax machine obtained no value from the device; as user numbers increased, the value of a fax machine grew.

Not all businesses display network effects. Webvan (an Aggregation) may gain a trusted brand and be able to stock a wide selection of groceries because it has a lot of customers, but people shop there for the goods; the presence of other customers makes no material difference to the value proposition for a shopper. GM's Web-enabled Value Chain will reduce costs and improve quality and responsiveness. This will be great for the company and its customers, but it's not necessarily an example of network effects.

Many b-webs add Alliances to their mix (see chapter 9) in order to enhance their value propositions with network effects, increasing benefits for all participants. Some of these Alliances are purely virtual communities—the Internet equivalent of talk radio—where people simply hang out online and gossip. Such communities are just one end of the Alliance b-web continuum. At the other end, the "customer" communities of open source and Wintel actually create and distribute valuable products. In all these cases, from the lonely hearts on America Online to a farmers' co-op on Agriculture.com, from distance learners to PalmPilot users, customers gain more value from an Alliance b-web as their numbers increase.

Network effects, when deployed effectively as in the Linux Alliance, synergistically link all three forms of digital capital: multi-way relationship capital, cross b-web human capital, and structural capital's networked knowledge and processes.

Intentional Emergence

Network effects alone do not account for the Linux phenomenon. You can get more value from a telephone network when millions of people use it. But you will not likely want to talk to any randomly selected person on the network, nor will all telephone users collaborate to design an operating system.

Kevin Kelly and others have explained Alliance-like models of innovation through *emergence*, the science of understanding how meaningful patterns emerge from complex, apparently random systems, as a result of the presence of a few, often very simple rules.[8] Emergence has captured the imagination of scientists, researchers, and analysts in a variety of disciplines, including biology, mathematics, and economics.

D. R. Hofstadter's metaphor of the ant colony illustrates the concept.

> *The behavior of individual ants is remarkably automatic (reflex driven). Most of their behavior can be described in terms of the invocation of about a dozen rules of the form "grasp object with mandibles," "follow a pheromone trail [scents that encode the messages "this way to food," "this way to combat," etc.] in the direction of an increasing (or decreasing) gradient," "test any moving object for colony-member scent," and so on. This repertoire, though small, is continually invoked as the ant moves through its changing environment. The individual ant is at high risk whenever it encounters situations not covered by the rules. Most ants, worker ants in particular, survive at most a few weeks before succumbing to some situation not covered by the rules.*
>
> *The activity of an ant colony is totally defined by the activities and interactions of its constituent ants. Yet the colony exhibits a flexibility that goes far beyond the capabilities of its individual constituents. It is aware of and reacts to food, enemies, floods, and many other phenomena, over a large area. It reaches out over long distances to modify its surroundings in ways that benefit the colony, and the colony has a life span many times longer than that of its constituents. To understand the ant, we must understand how this persistent, adaptive organization emerges from the interactions of its numerous constituents.[9]*

As noted in chapter 1, we believe that ecosystem and emergence theories of digital innovation are insightful, but miss an essential point. Human communities differ from ant colonies. Individual humans are not just automatic and reflex driven. Humans exercise deliberate choice, based on ideas, needs, and wants. In a word, humans display intentionality.

Linux is a product of *intentional emergence*. Its community participants chose to cooperate in processes that led to an agreed-upon outcome: a coherent, functioning operating system artifact. Returning to Eric Raymond's statement at the beginning of this chapter: "The [open-source] world behaves in many respects like a free market or an ecology, a collection of selfish agents attempting to maximize utility which in the process produces a self-correcting spontaneous order more elaborate and efficient than any amount of central planning could have achieved." The selfish agents do not merely obey instinct, but consciously work toward an end, which Raymond describes as maximizing utility. We might also say that the open-source movement consciously draws on the power of relationship capital (e.g., the community of Linux programmers and users) to convert its participants' human capital (their networked software knowledge) into a shared resource of structural capital (networked intelligence in the form of working Linux code). Neither ants nor freeway drivers exhibit such thoughtful, planned-out behavior.

Intentionality can also hurt. Unlike ants, people decide to make antisocial choices. Some b-web participants could develop a proprietary version of Linux, incompatible with the mainstream, just as Unix suppliers did in the 1980s. Linux observers—both supporters and competitors—have wondered why it has managed to avoid such fragmentation. Microsoft's insightful analysis suggests that the very inclusiveness of the Linux community deters differentiation.[10] Microsoft compares Linux with another version of Unix, BSD. Membership in the BSD community of contributors is restricted, and outsiders feel left out. For this very reason, Microsoft argues, some BSD developers have struck out in new and incompatible directions.

The open Linux community has a saying: "He who has the best code wins." Status, and therefore the ability to "homestead" a bigger piece of Linux, depends on the quality of contributions. Recognized contributors get to parlay their human capital into structural capital; the result is that over time, the Linux Alliance becomes increasingly institutionalized. Also, because Linux is free, differentiation provides no economic benefit. Intentional emergence works when Alliance participants have good incentives to stick with b-web standards.

Network Effects and the New Design Paradigm

How does such a loose collection of well-meaning souls manage to achieve coherent results? Designers, whether of physical goods (like cars and toothbrushes), technology (like computer software), or of abstractions (like business strategy), tend to have a linear view of the design process. Define your needs, do a high-level design, and then do a detailed one. Create a prototype, then the item. Test before deploying on a large scale. And for heaven's sake, keep the team as small and as focused as you can, because there is a law of diminishing returns in design teams. Software engineering has for nearly thirty years sworn by Brooks's Law, which states that as the number of program developers increases, the number of bugs increases exponentially. Beyond the minimum number required to get the job done, adding people produces a result that is late, of inferior quality, and over budget.

How did the motley Linux crew overturn Brooks's Law? Raymond proffers three design process principles to explain this phenomenon:[11]

1. Treating your users as codevelopers is the least-hassled route to rapid code improvement and effective debugging.

2. Release early. Release often. And listen to your customers.

3. Given enough testers and codesigners, almost every problem will be identified quickly; the fix will become obvious to someone.

Raymond describes the difference between what he calls "cathedral builders" and the "bazaar" style of development:

In the cathedral-builder view of programming [think "design" in general], bugs and development problems are tricky, insidious, deep phenomena. It takes months of scrutiny by a dedicated few to develop confidence that you've winkled them all out. Thus the long release intervals, and the inevitable disappointment when long-awaited releases are not perfect. In the bazaar view, on the other hand, you assume that bugs are generally shallow phenomena—or, at least, they turn shallow pretty quick when exposed to eager co-developers pounding on every single new release. Accordingly, you release often in order to get more corrections, and as a beneficial side effect you have less to lose if an occasional botch gets out the door.

For-profit software companies have recognized the power of the Net-enabled bazaar model and, in 1998, began to adopt it. Sun opened its Java offering to customer innovation, and Netscape published the source code to its Web browser.

Arguably, bazaar-style software development is a special case—it's a gift economy (see next section) in which producers (developers) improve their tools as they use them. They fix bugs because they need to use the software personally. They are pure "prosumers."

How might Alliance b-web bazaars change your business? Gary Hamel suggests that organizations bring as many as thousands of people into the process of making business strategy: "There is an inflection point where the quest for divergence is transformed into a quest for convergence, and a new collective point of view emerges."[12] If thousands of people can productively design business strategy, why not other products?

Consider these scenarios:

- General Motors collaborates with its b-web to design cars using three-dimensional visual prototypes that it distributes via the Web. Participants include style-conscious customers, fleet buyers, knowledgeable service technicians, supply-chain partners, dealers, car buffs, and industrial designers. These participants are motivated to provide the "gift" of their advice because they love cars, enjoy interacting with the b-web community, and gain pleasure from influencing the design of a future car. When General Motors adopts an idea, it publicizes the news to the community, enhancing the reputation of the contributor. The manufacturer returns the favor by providing buyer rebates based on quality and quantity of contributions.

- Columbia Sportswear recognizes that its millions of customers have thousands of ideas that are better than anything that its in-house designers could dream up. It decides to "open source" the design of an entirely new line of clothing, producing both three-dimensional electronic and physical products in real time, based on the contributions of its panel of consumer experts. These prosumers debug the designs in their sports outings. Panel members get test items for free and gain reputational pride as well. Top contributors gain fame and glory—they appear in advertising, and some have products named after them. As early adopters, they also play a critical role in seeding the market.

If you can imagine such a model working for automotive design and sports equipment, how about surgical instruments, shrink-wrapped foods for gourmet recipes, hotel room design, urban planning, or multimedia computer games?

GIFT ECONOMIES: THE GOLDEN RULE

Online or off, money makes the world go around. An Agora supports its price-discovery mechanism. In an Aggregation, price is usually fixed. In a Value Chain, cost is a key performance measure. By contrast, in Alliances, more often than not, people and organizations freely contribute with no expectation of payment.

How and why does a gift economy work? What motivates its participants? And what is unique about Alliances that causes them to function as gift economies? Gift economies turn the Golden Rule—do unto

UNIX AND OPEN SYSTEMS: HOW ALLIANCES FAIL

During the 1980s, a computer operating system called Unix crystallized the open-systems movement. A collection of upstart companies, including Sun and Silicon Graphics, had formed a loose coalition with established players like Hewlett-Packard and big customers like Boeing, General Motors, and several government agencies to break the lock-in of then-dominant "proprietary" vendors—principally IBM, but also Digital Equipment Corporation (DEC), Burroughs, Honeywell, and others.

The battle surged around the costly and complicated mainframe and minicomputers that defined data processing from the 1960s into the 1980s. Each manufacturer had developed proprietary operating systems compatible with only its hardware and applications. Software and information designed for an IBM computer would not work on DEC equipment, and vice versa. Once committed to a particular product, customers could not easily switch. Each manufacturer was a small monopoly that extracted predatory pricing.[13]

In contrast, Unix offered many advantages. Clean, elegant, and modular in design, it appealed to creative programmers. Leading-edge customers and suppliers noticed how they could easily transfer applications and information others as you would have them do unto you—into a system for creating sustainable value.

In an essay on the economics of online cooperation, Peter Kollock synthesizes the strands of research on this topic.[14] He defines a gift as the obligatory transfer of inalienable objects or services between interdependent and mutually obligated transactors. A gift economy gains from improving the "technology of social relations."

A gift transaction implies an *unstated obligation to repay the gift* sometime in the future. The moment of giving is not the time to demand that future repayment. But, without reciprocity, a relationship is not likely to last. Millions receive Linux for free; the Linux community expects those thousands who improve it to share their enhancements. In contrast, in a commodity transaction involving payment, you have no future obligation: Since you pay for Microsoft Windows, no one expects you to share your improvements to it.

---

from an IBM-brand personal computer to a Compaq. Why not enjoy the same flexibility with minicomputers and mainframes? And why not through Unix? Unix computers from a variety of upstart suppliers invaded the marketplace. Thousands of technology managers bought into the low cost, quality, and performance of these machines. Open systems became a modest mass movement; Hewlett-Packard and then IBM and DEC downgraded their legacy products and embraced the cause.

The glitch? Unix had shaken but not broken the proprietary mind-set of the computer industry establishment. Few Unix vendors adopted truly open practices; each manufacturer added its own features to the operating system, limiting application portability. Confusion and rancor split up the open systems movement. Meanwhile, Microsoft successfully launched NT as an alternative.

The Unix story shows how to wreck an Alliance b-web: Let the participants compete on petty, parochial, and proprietary differentiators; shun common rules and standards; and ignore customers as both contributors and consumers.

A gift is also *inalienably linked to the giver.* It's not just any kernel, but the kernel that Linus Torvalds created, gave away, and is enhancing collaboratively. A commodity has no such hidden meaning: Windows has a strong brand, but few users feel as if they owe Bill Gates a debt of gratitude or reciprocity.

Gift exchanges typically occur among people who have *interdependent relationships:* Linux users can count on one another for help. Commodity exchanges, however, occur between self-interested, independent transactors. For help with Windows, you will probably need to pay someone.

A gift economy depends on the range and diversity of its social network—*the technology of social relations.* As the Linux community grows, more people, with a greater diversity of skills, can contribute and develop meaningful friendships. More contributors, who care for one another, produce better results. On the other hand, traditional commodity economics focuses on the technology of production. A typical software business mainly seeks productivity—getting more software from fewer developers—and will readily hire low-cost, faceless offshore programmers if feasible.

The Internet is home to millions of gift economies. Most are Alliances: chat groups, mutual help forums, multi-player games, and design collaboratives like Open Source and the Human Genome Project. In many of these, people contribute gifts to community friends and anonymous recipients alike, assuming that eventually someone will return the favor. Such a network-wide accounting system is known as *generalized exchange.* It applies in the physical world, too. When you help a stranded motorist, you do not expect that particular motorist to pay you back, but you hope and expect that, should you ever have a similar mishap, someone else will bail you out.

In the physical world, we do not encounter many large-scale gift economies. The volunteer sector is the closest example. Is the Internet more suited to gift economies? We think so.

The Internet makes it easy, cheap, and convenient to create information goods, whether a posting on gladiola cultivation, an MP3 music track, or a new patch for a Linux routine. It is easy to send such goods to any number of recipients—in myriad locations—with the press of a key. Online discussion groups and e-mail provide convenient ways to coordinate processes and make decisions. It's not even necessary for everyone to be present at the same time.

Digital information goods typically retain their value, no matter how many people use them. A single individual or small company—a regular contributor to a discussion group on oral cancer, a Linus Torvalds, or Netscape releasing its first Web browser for free—can ride the infrastructure to change many lives.

An Alliance leader can form and galvanize social networks (relationship capital) in ways that were heretofore impossible. Are you a corn farmer who wants to compare notes on the latest pest to invade the prairie crops? A campaigner gathering a petition for gun control? Perhaps a steel industry executive trying to build a coalition to change import tariffs? The Internet enables you to find—or create—the social network that you need.

Some people ride free and take more than they give. Such individually rational behaviors devastate a gift economy. Given the free-rider temptation, why would anyone contribute to the greater public good?

First, the Internet cost-benefit equation is so compelling that free riding becomes redundant. Everyone can share in the benefits of Internet gift economies. The second reason is self-interest: The public good corresponds to a participant's need or desire. For many technology companies and individuals, the Linux gift economy provides both a better mousetrap and effective competition against Microsoft. Third, some contributors may join in to enhance their personal reputation or their corporate brand. Fourth, participants may contribute because they feel attached or committed to the relationships they form in the group. Finally, as Eric Raymond points out, we live in an economy of growing abundance:

> Gift cultures are adaptations not to scarcity but to abundance. They arise in populations that do not have significant material-scarcity problems with survival goods. We can observe gift cultures in action among aboriginal cultures living in eco-zones with mild climates and abundant food. We can also observe them in certain strata of our own society, especially in show business and among the very wealthy. Abundance makes command relationships difficult to sustain and exchange relationships an almost pointless game. In gift cultures, social status is determined not by what you control but by what you give away. Thus the Kwakiutl chieftain's

potlatch party. Thus the multi-millionaire's elaborate and usually public acts of philanthropy. And thus the hacker's long hours of effort to produce high quality open source.[15]

Gift economics are not for everyone. Production- and distribution-oriented Alliances—in which goods are built and money changes hands—tend not to be gift economies. But in the digital economy, this mode of production emerges as a potent force. Expect to see more gift economies, maybe even in your industry.

TYPES OF ALLIANCES

Concepts like free contributions, community, and such, can be a bit disconcerting to a business manager or strategist. What's the value? Where's the money? Figure 5-2 provides one useful way to think about Alliances. The Alliance's value proposition can draw primarily on a communication event, such as an online forum, a game, or a technical support service. Or, the Alliance might exist to produce a tangible output, such as scientific research or computer software. We have identified six types of Alliances: social, discussion, help, design collaborative, production, and games.

Social Alliances

Social communities, which foster conviviality for its own sake, are a big part of what makes life worth living. They include dinner parties, gossiping neighbors, and the "random" and "romance" online chat areas on countless Web sites, AOL discussion groups, and Usenet forums. Conversations tend to be free-form and open-ended. Drawing power from the creativity, common sense, needs, cravings, and impulses of ordinary people, social community outputs run the gamut from smut and schlock to genius and poetry. The value proposition of a social community is the communication event itself, which is typically a gift. Some people sneer that the Internet is a refuge for the bored and the lonely. Certainly, many such people live in our world; before the Net, many passed hours and days alone. Online social communities also provide positive, tangible benefits. Online teenagers can learn to communicate and think for themselves at well-lit social sites. And untold lifelong romantic partnerships began on a chat line.

In the parlance of Net marketers, online communities are sticky. Stickiness indicates passionate, interested, committed participants. Stickiness often depends on less, rather than more, context-provided content. But the aimlessness of a purely social community can make it more slippery than sticky. Nevertheless, gossip and chatter are big draws, worth considering as a feature of any consumer-oriented b-web.

Discussion Alliances

Discussion communities focus on topical matters—whether the hidden meaning of the *X-Files*, the latest gaffe by a political candidate, the

FIGURE 5-2   Alliance Design Options

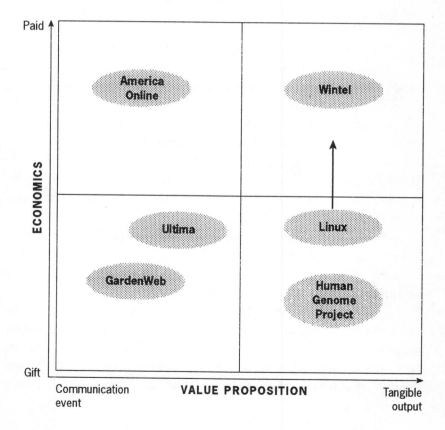

merits of Linux versus NT, or the nuts and bolts of a new steel production process. The value proposition combines learning with social interchange—increasing the stickiness of this format. Like social b-webs, discussion groups derive value from the communication event itself and typically function as gift economies. However, the focus can draw and keep a repeat crowd. It can also contribute to buying decisions: more *X-Files* viewers, changes in voters' opinions, operating-system implementations, even billion-dollar steel mill investments.

For some Web businesses, such customer-created content draws other customers to the site, again to contribute content of substance and value, in a well-defined area of focus. At GardenWeb, which served more than three million page impressions per month in 1999, users provide the majority of the content through forums that cover ninety plants, growing regions, and other themes. The company claims more than two-thirds of all messages posted to Internet garden-related forums and news groups. Another dimension of user-contributed content is GardenWeb's exchanges, in which gardeners barter seeds and plant cuttings. The site's revenues come from advertisers who target its audience of upper-income, primarily female homeowners.

Discussion communities can also build brand cultures—patterns of self-expression on shared themes and interests. Harley-Davidson sponsors the Harley Owners Group (HOG), the world's largest factory-sponsored motorcycle organization, with more than 450,000 members and over a thousand local chapters around the world. HOG organizes rallies and racing events just about every week. It brought its enormous physical-world community Alliance online with the launch of hog.com in 1999.

Fans, packagers, and trinket sellers build amateur online Alliances that often dwarf official initiatives. In January 2000, Yahoo! listed 57 sites devoted to the television series *ER*, 616 to Harley-Davidson, 258 to Beanie Babies, and 671 to the *X-Files*. Participants in these communities contribute "shrines" to individual characters in a movie or series, television episode guides, fan fiction (made-up stories and novels based on the movie's or program's themes), games, humor, multimedia—the list goes on and on. These intensely active communities are full-fledged Alliances that have moved well beyond social and discussion activities into the design and production of new value based on the themes and standards of the core brand.

Help Alliances

Help communication, in which the participants exchange advice and experiences, helping one another solve the myriad problems of life, is a gigantic category of Alliance b-web. GardenWeb's forums allow visitors to tap the collective wisdom of the thousands of users who visit its site each day. Investors join the Motley Fool's forums and workshops to trade tips and debate strategies.

Amazon.com uses collaborative filtering to help customers choose books. Its software creates anonymous "recommendation" communities of readers and music fans who share similar interests. It produces a reading list just for you, culling purchases by other customers who bought the same books that you did.

Cisco's engineers monitor and contribute to various online technical support forums in which its customers provide one another with tips and advice. This is in addition to the large volume of online documentation that the company provides on its own Web site. Cisco's help Alliance increases customer engagement and loyalty while reducing its costs; the company estimates that its online support environment enables it to avoid hiring four hundred engineers each year.

In all these cases, value comes directly from the communication event itself. The ultimate benefit, however, is the tangible action that the participants take after they sign off from the discussion. Help resources can include peers (Amazon.com), mentors and veterans (GardenWeb), and experts (Cisco).

Design Collaborative Alliances

In design collaborative Alliances, participants do more than chat. They actually design a tangible output like a piece of software (e.g., Linux and the Internet itself) or a scientific breakthrough (e.g., the Human Genome Project). Open Source is proof positive that when the conditions are right, a superior and complex—industrial-strength—design becomes feasible when motivated participants contribute, in a nonhierarchical process, to the development of a new standards-based product or service.

Production Alliances

Production Alliances differ greatly from others, whose communication event is intimately bound with the outputs. Instead, a production Alliance (like Wintel) generates real cash in exchange for tangible value (Windows-compatible solution). The participants create collections of modular goods, which match needful users to an integrated outcome. Each participant is an autonomous producer (typically supported by a Value Chain). The producers adhere to common standards to ensure compatibility and connectivity. When a pipe bursts in your basement, you can confidently walk into any hardware store and buy a part that fits, thanks to an Alliance among plumbing suppliers who adhere to the building code's standard sizes. You can phone a colleague on the other side of the world, because telecommunications companies have an Alliance b-web for telephony standards.

Online and Video Games

Online and video games are another unique category of Alliance b-web. Gaming is an Alliance-type phenomenon, because its participants collaborate and compete to create a compelling, shared experience. The online gaming industry is growing fast (projected to hit $1.4 billion by 2002). It is a domain of continuous, fertile innovation—in technology, game design, aesthetics, social interaction, and commerce. Its categories include online versions of traditional pursuits like checkers and bridge, electronic versions of traditional physical games like golf and baseball, fantasy sports leagues, new multimedia games, gambling, business simulations, and fantasy adventures, both text-based and multimedia. Ultima Online, by Electronic Arts, is an addictive fantasy adventure world whose 150,000 b-web participants help build and customize the narrative, landscape, and play pieces. Participants pay $39.95 for the software, plus $9.95 a month to play. A character may go through all the cycles of a natural life, including a career that earns a high, virtual, disposable income. Play has crossed into the real world of commerce: In January 2000, eBay was hosting auctions for over six hundred Ultima Online bid lots, from characters and pieces to entire game accounts— priced from $5 to $4,000.

KEY SUCCESS FACTORS

An Alliance is the most virtual of b-webs, achieving high value integration in the absence of hierarchical management. The value proposition of an Alliance b-web is creative collaboration toward a goal shared across a community of contributors. Alliance b-web participants are members of a community that designs or makes useful goods and services, creates and shares knowledge, or simply produces dynamic group experiences. Linux illustrates how an Internet-enabled Alliance b-web can design, produce, and support a robust, highly complex product. Alliances depend on principles of intentional emergence. Alliances are unique in that many (though certainly not all) function as gift economies.

In designing and facilitating Alliance b-webs for success, pay attention to the technology of social relations, not just the technology of production, and do the following:

Ensure that the participants' self-interests are aligned—people won't focus on the greater good unless it is in their interest to do so.

Define whether the Alliance is a gift or commodity economy, based on proprietary or open standards.

Enhance leadership credibility by sharing power among Alliance participants.

Award stature on the basis of the quality of contributions, rather than entitlement. Alliances work best as meritocracies.

Keep interactions lively and moving forward. Encourage fast-paced, continuing innovation.

Share information as openly as you can.

Recognize and reward contributions through public recognition, financial rewards, and enhanced authority within the Alliance.

Keep rules and rule-making as transparent and democratic as possible. Foster open discussion and debate on rules, norms, processes, and value appropriation.

Ensure that the contributors perceive value appropriation to be fair.

Design the architecture of the Alliance's outputs in a modular way, so that participants can easily plug in their contributions.

LEADER'S GUIDE TO ALLIANCES

Definition: The core value proposition of an Alliance b-web is creative collaboration in aid of a goal that is shared across a community of contributors.

Significance: Alliance participants often do not get financial payback for their contributions, but they can exploit the outcomes of the Alliance's work. Thus, each is motivated to contribute his or her best, with reasonable expectation of realizing downstream benefits. The design architecture of the value proposition is modular; each contributor can work on a manageable chunk that will readily plug into the overall design. Some, but by no means all, Alliances function as gift economies.

Types: Alliances display many shapes and benefits:

- Social communities foster conviviality for its own sake.

- Discussion communities focus on topical matters. The value proposition for participants combines learning with social interchange—increasing the "stickiness" of this format.

- Help is a gigantic category of Alliance b-web in which participants exchange advice and experiences, helping one another solve problems in every sphere.

- In a design Alliance, participants design a tangible output like a piece of software or a scientific breakthrough.

- Production Alliances are about generating real money in exchange for tangible value. Participants create collections of modular goods, which connect with one another to provide users with an integrated solution to a need. Each participant is an autonomous producer (typically supported by a Value-Chain-production process).

• Online and video games include online versions of traditional pursuits like checkers and bridge; electronic versions of traditional physical games like golf and baseball; fantasy sports leagues; new multimedia games; gambling; business simulations; and fantasy adventures, both text-based and multimedia.

Key transformation: Enabled by the Internet, Alliance models are coming into their own as a powerful approach to value creation. Successful Internet businesses are initiating Alliance b-webs to add network effects to their value proposition, dramatically increasing the benefits for all participants.

6 distributive networks

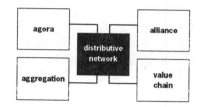

Before Distributive Networks, the world was a collection of isolated and lonely places. Distributive Networks—like telecom operators, courier and postal services, and bank deposit and lending facilities—make possible the global economy and the global village. Their value proposition is to facilitate the exchange and delivery of information, goods, and services. Industrial-age Distributive Network monopolies (such as integrated power companies) now face deregulation, disaggregation, and disintermediation—fundamental transformation. While their core offerings slip into commoditization, new and agile competitors turn out premium-priced value. Every b-web needs a Distributive Network strategy, and every Distributive Network business needs a strategy for the world of b-webs.

NETWORKS IN YOUR LIFE

Distributive Network businesses are the infrastructure of the entire economy. If you are in one of these businesses, your old industry model is being radically transformed. New competitors appear on the scene, devising value propositions that didn't even exist a few short years ago. You need a game plan for the new rules of the digital playing field.

Whether in an infrastructure business or not, you depend on Distributive Networks to power your operations; communicate with customers, suppliers, partners, and employees; distribute goods and services; and facilitate money flows. Your b-web strategy depends on the new Distributive Networks of the digital economy. And maybe you have opportunities to generate new value and wealth by jumping into a digital Distributive Network business.

Distributive Network services typically eat up a large portion of any company's operating costs. Often, companies manage such services poorly and receive less than optimal results. Instead of treating them as enterprise-wide or b-web-wide utilities, companies inefficiently leave the management of these services to ill-trained personnel in individual business units.

You are squandering opportunity if you fail to redefine the ways that you organize and source the services that Distributive Networks provide. If you are in a Distributive Network type of business, you should rethink your core value proposition to capitalize on the potential of b-webs. The following are the types of questions to ask:

- Rather than pay fees to or leave funds with banks, could you manage your—and your customers'—cash flows, financial requirements, and investments more effectively? (If you are a bank, then are you helping all your customers figure out how to achieve this?)

- Do your physical distribution services achieve maximum flexibility at minimum cost? How quickly do they respond to changes in supply and demand? Can you track activity in real time? (If you are in the distribution business, can you provide such services to customers on a turnkey basis?)

- Who is in charge of your "private" (power, telecom, or transportation) utility? Are you ready to capitalize on deregulation? For example, is anyone looking at ways to generate some of your own power in a cost-effective way? Should you consolidate and assign the activity to a b-web service provider? (If you are a power, telecom, or transportation company, do you see these questions as an opportunity or a threat?)

- Do you have strategies for managing Distributive Network services across your b-webs?

DISTRIBUTIVE NETWORKS DEFINED

Value Chains and Alliances add value by converting raw materials or ideas into finished "goods." Aggregations and Agoras select, package, and price goods for markets that they seek out. Distributive Networks, in their purest forms (which is not always how you find them), service b-webs by allocating and delivering goods—whether information, objects, money, or other resources—from providers to users. The core value proposition of a Distributive Network is to facilitate the exchange and delivery of information, goods, and services. Distributive Networks typically provide commerce or infrastructure services to customers, context providers, and content providers.

A Distributive Network uses *mediating technologies* to facilitate exchanges across space and time.[1] Industrial-age transportation companies use trucks and roads. Federal Express zipped ahead with an intelligent software-enabled air–truck network. Then, in late 1998, FedEx declared that its physical distribution system of trucks and airplanes was less valuable than its internetworked information resources: Its digital structural capital was gaining value over its physical capital. FedEx decided to focus on value-added context services like online package tracking and logistics outsourcing, and leave the "driving" to b-web partners. Essentially, the company started to dump physical capital in favor of relationship and structural capital. It began selling its transport network, marshaling a b-web of truck and air transporters to handle the physical delivery.

Distributive Network customers include both providers and consumers of goods: a bank's depositors and lenders, for example. In this way, Distributive Networks are like Agoras and Alliances. An Agora, like eBay or NASDAQ, treats buyers and sellers alike as customers. In an Alliance, community participants collectively create the core value that they consume, and the context provider facilitates the process.

A Distributive Network reaches its potential when it becomes truly multi-way, turning customers from passive recipients to active contributors of value. The electrical power grid, for example, is mostly a one-way network. Small-scale generation based on solar and wind power and hydrogen and fossil fuels will enable users to feed their excess power back into the grid. Similarly, Internet services like @Home and interactive television transform cable from a one-way to a multi-way network.

A Distributive Network "message"—whether a physical good or a piece of information—may traverse a variety of technologies and service providers. A telephone call or an e-mail from New York to Singapore traverses copper, glass fiber, and satellite networks, touching the facilities of several companies.

Because of their role as supporting infrastructure to the economy and their multilevel, layered structure, Distributive Networks depend on standards for their very existence. In Distributive Network industries from transportation to telecommunications, competitors co-invest in developing and implementing common packaging, pricing, process, information, and technology standards. Because proponents of a standard can gain market advantages, standards making can be competitive and political, sometimes resulting in lopsided dominance of a vendor-controlled standard or the confusing prevalence of multiple competing standards. When this happens—as a U.S. federal judge ruled in the 1999 Microsoft case—both providers and consumers can suffer. In another example, European and Asian wireless network operators have nearly all adopted the Global System for Mobile (GSM) standard for mobile voice and data communications. But in North America, GSM is the least popular among several competing options, so global travelers cannot readily use their phones everywhere. As a result, in early 2000, wireless telephony leaders like Nokia were providing more innovations for the big, unified European and Asian markets than for the fragmented settings of the United States and Canada.

INDUSTRIAL-AGE DINOSAURS?

The generic policy deal through which governments granted power and wealth to twentieth-century Distributive Networks had several parts. A company gained protected access to its markets and guaranteed rates of return. In exchange, it accepted regulation of pricing and profits, competition, investment, access, territory, performance and safety regulations, and more. Customers gained predictable service levels from reliable providers.

Enron and the Power Industry: Crisis and Transformation

The new environment of deregulation, price volatility, and customer dissatisfaction boggles many power companies. As regulated local monopolies with guaranteed 12 percent rates of return, they feasted for decades off the spoils of a gold-plated business model. One executive said, "This is the only industry where you could increase your profits by redecorating your office."

Such state-sanctioned fiefdoms, based on a distribution system (in this case the power grid) that locked customers in, typified Distributive Network industries for over a hundred years. They also reflected an old-fashioned, physical-capital, asset-based mind-set, a view that to deliver value to the customer, a company must own its entire value chain: generating facilities, transmission lines, local distribution networks, and access to end-customers. Partners, such as municipal power companies, were also monopolies.

Deregulation smashes the assumptions behind the asset-based mind-set, disaggregating the businesses of generation, transmission, and marketing, each potentially a distinct b-web type with unique management needs. A generation plant is a Value Chain, transmission is a Distributive Network, and power marketing is an Aggregation. Customers will buy from any generation source via Agoras. With small-scale generation, users will even sell power into the grid.

Because of this transformation, traditional utilities find themselves stuck with "stranded" facilities, whose operating costs are multiples of what an open market will bear. While professing support for open markets, many of these companies wistfully strive to protect and extend their local monopolies. Meanwhile, a wave of defensive mergers and acquisitions engulfs the industry.

With combined 1998 revenues of some $330 billion in the United States alone, power industry competitors have a lot to lose. The electrical market is growing faster than the gas market and will be worth $1 trillion early in the new century.

Enron Corporation takes a different tack. From a typical power industry executive, Enron evokes fear, anger, grudging respect, envy, and awe. The company stuns its competitors as it aggressively sells, deals, takes risks, gets in and out of trouble, and leaps into—and out of—market experiments and niches. The company leads the drive for deregulation—not just in the United States, but worldwide.

Enron charges ahead like an adrenaline-driven Silicon Valley entrepreneur. In one 1998–1999 twelve-month period, it entered and abandoned the competitive California consumer power market; tried selling its competitors' hydroelectric power to Oregon consumers; announced plans for several outside-the-box businesses (a telecom bandwidth exchange, a national Internet fiber-optic network for multimedia, a global water utility, and a weather futures exchange); opened a controversial multibillion-dollar power plant in India; and swapped out its huge Chinese and U.S. natural gas properties.[2] The Muhammad Ali of the power business, Enron floats like a butterfly and stings like a bee. The company believes that the power business will be sliced, diced, and globalized, and it intends to be the industry's number one global player.

Though it builds physical assets, Enron readily sacrifices its power plants, gas wells, and pipelines as pawns in a chess game of global strategy. In 1999, the company spun out its Enron Oil and Gas (EOG) subsidiary as an independent business, saying that in the deregulated North American market, such fixed assets were no longer strategic. The parent company, with a focus on resale, distribution, and customer service, would get better commodity prices in the open marketplace than from a captive internal subsidiary. In other words, the company responded to declining transaction costs by disaggregating production from distribution and capitalizing on market efficiency.

Enron's growth engine and 89 percent of its 1998 revenues of $31 billion derive from wholesale energy sales, which makes it North America's largest supplier of electricity and natural gas. This business consists of (1) the marketing, resale, and delivery of energy commodities and (2) an energy asset investment operation. Customers include business users and power utilities. Enron learned these trades as a natural gas marketer and became America's top power marketer in the late 1980s.

Enron sells power from anyone to anyone and is just as happy to deliver via a competitor's network as its own, drawing on the structural capital of the entire industry. Its trading staff (human capital) use sophisticated, computer-based risk-management analytics, combined with networked market applications and trading and delivery systems that encompass thousands of suppliers, channels, and end-customers: a b-web for the energy marketing business. Traditional power companies, hoping to squeeze more returns from their physical capital legacies, self-deal prices that support their stranded facilities and bloated bureaucracies. Enron draws on b-web digital capital to help users get much closer to a fair market price.

Enron has several new ventures attuned to the world of b-webs: a telecom bandwidth exchange, a weather futures exchange, and a national Internet fiber-optic network for multimedia. All reflect the company's risk-management core competency. The fiber-optic network, an initiative of Enron Communications, transmits TV-quality videoconferences. Again, however, Enron is less concerned about owning the end-to-end asset than about delivering the customer service. As Enron Communications CEO Joe Hirko told us,

> *In the telecommunications industry, companies say they can only give you quality of service because they own the network end-to-end. It's an asset-focused view. We're going to link our networks together at a software layer so that we can deliver the same quality of service end-to-end. But we will do it over multiple networks, invisible to the content provider.*

Enron has also started an energy-management outsourcing business, positioning itself as a value-added infrastructure services provider. For most businesses—even some manufacturers whose energy costs can be 15 percent or more of total expenses—power management is an afterthought. Enron views customer-owned on-site assets like boilers, chillers, lighting, and controls as totally unregulated private utilities. It estimates the value of this market to be $240 billion in the United States alone. Enron wants to outsource the entire energy-management function, including asset capitalization and risk management, on long-term pay-for-performance contracts.

Enron displays many characteristics of an innovative b-web-oriented Distributive Network business:

- It views power and telecommunications as virtual core-value content, whereas the Distributive Network that enables delivery is an incidental commodity service.

- It finds effective ways to add value to these commodities, whose margins as pure bulk goods are in dramatic decline.

- It positions itself as a dominant b-web context provider (energy marketer) by taking control of customer relationships and defining the value proposition. In the process, asset-oriented industrial-age competitors become relegated to commodity suppliers of content (bulk power) or infrastructure (transmission) services.

• It applies advanced risk management and optimization analytics to reduce costs and increase customer value: an opportunity inherent to the nature of Distributive-Network-type businesses.

DISTRIBUTIVE NETWORK EFFECTS

Distributive Networks also have a feature that makes them drivers of any economy: they enable network effects (chapter 5). Nineteenth-century railways and telegraph networks gained exponential value as their coverage expanded, enriching robber barons like Andrew Carnegie and seeding telecom dynasties like AT&T. More important, these networks drove the Industrial Revolution by opening up and speeding the flow of goods, information, and transactions. The networks enabled Sears and other national retailers to create a new business model, using mail order to sell and deliver directly to farmers, disintermediating small-town general stores across the United States in the process.

Two forces encourage Distributive Network businesses to expand as much as possible. The first, and strongest, is network effects: The bigger the network, the greater its value. The second is regulation: Many governments expect Distributive Network monopolies to service everyone. As regulation has ebbed, Distributive Networks have worked even harder to capitalize on network effects through build-outs, mergers, and acquisitions.

Network Optimization and Arbitrage: Special Features of Distributive Networks

Network optimization is a complex challenge. All customers expect to be treated well and fairly, and at the time and place of need. But servicing some customers is especially costly (as with rural residents) or risky (as with loan defaulters). Also, keeping the network responsive and efficient—capable of handling routine service levels, unexpected demand spikes, and unruly performance glitches—is a complex optimization problem. Airlines call the solution yield management, banks call it risk portfolio management, and telecom operators simply call it network management.

Outliers—unexpected extreme shifts in supply and demand—provide Distributive Networks with unique challenges and opportunities. Enron set up a weather futures exchange after the short-term price of electricity increased 500-fold during a 1998 heat wave in the North American Midwest. Now, companies that depend on the weather can hedge their risks against hurricanes and droughts.

As the resources and mediating technologies that a Distributive Network optimizes become tradable, opportunities for arbitrage appear. The basis of arbitrage is that some goods are cheap in one market and dear in another. The arbitrageur profits from the spread between the two markets. As markets converge in time and space (whether physical or virtual), arbitrage opportunities decline. A classic example of this phenomenon was the 1960s craze for Levi's blue jeans in the Soviet Union. Travelers could buy a pair of pants in New York for $15 and sell them in Moscow for $75. Arbitrage may be good for a Distributive Network company, but at a cost to customers.

Two kinds of arbitrage exist: information arbitrage and allocative arbitrage. With *information arbitrage,* the Distributive Network benefits from asymmetrical information: It has better knowledge than do other market participants. We deposit our savings in the bank and rely on the bank's special skills to evaluate loan-related risk. In exchange for security and various services, we accept that the bank pockets the spread between the low interest rate it pays us, and the higher rate it charges borrowers.

Allocative arbitrage, as with Levi's blue jeans in Moscow, capitalizes on differences in the physical availability of a good. Cable TV networks have historically been able to charge high rates for access to TV channels because they were the only game in town.

Arbitrage in financial markets involves a bit of both. Arbitrageurs use their special knowledge (information arbitrage) to place bets on the relationship between the price of a futures contract and the price of the assets that underlie the contract (allocative arbitrage). Customers of industrial-age Distributive Network companies (all of us) often end up paying arbitrage-driven fees for inflexible and disappointing services. The low cost of Internet telephony gives phone companies an opportunity to play an arbitrage game for the next few years: charging regular long distance rates and using the Internet to transmit the calls.

The transparency, immediacy, ubiquity, and smart software tools provided by digital networks empower Distributive Network customers to recover some or all of their arbitrage costs. Knowledge, analysis tools, and access to goods and services that were formerly available only to specialists now become available to everyone. Business-model innovators are enabling customers to capitalize on this new transparency. Enron's value proposition, for example, empowers customers to participate in a price and services definition game that was formerly the exclusive preserve of monopolies.

DIGITAL DISTRIBUTIVE NETWORKS

Distributive Networks include three primary categories, which we call slice and dice, store and forward, and park and lever.

- *Slice-and-dice* networks amass and distribute continuous-flow, divisible goods like power and natural gas.

- *Store-and-forward* networks include shipping and postal services, travel facilities like airlines and highways, the content-delivery functions of telecom networks (both voice and data), and the Internet itself. These networks deliver their goods intact and mostly untouched.

- *Park-and-lever* networks include banks and insurance companies. These networks accumulate capital, slice and dice it, and "lever" the value by lending it for interest or guaranteeing and paying off risks. B-web "infomediaries" also qualify as park-and-lever Distributive Networks.

Slice and Dice

These industries have begun to transform themselves but remain in the early stages of change. The asset-based mind-set is a big inhibitor.

Challenging the dominant industry model, Enron Communications set up an exchange b-web marketplace intended to commoditize the sale and pricing of telecommunications bandwidth. Enterprises will be able to reserve bandwidth for high-bit-rate applications like streaming media and Internet videoconferencing. "The trading of bandwidth will supercharge the entire Internet industry by dramatically increasing the efficiency of bandwidth provisioning and deployment," argues Tom Gros, Enron's vice president of global bandwidth trading. "Bandwidth trading levels the playing field for communications companies by making bandwidth more cost effective and more readily available."[3] Service providers benefit because they have access to a reserve of capacity when their customers need it. End users benefit because market forces will drive down the price.

The power industry is also feeling the effects of disaggregation. California has legislated structural separation between electrical power generation and transmission. Pacific Gas and Electric (PG&E) customers can buy power from competing generation companies. The California Power Exchange publicly prices and trades kilowatt-hours. The start-up company utility.com, which buys power through the exchange, guarantees its consumers a minimum 10 percent saving over "monopoly" pricing.[4] An Internet-enabled power management service, ModernMeter, tracks customer energy usage and transmits the information back to utility.com, which then provides advice on how to achieve cost savings.

Despite all this change, the power business—like most slice-and-dice Distributive Network industries, with a few exceptions like Enron—still behaves as if wedded to an asset-based, vertically integrated model. In our scenario, the power industry is a collection of competing b-webs, with businesses in each of the five areas of table 6-1. Internet applications make "smart" power management decisions. Vertical integration is virtual; businesses in each layer compete for deals with those in other layers. Consumers can go to an online hub to choose among a variety of power offerings, with pricing packages that depend on usage, term, timing, power source, and so forth. Agent-enabled home appliances negotiate price and terms of use in real time via the Net. A dishwasher seeks out and bargains the best available deal for the night's load. Customers

TABLE 6-1   Disaggregation of the Power Industry

Horizontal Component	B-Web Type
Power generation	Value Chain (routine production)
Transmission	Distributive Network (slice and dice)
Power services marketing and delivery	Aggregation
Energy management and advisory services	Value Chain (both project-based and routine production)
Online power services "hubs"	Aggregations with Agora dimensions

and small-scale generating plants provide 10 percent of the grid's power. In this world, as Hirko suggests, "energy sells at the lowest possible cost."

Store and Forward

In contrast to slice-and-dice industries, store-and-forward Distributive Networks have raced to provide commerce and infrastructure services for the thousands of b-webs now coming to life. These businesses enable the core commerce and infrastructure of the digital transformation. If the financial services industry manages other people's money, then store-and-forward Distributive Networks deliver other people's goods, both digital and physical.

Telecom networks—telephone, cable, and wireless—provide the new infrastructure. Physical fulfillment industries, including courier, postal, and shipping, have also responded quickly. Federal Express and UPS have aggressively adapted their offerings to the demands of digital business. The responses of the airlines, which carry the human cargo of the global economy, have been mixed. American Airlines, a leader, now offers both an online travel service (Travelocity) and a slick site for its own customers. Delta was an early investor in and supplier to Priceline.

But the asset-based mind-set and information arbitrage are alive and well in store-and-forward Distributive Networks. In the airline industry, yield management systems create perceived and real value inequities for customers. Priceline capitalizes on this perception (chapter 2). Telecom operators have wisely gotten out of equipment manufacturing. But several telecom companies have entered the "content" business, buying into TV networks or (like AT&T) into Internet portals and digital publishing. Many still act as if they need to own the industry value chain, rather than recognizing the b-web opportunity; the January 2000 merger between AOL and Time Warner is to date the most spectacular example of this mind-set.[5]

Focus is the key to success in store-and-forward Distributive Networks. Consider telecommunications, for which the upheavals of the 1990s will pale in comparison to what is coming. During the next decade, three changes will transform the industry.

First, the economics of telecommunications will turn upside down. The price/performance curve will plummet, enabling networks to cheaply deliver high-quality interactive multimedia—based on Internet communications protocols—to homes and offices. Telephone calls will be less than 1 percent of what these networks carry, and long-distance revenues will collapse.

Second, as the Net becomes ubiquitous, applications become more interesting. Software technologies like Bluetooth (which enables ad hoc wireless connections among many kinds of devices, from digital Barbies to PCs, cameras, Cadillacs, and Jeeps) will engage multiple devices in transactions with one another. "Hosted applications" on the Net will transform the economics of the software business.

Third, the future is wireless, ubiquitous computing. Mobile phones will transmogrify into compact tools that combine the features of telephony, personal organizers, and the Internet. PCs, Internet tablets, electronic books, security devices, smart cards, music-on-demand players, Coke machines—you name it!—will communicate via a wireless infrastructure. New entrants, unencumbered by the capital costs of still-necessary wire-based assets, will enter the market. Power companies, with hydroelectric lines flowing into and through every house and office building, may even find a technology that enables them to compete with telecom companies in a cost-effective way.

Telecommunications providers face a huge upside opportunity from all this. But they also face challenges. Telecom companies that have traditionally established branded relationships through their lock on the user's experience—from dial tone to superficially value-added services like voice mail—face brand slippage. This happens to your brand when someone else becomes the context provider, the most visible gateway for the user's experience. Wireless data will include a full gamut of user services, ported over from next-generation Web applications, so the interesting context could be a browser (say, Palm or Windows CE) or a portal (one can already do voice mail and faxing via the Excite @Home site), or just about any sort of service provider.

In such a world, how do you come up with a profitable business model—one that provides the greatest return on assets? Many telecom players are pursuing the old asset-based infrastructure model by other means—acquiring or building brute-force, global, end-to-end facilities and services from underground wires to Silicon Valley software and Hollywood content.

AT&T Corporation subsidiary AT&T Solutions is among the first and largest of a new breed of "networking integrator" focused on adding value to the traditional "transport" functions of telecommunications. The company's offerings include professional services (b-web strategy and network infrastructure design), network construction and implementation, and ongoing operation. Like an Andersen Consulting, AT&T Solutions uses gray-matter strategy consulting as an entrée to large-scale systems deals. Unlike Andersen, which specializes in software applications, AT&T Solutions has a new kind of focus: global internetworking as an enabler of b-webs.

Rick Roscitt, president and CEO of AT&T Solutions, describes the challenges that asset-based telecom companies face in moving upstream:

> The telcos of the world have got their hands full. They need to do much more than deliver broadband. They must get their cost structures down through a combination of technology-based, systems-based, and people-based efficiency moves. They need to go global because that's what it takes to service customers. If that weren't bad enough, they also need to expand their capabilities. . . .
>
> A professional services firm doesn't say, "I can fix what your problem is as long as it's a fever." It diagnoses what you need from a clean sheet of paper and applies the right dose of medicine at the right time, precisely for your individual needs. Product-driven companies hate that: they want to build something once and scale it up to millions or billions of people.[6]

Roscitt points out that to achieve this transition, a Distributive Network company must shift its value focus from physical to human capital:

> A traditional telecom executive loves the network because it's like a cash register. If he can't sleep at night he just says to himself, "I wonder how much we're ringing up tonight." It just keeps functioning. It's an automated wonder. This doesn't work very well in a professional services business. You need people working around the clock, so you run work centers around the world to follow the sun—Amsterdam, Bangalore, Singapore and Shanghai, then North Carolina and Ohio. It's not just the network ticking along—it's all those people surveying, monitoring, and working. Everybody likes to say people are your most important asset, but in professional services they're really your prime asset.

Clearly, someone needs to be in the business of providing physical infrastructure and services. But do *you*? If that is what your business excels at, then do it, recognizing that it is increasingly a competitive, commodity-priced service. To win, you will need to focus on network effects, acquiring as many points of presence as possible. But draw a line between your network and the content that it distributes, or you will soon find yourself competing with your customers.

On the other hand, if you can carve out one, or several, areas of value-added focus, your return on capital is likely to be substantially higher than if you try to do it all. Even a seemingly non-differentiable industry like telecommunications is disaggregating into a portfolio of b-web services.

Park and Lever

Arbitrage is the essence of banking. Depositors "park" their money in banks in exchange for the "leverage" of interest income and payment services. Banks also "lever" depositors' money by lending it to borrowers for a higher interest rate. Banks live off the spread, the difference between lending rates and the savers' interest rates.

The banks' expertise in evaluating and managing the risks entailed in lending and cash-flow management theoretically justifies their arbitrage profits. During the 1970s, when inflation and lending rates soared, customers began to disintermediate the banks and put their money into securities markets: mutual funds and commercial paper. Networked computer technology turned these instruments into sophisticated mobilizers of capital. In 1960, U.S. banks' share of household financial assets was 40 percent; by 1997, their share had declined to 14 percent.[7]

Money has a number of unique properties as an object of arbitrage. First, unlike other goods that Distributive Networks convey, like electricity or UPS packages, money is pure information, easy to distribute as a stream of bits. Second, unlike other information goods like e-mail messages, money is a pure commodity. Third, a Distributive Network as temporary holder can gain value from the money itself (e.g., by backing a loan that attracts interest) without diminishing its worth to the depositor, its true owner. Like the burning bush of the Mosaic fable, money can cast off heat and light without being consumed.[8]

On the one hand, these properties of money explain why financial intermediaries capture extraordinary benefits from their privileged roles. On the other, they also explain why depositors, the true owners of capital, find it both attractive and easy to park their money elsewhere. Now, the digital economy poses new challenges.

Witness how easy it is to apply for and receive a loan online. New, Internet-based "investomediaries" will manage this service at near-zero transaction costs. They will invite depositors to lend money directly to borrowers, splitting the loan spread and increasing liquidity throughout the economy. Network effects, indeed!

Banks and post offices are moving to prevent Internet start-ups from capturing the emerging electronic bill presentment market. But why can't businesses simply use secure e-mail to transmit their e-bills themselves? All they need is a third-party certification authority to vouchsafe the authenticity of the transmission.

Is consolidation the solution? The traditional local bank is rapidly disappearing, under the watchwords "economy of scale" and "economy of scope." Economy of scale views a bank as a factory, where return on investment (e.g., for soaring information technology and marketing costs) increases when two banks combine. Economy of scope suggests that it is more profitable for one bank to offer a variety of services than it is for two different banks to offer different services—since customers presumably prefer one-stop shopping.

Consolidation may be only a temporary fix, however. The banks may need *economies* of scale, but more important, as their role changes from face-to-face savings and loan services to networked transaction enablement, they need pure *scale:* as many electronic points of presence as they can get.

With the 1999 repeal of the Glass-Steagal Act in the United States breaking down the walls between banking, brokerage, insurance, and other financial services, these institutions' drive toward economies of scope will likely take off. But are they missing the b-web point? Consumers certainly prefer the convenience and sense of control offered by one-stop shopping for financial services. However, one-stop shopping does not require one-source services content. Citibank's Web site provides thousands of securities to choose from—including (obviously!) those of its competitors. When in the market for personal banking, a loan, or a mortgage, however, Citibank customers can only select among

Citibank offerings. A new class of "investomediaries" will be broad financial-service context providers, enabling us to choose among global (and local) brands in any service content category. Examples of these services include the following:

- *Managing wealth through an online broker context.* Well before the Internet explosion, many brokers followed Merrill Lynch into checking, credit card, and other banking-type activities. Online brokers, including Schwab, E*Trade, and Fidelity (on- and offline) did the same. By early 2000, some online brokers were nicely integrating these two sides of the personal financial management process. But with the exception of TD Waterhouse (an acquisition), banks' online brokerage services lacked pizzazz. Evidently, it's more complicated for a Wells Fargo to build a robust online broker than for a Schwab to add checking services to its existing brokerage. But it's also true that because of their love of spreads, banks don't really want customers to put money into securities. The holy grail of wealth management is an anytime/anyplace confidential resource that tracks a customer's entire financial portfolio; it matches advice and products (from whatever source) to the customer's changing needs.

- *Empowering customers to do their own arbitrage.* In 1997, Richard Branson's UK-based Virgin Group company launched the Virgin One account as a telephone bank. The account pools customer income and debts, including credit card charges and home mortgages. Each customer receives a line of credit, secured against his or her home. Virgin One is revolutionary. First, loan and deposit interest rates are identical: no spreads. Second, the customers may repay loans at their own pace. They are neither penalized for paying off a mortgage quickly, nor for slowing payments down. The Virgin model gives customers transparent control over the distributive side of personal money management.[9] How about an online offering that matches individual lenders to individual borrowers, enabling them to "split the difference" on traditional bankers' spreads?

- *Intermediating investments, or "investomediating."* Online mortgage brokers have built b-webs that presage the investomediary concept described above. These businesses provide competitive quotes from banks both large and small. Some, like IOwn.com, are stand-alone sites that function purely as brokers. Priceline takes this function a step further, encouraging borrowers to name their terms for mortgages, home refinancing, and equity loans. Others, like Realtor.com and Microsoft Home Advisor, embed mortgage brokering in an integrated home-buying automated service.

Two lessons can be learned from the banking industry. First, if you are profiting from information arbitrage, expect someone to come up with a business model that challenges your advantages. Second, change the value proposition by providing customers with the information and tools they need to make their own informed choices. Assume that if you don't provide such a service, they will get it from someone else.

Infomediaries: A New Park-and-Lever Opportunity?

Information, or knowledge, is a "good" that can be parked (stored) and levered (increased in value without being diminished). Though a knowledge asset can be shared widely without the diminishment of its intrinsic value, such distribution can be costly or harmful to the original owner, who may lose privacy or control over intellectual property rights.

Although John Hagel and Marc Singer popularized the concept of infomediaries, in some ways their book *Net Worth* does not describe the full potential of this concept.[10] First, they define the term narrowly. Dozens of others picked up the word, because it is such a good one, and gave it their own definitions. As a result, the term has become a bit meaningless. We believe that *infomediary* should refer to *an entity that captures trusted information from customers and manages it on their behalf for potential reuse.*

Second, although Hagel and Singer's starting point is good, they recommend a business strategy for infomediaries that weakens the core idea. They say that an infomediary works for consumers "to aggregate their information with that of other consumers and to use the combined market power to negotiate with vendors on their behalf." But they go on to argue that infomediaries "will become the custodians, agents, and brokers of customer information, marketing it to businesses (and providing them with access to it) on consumers' behalf, while at the same time protecting their privacy."[11]

But why should the consumer trust an infomediary that works for (is paid by) businesses who want his or her personal information? Consumers confide their most confidential personal information—say brand preferences or a medical condition—based on the assumption that the infomediary will "negotiate" on their behalf. Then, the infomediary makes money from marketing and providing that information to businesses. Though they describe the importance of privacy rights, Hagel and Singer ultimately define the infomediary as a matchmaker that controls the prospect list, which it flogs to vendors—a kind of digital asset-based mind-set where the infomediary holds the cards.

Let's imagine another approach, one of many possibilities. Consumers (and businesses as purchasers of goods and services) pay the infomediary. The infomediary is accountable to the customer for ensuring quality of service and privacy. Infomediaries enable consumers to manage their own personal b-web through services that could include the following:

- Maintaining and managing access functions and privileges (user IDs, passwords, credit card information, etc.)

- Maintaining and managing transaction records

- Building and maintaining preference profiles in various subject areas (books, music, health, food and drink, technology, etc.)

- Managing confidential profiles for user-authorized sharing with suppliers (health care record, investment portfolio, credit history, etc.)

- Forming spontaneous, anonymous buyers' groups on the fly

- Representing the customer's intentions and preferences as a buyer of goods and services

Instead of making money on the "spreads" of information arbitrage between the buyer and seller, an infomediary represents the buyer. The infomediary is more like a broker—executing the customer's orders for a fee—rather than like a bank, which levers the customer's money on its behalf.

The core issue is this: What is the business model for capturing and managing this most trust-critical dimension of relationship capital?

Thousands of infomediaries—including credit agencies, health care institutions, and retailers—already exist, most operating without consumer consent.

B-WEB ENABLERS

As we have said, Distributive Networks provide the commerce and infrastructure services foundation of the digital economy: telecommunications, financial services, distribution and logistics, air travel, and power. However, a business or entrepreneur embarking on a digital strategy is unlikely to place its first call to someone in one of these industries. It is more likely to contact a Web site developer, a consulting firm, an advertising agency, a systems integrator, or a software company. Webvan did begin with logistics and seems to have made the right, albeit countercultural, decision (chapter 3).

Leading-edge Distributive Network context providers, like Enron, UPS, and AT&T Solutions, operate as enablers, not just of e-commerce, but of business webs. They specialize in weaving together networks of companies, adding value through visibility, speed, and agility.

A critical competency for b-web-enabling Distributive Networks is real-time event-driven responsiveness, supported by highly optimized distribution processes. On the flip side, aspiring b-webs that fail to mobilize such optimized Distributive Network services are unlikely to succeed. Cisco's single-enterprise b-web depends on the responsiveness of its logistics partners. Online grocers Peapod and Streamline faced untold headaches and costs in trying to solve the complex distribution problems of the consumer marketplace.

An untapped opportunity is the formation of b-web-enabling commerce and infrastructure networks that crisscross Distributive Network industries. Such "Distributive Network solutions" could break many of the logjams in the way of b-web effectiveness. For example:

• *Fill your trunk and your tank.* A b-web partnership between a bank, a telecom provider, a delivery service, and an oil company provides shopping, delivery, and pickup services for a broad cross-section of retailers, using neighborhood gas stations as drop points.

- *We deliver anything, anytime!* A similar b-web leaves out the oil company, but joins with the power company to provide a secure, three-level, temperature-controlled (frozen, cold, and room temperature) box for grocery and other deliveries in consumers' garages. With such a box, consumers need not be home when the e-groceries are delivered. Streamline offers such a service today, but only for its own products.

- *Plug-and-play e-supply chain.* Distribution, software, telecom, consulting, and financial services companies partner to provide turnkey solutions for digital supply-chain enablement.

- *Digital destinations.* A telecom company, an airline company, a limousine service, a travel agency, and a package delivery company partner to provide concierge services that ease and simplify the lives of frequent travelers.

Such opportunities mean forming b-webs that enable b-webs. It entails a focus on customer value and on "horizontal opportunities" through partnerships, rather than asset monopolization.

KEY SUCCESS FACTORS

Enable b-webs. In the digital economy, customers who act on b-web opportunities are most likely to succeed. Such customers are also in greatest need of your services. They understand the need for partnership, and so are more likely to turn to external providers of commerce and infrastructure services. They also need a vast, high-performing, yet efficient set of distributive services to link up with their own ever-changing array of customers and partners.

Choose between commodity infrastructure services and value-adding "slices." Some telecom companies, like Global Crossing and, arguably, MCI WorldCom, are "bit haulers" that focus primarily on physical facilities and commodity services. AT&T Solutions has taken a value-added approach.

Cut customers into arbitrage deals. Arbitrage is fine when customers accept it. But in the digital economy, instantaneous and distributed information gives customers knowledge, choice, and process transparency. Arbitrage won't disappear, but you may do well to split the proceeds with customers. When you play the game right—as Enron has done—you will more than make up for it in volume.

Enable event-driven responsiveness and optimization. Event-driven operational effectiveness is the price of admission in the digital economy—akin to good blocking and tackling. It is a necessary, but not a sufficient, condition to b-web success.

Maximize points of presence. Network effects drive value in Distributive Networks. The more locations and customers that you serve, the more value you will deliver to your customers.

Beware the asset-based mind-set and think b-webs. Just because you need to maximize points of presence, you don't need to own them. As FedEx works with third-party truckers and airlines, you can control the b-web information highway, and let your b-web partners drive.

LEADER'S GUIDE TO DISTRIBUTIVE NETWORKS

Definition: The core value proposition of a Distributive Network is to facilitate the exchange and delivery of information, goods, and services.

Significance: Distributive Networks provide key commerce and infrastructure services to all businesses. Every b-web strategy requires a state-of-the-art strategy for Distributive Network services; every Distributive Network business needs to perform as an enabler of b-webs.

Types: Distributive Networks include the following types:

• Slice-and-dice networks amass and distribute continuous-flow, divisible goods like power, gas, and telecommunications bandwidth.

• Store-and-forward networks include shipping and postal services, travel facilities like airlines and highways, the content-delivery functions of telecom networks (both voice and data), and the Internet itself. These networks deliver their goods intact and mostly untouched.

- Park-and-lever networks are typically banks and insurance companies. These networks accumulate capital, slice and dice it, and lever the value by lending it for interest or guaranteeing and paying off risks. B-web infomediaries also qualify as park-and-lever Distributive Networks.

Key transformation: Distributive Networks transform regulated, monolithic monopolies to competitive, disaggregated market players.

Part III

the human and relationship elements of digital capital

7 people:
the human capital
in the business web

Internetworked human capital raises challenges and opportunities for all businesses. Human capital now extends beyond the firm; people resemble molecules moving across the firm's porous membrane in ever-changing configurations. Companies need internetworked human resource management. Managers should define and communicate an explicit b-web culture to guide the deployment of human capital. While every b-web is unique, patterns and guidelines are emerging for fostering a high-performance b-web culture.

"Our people are our greatest asset." When Amazon.com CEO Jeff Bezos makes this statement, then to whom is he referring? Certainly his management team, the professionals maintaining the company's Web site, and its administration and distribution staff are great assets. But in Amazon.com's book business alone, the human capital base includes innumerable others:

• Countless authors and readers who generate online book commentaries for the Web site and participate in online chats

- Publishers that provide sophisticated content for the b-web

- Tens of thousands of Amazon associates, from a youngster in a Cleveland Little League to a professor in Houston, who hot-link to the site and participate in its extended sales network

- Trained personnel at Ingram Distribution, FedEx, and UPS who fulfill customer orders

- Staff at *Kirkus Reviews*, the *Library Journal*, and countless other book-review publications

Amazon.com draws most of its human capital from its b-web.

We are in the midst of a historic change, as human capital forms internetworks and extends beyond the boundaries of the firm. As discussed in chapter 1, human capital comprises the capabilities of individuals in the organization. It includes the skills, knowledge, intellect, creativity, and know-how that they individually possess. It is the capability of individuals to create value for customers. Peter Drucker pointed out in 1993 that such knowledge is not merely another factor of production like labor, money, and land—it is the only meaningful resource today. Consequently, the knowledgeable worker is every organization's greatest single asset.[1]

The b-web changes this asset fundamentally. No longer are a company's human resources restricted to traditional employees. As Steven Behm, Cisco's former vice president of global alliances, said, "We have 32,000 employees, but only 17,000 of them work at Cisco."

Indeed, Cisco works with a "human resource" that extends far beyond its own corporate boundaries. It treats its b-web as the central actor in value creation. The company does not outsource functions; it integrates partners. As integration tightens and focuses on customer value, the b-web grows faster. Cisco's human capital includes microchip designers innovating new technologies in teams that include, but do not primarily consist of, Cisco employees. This partly explains how this fledgling company stole massive market share from Lucent—a company that owns Bell Labs, one of the world's deepest reserves of human capital. Rather than just human resource (HR) management, Cisco has IHR—management of the *internetworked human resource*.[2]

THE MOLECULARIZATION OF HUMAN CAPITAL

An analogy from physics explains the human capital in b-webs. The individual is the basic component of human capital—not unlike the molecule in physical matter. A molecule is the smallest particle into which a substance, like water, can be divided and still maintain its chemical identity. Electrical forces attract molecules to one another. In solids, like ice, the electrical attraction is strong, allowing little molecular motion. When the electrical attraction is weakened (by the addition of heat), the molecules can move more, the result of which is the liquid state. And of course, when the attracting force is the weakest, the substance is in a gaseous state, that is, one in which the molecules move around the most. As conditions (temperature and pressure) change, so do molecular states.

A single person is like a molecule in a b-web. Some b-webs (Value Chains and Distributive Networks) under particular conditions (market, technology, industry, customer, etc.) can bind molecules tightly together. Certain conditions drive more dynamic relationships, as molecules combine, separate, and move into and out of b-webs. Turn up the heat on your people, and they'll leave. Change the forces that bind people, and they'll regroup.

How far is this trend going? Will disaggregation occur to the point that firms become networks of independent contractors?

In one extreme view, Thomas Malone and Robert Laubacher argue that in a couple of decades, we may look back on the integrated firm as a transitional structure that flourished for a brief moment in history. They suggest that the fundamental unit of the economy may be reverting from the corporation to the individual. Independent contractors, rather than full-time employees in big companies, will perform most work. Such networked *e-lancers* will join fluid and temporary webs to design, produce, market, and support goods and services.[3]

Malone and Laubacher acknowledge that the pace of merger and acquisition activities might lead one to the conclusion that the large industrial corporation is alive and well. However, they point to other evidence. During the 1970s, Fortune 500 companies employed one in five U.S. workers. Today the ratio is less than one in ten. Moreover, "the largest private employer in the United States is not General Motors, IBM or UPS. It's the temporary employment agency Manpower Incorporated."[4] They argue that the Net is returning us to a preindustrial organization model of independent journeymen.

The massive consolidation in Distributive Networks like telecom companies, banks, power companies, and other utilities is shrinking the number of traditional jobs. Meanwhile, the bulk of economic growth originates with small companies—increasingly in b-webs.

Certainly, many Alliance and Agora b-webs have already developed to a point at which individuals participate as full partners. Independent computer programmers around the world contribute to the Linux Alliance. Although many work for large organizations, few participate in the Linux b-web on behalf of their employers. Programmers solve day-to-day problems and share this knowledge with other b-web participants, handcrafting Linux to its formidable strength. Programmers at competing companies quietly help one another behind the scenes. Only in 1999 did large companies like IBM and Dell join the Linux Alliance. IBM treads lightly on the Linux culture, realizing that as a big company it could easily be resented and shunned.

Similarly, hundreds of thousands of individuals and small shopkeepers sell globally via the eBay Agora. Many now earn a full-time living through this channel. For buyers, a large part of the appeal is the opportunity to do business with fellow enthusiasts, collectors, and hobbyists.

Individuals contribute to the Amazon.com Aggregation more easily than to a typical bricks-and-mortar bookseller. Independent editorial contractors work from any location, and customers contribute reviews or join online discussions with authors.

For Value Chains—such as manufacturers—integrating armies of e-lancers is more difficult. But individuals and small firms frequently participate in less structured, more creative areas of shop production like industrial design.

There is already evidence that companies can acquire resources through human capital Agoras. In 1999 thousands of individual free agents auctioned their services on the Talent Market at Monster.com. On eBay, an entire virtual project team put itself up for sale.[5] These people aimed to shift from being independent molecules to a liquidlike structure posted on the Web; change to a solid, executing the project as a tightly knit team; and then revert to the equivalent of a liquid crystal, remarketing their capabilities as a strongly associated group of individuals. Had they experienced a disaster, the forces that bind them would have weakened and they would disperse like gas to reform with other molecules in a different situation.

Cynics could spin such developments differently. They might say that it was not a virtual project team for sale on the Net but rather a traditional company using the Net to sell itself to the highest bidder. Or that the Monster.com auctions are a gimmick to attract customers to its regular listings. Perhaps. But more likely, these events foreshadow bigger things to come.

Individuals and teams will acquire marketable reputations, like Wall Street analysts and eBay traders, based on their ratings and behavior as buyers and sellers. The next step? Reputations or personal brands (like Michael Jordan) will translate into market values. Over time such measures of human capital will become more sophisticated.

Consider this scenario:

Bob: "Let's try to get Greg Munro to work on this project. I just checked Monster.com, and he'll be available in a month."

Joanne: "Are you kidding? Have you seen what he's trading at?"[6]

From the perspective of the individual subcontractor, is molecularization of human capital a good way to earn a living? If you like working as an independent and you have truly marketable competencies, molecularization means freedom, variety, less bureaucracy, opportunities for skill enhancement and lifelong learning, and maybe even more income. Highly competent individuals will gain pride from their premium market valuations.

But this scenario has its downsides. Job security, as most people understand it, declines. Companies terminate contracts with individuals for infractions that would not warrant firing in the traditional employment model. The wealthy Silicon Valley programmer flitting from job to job is a glamorous but atypical stereotype. According to the U.S. Department of Labor, more than half of temporary workers do not have health insurance; almost half are women with children; few end up in full-time employment; and many report that they are treated worse than full-time workers. When you factor in the working conditions in many other countries, the list of grievances grows dramatically.

In the digital economy, where new business models and structures destroy entire companies and industries, job security has become a relic of a brief moment in human history. But managers must rethink the contract between firms and independents. Whether part-time, mobile, teleworking, contingent, contract, or all of the above, new working relationships based on ability to add value to the task at hand, clear expectations, mutual support, trust, and commitment will need to be forged.

As b-web opportunities grow, so does the number of people who choose to be independents. However, most workers are still employees. Some molecular clusters are small, such as in an entrepreneurial design firm. Some groups, loosely connected in larger firms like Manpower, provide individual units on a contract basis. Others, like EDS and Andersen Consulting, deliver tightly connected individuals and project teams with clear group-performance objectives. Such human-capital suppliers often take over entire business functions. Or, firms may partner in a b-web to cocreate and codeliver value. Regardless of how it is combined, human capital can be considered as molecules and clusters of molecules—within the firm and outside, local and global—to be rapidly deployed for customer value creation.

THE INTER-ENTERPRISE HUMAN RESOURCE

What are the implications of these ever-shifting dynamics for human resource management? In many companies, the HR function remains an obstacle to change. It lacks curiosity and covets old attitudes, ways of working, and legacy cultures. While some HR professionals rise to the challenge, too many do not. In integrated corporations, HR typically supplies services, such as benefits, staffing, salary negotiation, and performance reviews. But as we move into the world of b-webs, the HR profession must reinvent itself and attend to a vital new resource: internetworked human capital. It must create conditions for inter-organizational—b-web—effectiveness.

Rather than HR management, we need to think in terms of IHRM—inter-enterprise human resource management—human capital in its internetworked form. Companies must view the employees of their b-web's partners as extensions of their own capital, because competitiveness and customer value creation depend on accumulating and unleashing digital capital in all its forms.

Managers should not try to boss the people across their b-webs, however. Firms have fiduciary and legal obligations to their own employees. They have different obligations to people in partner firms. But several new factors merit consideration.

HR managers should rethink traditional functions like recruiting. B-web resources continually move across organizational membranes. When judging a prospective partner, a manager should evaluate its human capital, just as managers in the old closed corporation assessed a new hire. Rather than recruiting, HR managers should think about amassing internetworked human capital.

Cisco calls such activities "just-in-time recruitment." Rather than take months to evaluate a prospective employee, firms make decisions in real-time, particularly when the "employees" are e-lancers. Companies must court human capital to anticipate needs, develop and maintain reserves, make processes digital and networked, and develop new performance measures. Electronic recruiting, already an important new facilitator, is a multi-billion-dollar market.[7]

IHRM also applies to conflict resolution. The old corporation used a number of techniques to deal with conflict. Some, like day-to-day discussions, were informal. Others, like grievance procedures, were more formal. Now, new mechanisms that center on the market emerge in b-webs. For example, b-web price-discovery mechanisms for online recruiting change the way that organizations make decisions about compensation.

The b-web's total performance, not just the performance of one's own firm, determines success. Managers must motivate individuals across the entire b-web.

B-WEB CULTURE: NINE IMPERATIVES

In the past, smart managers deliberately fostered their firm's culture: the values, norms, and mission of the firm that grow from, reflect, and influence the thinking and behavior of its people. Outsiders see it as a modus operandi—ways of working and collaborating, strategic planning, business processes, approaches to staff development, HR policies, and management styles.

Like all organizations, every b-web has a culture, implicit or explicit. In the best b-webs, culture is robust and provides a healthy environment for value creation. Managers design their b-web culture to shape the evolution of internetworked human capital. Managers need to take steps to foster a high-performance culture.

1. Define and Shape B-Web Strategy and Values

The best b-webs share direction and values, although roles and relationships within the partnership vary. Participants who share goals demonstrate commitment, efficiency, and adaptability.

Sun Microsystems CEO Scott McNealy uses imagery, symbols, and humor to champion Sun's values and vision across its b-web. Sun presents itself as the open-systems company in contrast to an allegedly closed, autocratic Microsoft. Sun champions the values of customer power, vendor independence, and free enterprise. It positions its partnership with the U.S. Department of Justice as a crusade against monopolies and for entrepreneurship. Sun frees its knowledge workers to create new ideas and technologies like Java. Yet the company is hierarchical, and everyone knows who is in charge. McNealy communicates corporate values regularly through vehicles like Sun Talk Radio. (He describes himself to us as the Rush Limbaugh of Sun.) At one internal meeting, he was introduced as "Mr. Command and Control." No management jargon about learning organizations here. This CEO speaks and learns on behalf of the entire corporation and beyond to the b-web.

Communication of vision and values varies according to b-web and business conditions. Priceline poses a threat to anyone who sells anything, while positioning itself as an ally in liquidating unsold inventory—a mere bottom feeder. It tells sellers that it will help them realize opportunities online. Cisco's suppliers report that marketing hype permeates the company's b-web story. But they don't really mind. Cisco's vision helps hold this profitable b-web together. Preaching customer empowerment, E*Trade mocks stockbrokers in its marketing campaigns: "If your broker is so smart, why is he still working?" Michael Dell spends considerable time telling his direct-sales story to media and opinion leaders. His goal is not only to increase the stock price, but to invigorate a culture across his b-web.

To define and shape your b-web strategy and values, several steps are important:

- Align interests within the b-web wherever possible. Independent contractors and employees act in their own self-interest. Priceline must consider its suppliers, or it loses product flow. Everyone in the Nortel Networks b-web benefits from the company's growth and success.

- Decide the extent to which you want to involve b-web participants in business planning and formulating strategy. Alliances are highly consensual. Aggregations and Value Chains are more hierarchical, passing down vision and strategy. Performance-oriented b-web leaders behave as first among leaders rather than supply-chain bosses.

- Communicate, communicate, communicate. In the past, companies controlled their own cultures. Today, many employees use another company's Web communications system for large parts of their day, becoming immersed in someone else's culture through a very powerful medium. Some Solectron employees spend many hours on the Hewlett-Packard supplier site. As communication extends across the b-web, will you as context provider enhance the cultural context?

- Take into account national, social, and ethnic differences. Based as they are on the Net, many b-webs are global by definition. Internet-worked human capital speaks many tongues and appears in many colors. Sensitivity to language and cultural norms enhances collaboration. If you are creating a b-web for cosmetics consumers, how will your environments reflect the tastes and values of various customer nationalities?

2. Foster Open Relationships

Information transparency enables partnering and trust. In the old economy, suppliers were treated as external to the firm and relationships were combative. Company edicts told suppliers to reduce prices or lose their business.

Digital economy suppliers *participate* in the b-web. Competition is often b-web versus b-web rather than firm versus firm, and suppliers function as partners rather than adversaries. Suppliers have newfound power. In self-organizing b-webs like Agoras and Alliances, "suppliers" *are* the b-web. In Aggregations and Value Chains, some suppliers provide unique value that is unavailable elsewhere. This networked human capital external to the enterprise may be strategic, and irreplaceable, and therefore powerful.

Every b-web is a system with unique culture and dynamics. When the context provider is a juggernaut like Cisco, it exerts great power over suppliers. Sometimes Cisco pays a supplier more than market price, because it wants to develop a strategic partner. Other times it unilaterally tells its suppliers to cut costs or go elsewhere. It defines the b-web culture and determines its standards. It fosters discussion but rarely dissent.

This situation, however, differs from the old world, where Wal-Mart would dictate to its powerless suppliers. Cisco knows what its suppliers pay for components, labor, and facilities. It sees down through the Value Chain, decides what margins are appropriate for its partners, and balances its short-term interest in minimizing costs against its long-term interest in enhancing the robustness of its b-web. Like consumers, suppliers have a new kind of power derived, ironically, from their vulnerability. Transparency of information liberates them to detail the costs of their operation so that they get fair treatment on strategic grounds. The consequences of losing a b-web partner can exceed the consequences of Wal-Mart's losing the supplier of a hot toy or cool line of jeans. The loss of a strategic partner can cripple a b-web and its business.

"We are removing the boundaries of the firm. Everyone's business is everyone's business," says Celestica CEO Eugene Polistuk, describing how b-webs derive their power from openness and information sharing among participants. "Before, we had networks of data; now we have intelligent systems based on standards. The openness, the pervasiveness, the speed, and the sheer volume of information is redefining the way people work together."[8]

The faster information moves, the better. Undue secrecy between partners, win-lose negotiating, and an insistence on exclusive supplier/partner relationships characterize outmoded industrial-economy thinking. Cisco insists on open financial results with its supply-chain partners. The open sharing of information, combined with a single information system for all its supply partners, ensures that all b-web participants draw on the same data at the same time. This minimizes unnecessary inventory.

Polistuk underscores the implications of such openness and sharing: "Before, companies guarded and filtered information. Now we're all naked. It's like the CNN of business—instant availability."

Companies require a new level of professionalism and sophistication in managing information exchanges. "No room for bull," says Polistuk. "Internetworking squeezes out all the zero-value-added information, distortion, and ineffectual management." Managers who either hide or lack information about their own firm's operations cannot manage human capital and the transparent relationships within a b-web.

3. Focus All Participants on the End-Customer

Successful corporations focus on customers. But who is the customer? Your immediate customer may be the next link in the supply chain—but focusing exclusively on this customer can be a big mistake. B-webs should not be collections of partners delivering value to one another, based on the specifications of the next in line.

Consider the industrial-age auto industry in the United States. A simplistic, but more or less accurate view of its structure is as follows. The industry had a three-tier supply model. Tier-three companies (like U.S. Steel) made raw materials, which they delivered to tier-two companies. Tier-two companies converted raw materials into usable components, like seat frames, which they sent to tier-one companies (like Magna International). Tier-one companies built major subassemblies (like seats); they typically were the only ones who dealt directly with major manufacturers (like GM and Chrysler). Most supply-chain improvements happened initially with the largest tier-one suppliers. By the middle of the 1990s, only the biggest tier-one companies had begun to work with their tier-two suppliers to replicate programs like presourcing, target costing, structured supplier ratings, and motivational communications.[9] So although improvements for the Big Three were significant, they were a far cry from reinvention of their broad networks of relationships. And in this model, the participants in each tier tended to think of the customer as their buyer in the next tier. This helps explain the slow pace of innovation and the high costs that remain endemic in the auto industry.

Instead, as we have illustrated in descriptions of Dell and Cisco in chapter 4, an effective Value-Chain b-web keeps everyone focused—and fully informed in real time—on the needs of end-customers. Everyone must be accountable for contributing to end-customer value. A b-web must organize work processes to ensure customer satisfaction at each stage—from product design to post-sales services and support.

The customer's role is important in value creation in all five b-web classes. Customers become economic units creating and depleting value, exchanging value and setting value goals, which are met by value propositions.[10] In Agoras, customers typically create and deliver value themselves. eBay is the context provider for customers who define the content—the goods at the digital table. In Value-Chain b-webs, customers design and coservice the products. Customers are part of the Dell b-web, using the Premier Page to configure the product and initiate the manufacturing process. In Alliance b-webs, customers often create most of the value. Individual PalmPilot customers are active innovators and content providers.

4. Treat Employees and Contractors as Investors of Digital Capital

The old corporation compensated knowledge workers with salaries and bonuses and measured labor on balance sheets as a variable cost. Only senior managers received stock options. Today, we must think of people as investors of digital capital. This shift in perception changes how you reward and compensate people and how you behave toward them—both in your firm and in your b-web.

Throughout the 1990s, managers debated the wisdom of including intellectual capital measures on balance sheets. Stephen Wallman of the U.S. Securities and Exchange Commission has said that companies and lawmakers need to develop new measures of intellectual capital for this purpose. A firm's market value minus its capital assets is one of many possible measures.[11] Others believe that such measures are impossible and misleading.

Setting aside the debate, we know that humans, their brain power, and their know-how constitute a form of capital that in many ways surpasses the value of cash and other traditional capital assets. Regardless of whether we measure it on balance sheets, managers should rethink how to attract and retain human capital, especially in its internetworked form.

Some recoil at the notion of treating humans as capital. Isn't it a bit Orwellian, they say? Riel Miller, who wrote an Organization for Economic Cooperation and Development (OECD) study on human capital, disagrees: "What would you rather be, a cost or an asset?" He argues for "turning [people] costs into assets—something valuable, rather than a drag on the bottom line." Giving people the high status of capital doesn't dehumanize them—it implies that knowledge workers, more than money or factories, drive wealth creation and prosperity.[12]

Factor in demographics, and the case strengthens. As Internet-experienced youngsters—the Net Generation—enter the workforce, they have a high desire to participate in the wealth they create. They have grown up innovating and in many cases creating real value in the interactive world—building Web sites, contributing to online discussions, games, products, and services. The evidence suggests that they will not be satisfied with fat paychecks, but will want to participate in the wealth that they help build.

People bring digital capital to your firm and invest it. They bring their brains, know-how, energy, and capacity for innovation—human capital. They bring relationship capital as well—connections with customers, suppliers, and other partners. Many employees also have their own relationship capital in the form of a brand—"Did you hear who Webvan just hired?" They may also bring a strong experience with new business models. Rather than treating employees as a variable cost, we should think of them as investors of digital capital.[13]

In a typical publicly traded internetworked enterprise—and some not-so-typical ones like Microsoft—less than half of their stock was sold to investors. Digital capital bought the stock. Employees contribute digital capital in exchange for a share of the wealth that they create. Investors take risks and expect return on investment. But unlike traditional capital, there are risks other than financial ones. Investors of digital capital take personal risks when they throw their lot in with your firm or b-web. They give away their insights and ideas regarding how to create customer value and wealth. They risk their personal reputations, brands, and relationships, sometimes severing ties.

Stock-option and share-purchase programs and profit-sharing will dominate companies with lots of digital capital. Smart companies in b-webs expect the same of their alliance partners.

5. Define Governance and the Rules of Engagement

Who makes the rules and how? Who enforces them? How do you deal with people who break the rules? Within the old corporation, the bosses made and enforced the rules. Governments set minimum standards regarding relationships with external entities: "If you defraud customers, we will prosecute." The world of b-webs needs new mechanisms.

In a b-web, the context provider leads in defining governance mechanisms. Participants either comply or do not, based on their perceived self-interest. If you defraud someone on eBay, the user community banishes you by ruining your reputation and refusing to do business with you. To participate in the Linux and MP3 communities, participants must embrace the spirit of benefiting the Alliance or they become irrelevant. Participants in the volatile Java Alliance had considerable difficulty defining their self-interest, other than opposition to Microsoft. The ANX (Automotive Network Exchange) floundered because the competitive interests of the major automakers exceeded their shared interest in an industrywide b-web. The European-led wireless GSM telecom standard is an example of self-interests remaining aligned to help raise the standard to everyone's benefit—resulting in Europe's leapfrogging the United States.

In Aggregations and Value Chains, the leader sets the rules and enforces them through an array of rewards and penalties. The best leaders engage partners in setting and adjusting the rules of engagement. In the end, it's all about spirit and learning. Informed and voluntary compliance is the only way to govern a high-performance b-web.

Business practices differ across cultures. Sadly, many countries are paralyzed by graft and cronyism. The proliferation of b-webs around the globe provides a unique opportunity for leaders of the new economy to promote codes of ethical behavior globally. For example, corruption thrives in a culture of secrecy. Governance webs could make government procurement transparent—acting as an antibody for the culture of secrecy.

HR professionals and other managers must rise to the occasion to start establishing mechanisms for governance and new tools for value-creation management. When doing this, a professional should strive to accomplish the following:

- Consciously establish rules of engagement, and communicate them throughout the b-web.

- Match governance structure to b-web type and style.

- In setting rules, consult with the partners who will be affected and whose commitment and understanding are critical to success.

6. Manage Performance of Human Capital across the B-Web

In the old corporation, managers negotiated or assigned objectives for quality, delivery of projects, increasing outputs, and achieving sales targets. Consultants, subcontractors, and external partners were judged on the ability to meet project or other goals. In the world of b-webs, you must manage the performance of external entities as never before. Real-time capability depends on quick, effective decision making, problem solving, and collaboration at all points in the system.

Managing a contingent workforce presents unique challenges. For example, an employee on contract from an agency has special legal status. When one company we know learned that a contract employee had engaged in misconduct, it found it could not take corrective action, because, technically, she worked for another company. They had no choice but to have the agency replace—essentially terminate—her. A company HR manager told us, "We were forced to apply a blunt instrument because of the structure of the relationship." The corporation was only as strong as its weakest link.

Mirroring the multipath architecture of the Internet itself, b-webs are highly interdependent. They gain flexibility through redundant supplier relationships, while using only what is absolutely needed at any point in time. E*Trade has various partners who gather news and provide analytic modeling, ensuring that customers can choose whatever works for them. Cisco regularly assesses its partners' performance to make sure they can keep up with the company's growth plans. In 1998, concerned that parts-supply distributors would fall behind Cisco's growth, Carl Redfield, vice president of manufacturing, investigated partner inventory turnovers, cash flow, and other indicators of future capacity. He found the partners' financial health to be so robust that

Cisco actually trimmed from three main suppliers to two, deepening long-term partnerships and driving efficiency to higher levels.

HR and organizational effectiveness professionals require new tools to manage the creation of customer value between and among semi-independent work entities, enable interorganizational learning, and deliver real-time performance feedback to actors throughout the partnership universe.

7. Manage Knowledge across the B-Web

Knowledge management for internetworked enterprises means managing knowledge not just internally, but within your b-web. This is a new challenge. As explained earlier, structural capital is the organizational capability of a firm or b-web to meet market requirements. It includes knowledge captured by the enterprise itself, institutionalized, managed, and at the service of the organization. How do you translate human capital into structural capital when you do not own it?

Managers with titles like Chief Knowledge Officer know that knowledge management, while a good idea, has been slow to get off the ground. One impediment is that many people see knowledge as the basis of power and withhold it from colleagues. In b-webs, trust can be even harder to achieve.

A b-web achieves effective knowledge management when the context provider creates a culture in which the common self-interest of all participants is clear to everyone. A culture of authentication and trust—the sine qua non of digital capital—enables participants to share knowledge, to collaborate effectively, and to apply their human capital to value creation.

Another victim of this new environment is the not-invented-here syndrome, in which people and individuals reject new ideas unless they invented them. In many cases, Cisco prefers not to invent it. The Cisco culture favors acquiring technology and skillfully integrating it into existing product families. Cisco works on a number of customer-funded projects, evidence of their openness to outside input. If a customer will pay codevelopment costs, then Cisco assumes that this research probably matters more than Cisco's internal projects.

If you have long-term plans for your b-web, then consider a knowledge management program. Work with partners to develop systems that enable the b-web to marshal its collective resources to create and deliver customer value. Decide to what extent your company should expand its staff development, training, and educational programs to the b-web. Consider assigning human resources to manage knowledge across the b-web. Strategists should get their staffs working to build a b-web culture that shares knowledge.

8. Codify Culture in Process Objects

Business processes contain implicit norms, values, and business practices that govern the deployment of human capital. Such processes—comparable to Lego-like software "objects"—are increasingly standardized and reusable in different situations.

This standardization and reusability can now be applied to business processes that extend beyond the firm. In the industrial economy, business processes were generally considered to be contained within the enterprise. The popular management book *Reengineering the Corporation* discusses how companies can cut costs and improve effectiveness by redesigning their core processes.[14] However, as the focus shifts from the enterprise to the b-web, companies need to develop new competencies in redesigning their inter-enterprise business processes.

Consider the shift away from EDI (electronic data interchange). In the past, companies used EDI to develop highly specialized and customized interfaces for data exchange. Based on EDI, technology firms also needed to cooperate to create customized business processes governing the exchange of data, money, and work activities. The Net is standardizing such technical hookups. Companies will soon organize the interchange of critical data in days and hours rather than years.

Similarly, standardized business processes are emerging. Firms and b-webs will soon draw from a repository of such business process "chunks." The focus on business process reengineering changes to inter-enterprise business process assembly.

When companies "assemble" inter-enterprise business processes from standardized parts, they implement new business models more rapidly. But they can also rapidly deploy an implicit b-web culture. For example, many business processes govern both customer and supplier use of the Dell Premier Page. Process objects embody the Dell customer-centric culture and enable its adoption by the b-web.

9. Embrace the Net Generation

The revolution in Net-enabled business models is intersecting with a demographic revolution, which is changing the culture of work. The biggest generation ever, the baby boom echo, is entering the workforce. The 88 million offspring of the North American baby boom, kids who in the year 2000 are aged two to twenty-two, now outnumber their parents by a healthy margin. The population is not aging but becoming bimodal. This demographic tsunami will profoundly change the workforce and the challenges of HR management in the firm and in the b-web.

Call them the Net Generation, the first generation to be bathed in bits—the first to grow up in a multimedia, multitasking, interrupt-driven world and with a different psychology from their boomer parents.[15] Your teenage daughter probably surfs the Net while responding to e-mail, talking on the telephone, watching TV, and reading a magazine.

Now imagine the impact of millions of these fresh-thinking, energized kids, armed with the most powerful human capital in history, hitting the workforce. This wave has just begun. The Net Generation ("N-Gen") will transform the nature of the enterprise and how wealth is created, as their culture becomes the new culture of work. This generation is exceptionally curious, self-reliant, contrarian, smart, focused, able to adapt, high in self-esteem, and globally oriented. These attributes, combined with the Net Generation's ease with digital tools, should threaten and challenge the traditional manager and traditional approaches to strategy. This generation will create a push for radical changes in existing companies and established institutions.

Unlike their parents, the young people in this generation thrive on collaboration and abhor the notion of a boss. Their first point of reference is the Net. They strive to innovate and require fast results. They love hard work because work, learning, and play coincide. They are creative in unimaginable ways. A bigger proportion than of any other generation will seek to be entrepreneurs.[16]

Smart organizations can learn from them. Finland has hired thousands of children to teach the teachers how to use computers and the Net. One Procter & Gamble manager implemented a reverse mentoring program in which young hires mentor P&G managers in the new media and the new youth culture. When P&G decided to spin out its

Reflect line of cosmetics and skin care into a separate company with its own b-web and dot-com structure, it searched the firm for young people who were fluent with the Net and comfortable with b-web thinking. Says Alan Lafley, the venture's interim president, "We decided to let the kids drive this, and it worked."

8 marketing:
relationship capital in the web

B-webs change most aspects of marketing. When customers participate in a b-web, everybody communicates—in multiple directions—and marketers can no longer control customer perceptions. The brand is no longer an image established through print and broadcast media; it functions as a measure of relationship capital. Customers gain new power: The seller, the hunter of old, becomes the hunted. Dynamic pricing challenges fixed prices. Buyers, not just sellers, establish prices. Rather than tout products, firms must build relationship capital via comprehensive communications strategies.

Twenty-nine-year-old Nicole is watching the sequel to the movie *The Saint* on her interactive television. In one scene, the character Simon Templar is driving his Volvo. Since she is in the Volvo demographic and needs a car, Nicole establishes herself as a market by clicking to pause and ask: "Cool car. What is it?"

Simon steps out of the vehicle. "It's a Volvo," he replies. Instead of adding, "Volvo is the Safety Car," he asks, "What do you like in a car?"[1]

Nicole: Performance, dude.

Simon: Yes, if I lived in Denver like you, then I'd want a peak performer, too. You'll probably want a turbo engine because of the high altitude.

Nicole: Do turbos perform better at high altitudes?

Simon: Absolutely. Would you like to attend the Denver Volvo owners' forum on how turbos perform in your city, or go into an independent rating system that compares Volvo's performance to other cars? Or maybe do a test-drive animation on the screen so that we can talk while you drive? Or design your own car right now, and we'll do some pricing scenarios?

One year later, Nicole owns a Volvo. Volvo is now her trusted mobility and lifestyle adviser. As a participant in Volvo's b-web, she gets a range of services. Volvo picks up her car for regular service and software upgrades, insures her, teaches her teenage sister how to drive, helps her plan trips (including routes and all entertainment and education modules for her kids in the back seat), organizes teleconferences, and calls 911 when she has had an accident. She happily pays for these services.

Welcome to b-web marketing.

THE DEMISE OF THE FOUR P'S

Every business school graduate and marketing manager has learned the four P's of marketing—product, price, place, and promotion. The paradigm was one of control, simple and unidirectional: Firms market to customers. *We* create products and define their features and benefits; set prices; select places to sell products and services; and promote aggressively through advertising, public relations, direct mail, and other in-your-face programs. We control the message. B-webs transform all these activities.

Products: Infused with Knowledge of Customers

Products are now mass customized, service intensive, and infused with the knowledge and the individual tastes of customers. Companies must constantly innovate, and product life cycles collapse. Customers now participate in creating products. Through b-webs, customers co-create products and services. Products are becoming experiences. The old industrial approaches to product definition and product marketing die.

Price: Going Once . . .

Enabled by Agora b-webs, dynamic markets and dynamic pricing are challenging vendor-fixed pricing. In these early days of new price-discovery mechanisms, we question even the concept of a price, as customers gain access to mechanisms that allow them to state what they're willing to pay and for what. As John Sviokla points out, price is a crude measure. It reflects in a single number all the attributes that customers may value in a product—time, effort, craftsmanship, innovation, fashion, status, rarity, long-term value, and so on.[2] Customers will offer various prices for products depending on the conditions specified: "If you deliver this afternoon, then I'll pay A. If I can buy this quantity, then I'll pay B. I'll accept certain defects and pay C. If someone else will pay D, then I'll pay E." Buyers and sellers exchange more information, and pricing becomes fluid. Markets, not firms, will "price" products and services.

Place: Introducing the "Marketspace" and "Marketface"

Every b-web competes in two worlds: a physical world (marketplace) and a digital world of information *(marketspace).*[3] B-webs enable firms to focus on the marketspace, by creating not a great Web site but a great b-web and relationship capital. Hearts, not eyeballs, count. Within a decade, the majority of products and services in many developed countries will be sold in the marketspace.[4]

A new frontier of commerce is the *marketface*—the interface between the marketplace and marketspace. For example, some Aggregations have both an online presence and physical stores (so-called clicks and bricks). Customers of the Gap can buy clothes online; if they don't fit, then they can return items to the store. Or they can browse the Web at their leisure and take printouts of desired items to the store. Gap has even installed Web lounges in some stores, where customers can place orders. Consumers like the greater choice and convenience.

Promotion: The End of an Era

Advertising, promotion, publicity, public relations (PR), and most other aspects of corporate communications are archaic concepts. They exploited unidirectional, one-to-many, and one-size-fits-all media to communicate messages to faceless, powerless customers.

The b-web upends control. Friction breaks down among customers and between you and your customers. They often have access to near-perfect information about products, and power shifts toward them. Customers, no longer external entities, participate in your firm's b-web through multidirectional, one-to-one, and highly tailored communications media. They control the marketing mix, not you. They choose the medium and the message. Rather than receiving broadcast images, they do the casting. Rather than getting messages from earnest PR professionals, they create "public opinion" online with one another. Marketers are losing control.

THE RISE OF RELATIONSHIP CAPITAL

The wealth embedded in customer relationships is now more important than the capital contained in land, factories, buildings, and even big bank accounts. Relationships are now assets. This relationship capital accumulates and provides a new foundation for marketing and sales revenue. A firm's ability to engage customers, suppliers, and other partners in mutually beneficial value exchanges determines its relationship capital.[5]

The customer-facing aspects of relationship capital cause a profound rethinking of marketing. For the first time, companies can forge two-way, interactive, personalized relationships with all customers on a mass scale. While the virtue of deep relationships was always self-evident in theory, it wasn't always practical in reality. But now the ubiquitous, cheap, and interactive Net, coupled with enormous, low-cost databases, enables producers to develop a meaningful, direct relationship with each customer. Sellers and buyers have ongoing dialogue. Customers expect you to tailor each iteration of your product to their needs and wants.

Add the word *relationships* to the digital economy buzzword lexicon. We are said to develop relationships with people online, with Web sites, with companies, and even with inanimate objects like mobile telephones, computers, and automobiles.[6] (How's your relationship with the Internet these days?) Sales personnel are now "relationship managers." Customer relationship management (CRM) is a hot new class of software.

As we have noted, the Internet slashes transaction costs. A customer buys a book from an online bookstore (an Aggregation b-web) because of low transaction costs—search costs, for example. She can request all books on a certain topic or by a certain author. She can indicate authors she likes and find out what other authors are enjoyed by customers who share her views. She can request a bestseller list in a category or ask for a book's daily sales status. Some neighborhood boutique stores deliver a few such value-added services, but such stores are disappearing. The costs are too great relative to the revenue received.

But this is just one part of the equation. As illustrated in figure 8-1, in the physical world, relationship costs between customers and businesses are even greater than transaction costs. These costs hinder personalized service and the creation of relationships. But in the interactive world, you can get to know your customer, educate her, inform her proactively, and deliver value-added services on a personal basis. The astute online bookstore e-mails a customer when a new book fits her personal profile. The relationship is mutual—she creates value for the seller and for other participants by contributing her views. She establishes her personal profile (makes a relationship investment) that includes registering gifts she would like to receive. She complains about something and receives a personal note within an hour, telling her how the problem has been fixed. She and the vendor develop a relationship. Both invest by exchanging customized information and knowledge. The more she invests time and effort, the more personal the bookstore becomes. She builds loyalty to this company, not just because of the services it provides, but because of the effort required to re-educate another company about her. For both buyer and seller, this networked relationship constitutes capital.

POWER TO THE PEOPLE?

Like computer power, human intelligence shifts outward on the Net—to customers and the new kinds of networked producers described in this book. The balance of marketplace power shifts control to consumers.

Consumer perceptions and preferences decreasingly depend on what a company says about itself. Managers who continue to budget resources for controlling message content, flow, and timing should brace themselves. Influencing customer tastes and behaviors depends on developing relationship capital.

Third Voice, a free plug-in for Microsoft's Internet Explorer Web browser software (motto: "Your Web. Your Voice"), lets you attach electronic "sticky notes" to any site. When other Third Voice users visit, they see little red triangles that link to your (and others') annotations.

The targeted Web site itself has not changed. Third Voice computers store its users' comments separately. So Web site managers can't stop it. Commentators originally damned the software as junky electronic graffiti, particularly since the notes tended initially to be juvenile or abusive.[7] Then the designers added a feature that lets users form private Third Voice common-interest groups.

Consider the possibilities. Union members annotate employer sites to highlight untrue statements or expose grievances. Sites of companies with controversial products become protest rallying points. An automaker trumpeting a gas-guzzling sport utility vehicle faces environmental groups plastering complaints, petitions, and calls to action.

Consumers arm themselves with other information weapons. Web "reputation managers" solicit advice from consumers about which products are good or bad. Databases containing millions of comments from knowledgeable users provide advice to buyers of bread makers to CD players. Epinions.com, the most ambitious, builds databases so detailed that the company can offer advice on the best dry cleaner or dentist in

---

FIGURE 8-1   Relationship Costs versus Transaction Costs

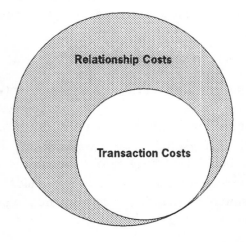

a neighborhood. As the Internet grows, all businesses, no matter how small, will have reputations accessible to anyone in the world.

Marketers complain that traditional broadcast and print media now lack punch. The media help establish awareness, but they don't build relationship capital. Agent technology provides customers access to near-perfect information, weakening powerful brands. As John Mac-Donald and Jim Tobin have said, "New technologies equip the hunted with better camouflage—perhaps turning the tables completely. The hunted becomes the hunter."[8]

In 1996, Walter Wriston, former chairman of Citibank, asked, "Who will create the financial services supermarket? Will it be something called a bank? I think not."[9] His statement was prophetic, as today's software companies and telecommunications firms lead the transformation of banking. Banks need to aggregate best-of-breed products together, taking a view of all the customer's financial needs, not selling individual products in isolation.[10] Wealth management revolutionizes investment banking. Smart, proactive investors become free agents. Technology gives them competitive knowledge-trading abilities. Power moves from the bank to the investor. Banks and other financial institutions must compete for customers' scarce attention with an array of innovative, customized products and services. As explained in chapter 6, the old sources of profit based on proprietary knowledge disappear, as service providers scramble to find new ways to add value.

In music, hit singles—not site hits or clicks—start in b-webs. The Net Generation first met teen music idol Britney Spears online. The movie phenomenon *The Blair Witch Project* got its start among Net Generation sites and chat rooms long before it was known to the public or broadcast media.

Such shifts in power affect every industry. Prudent managers will reassess the power relationships between their firm and customers and act accordingly.

THE NEW PRACTICE OF MARKETING

If the four P's and the traditional categories of advertising and PR no longer provide a useful framework for marketing, then executives need new practices, and fast. In a b-web, everyone and everything communicates—

two-way, multi-way, and all the time. Marketers become interactive communications vigilantes whose job is to accumulate relationship capital.

Think of customers as individual molecules rather than mass markets, and the picture becomes clearer. B-webs group their economic units to create value just as in physics molecules cluster to form a substance. A b-web is a collection of molecules held together by economic, personal, technological, cultural, demographic, and other forces. Customers are molecules in the b-web. The new challenge of marketing is engineering the forces that attract and bind customers.

The brand is no longer an image established through one-to-many communications. It is also more than a symbol of a relationship, like a wedding ring. It is a measure of relationship capital.

In the last fifty years, upward of $3 trillion has been spent to establish and maintain brands. Many say that the brand is safe as the key to success in the digital economy: Shoppers look for trusted brands, especially in the unfamiliar environs of cyberspace. Successful online companies, such as Amazon.com and E*Trade, create a comfortable brand and ubiquitous presence. They play on consumer fears of being stranded with a loser. Online shoppers would rather pay a little more to do business with a company they believe will be in business for a long time.[11]

This view is fundamentally wrong. Mass communications created the brand and continues to do so. Using one-way broadcast and print media, marketers convinced people through relentless exhortations to "Just do it!" If you say "Things go better with Coke" enough times, then you associate anticipated experiences with a brand. The brand was an image, or as marketing teachers say, "a word in the mind." Conventional wisdom used to be that time, money, and a quality product could establish any brand.

The experience with Netscape flips this thinking on its head—it became an instant brand through "word of mouse" and through forging a b-web. Netscape predecessor Mosaic was passed along from person to person on the Net, and when Mosaic turned into commercial-quality software, branding was instantaneous. Within eighteen months, Netscape had forty million users.

Brands can also be instantly destroyed. Microsoft's relationships with a hundred million PC users enabled it to squeeze Netscape off the desktop. Intel also learned about brand vulnerability the hard way when a rumor spread on the Net like a kind of reverse "viral marketing," alleging that the Pentium chip was having trouble doing floating-point calculations.[12] Intel had to stop production, writing down $470 million. The Pentium brand evaporated and Pentium joke databases appeared on the Net. (What's the difference between a nine-year-old and a Pentium chip? A nine-year-old can do long division.) Yet with some attentive relationship building and old-fashioned advertising, the Pentium brand stormed back and most people forgot the incident. The brand image is here today, gone tomorrow, and back again the next day.

Dynamic pricing drives much of the challenge to brands. When you offer $100 to book any four-star hotel in San Francisco on Priceline, you are blind to the brand. Priceline fosters a mind-set of brand equivalency. The same occurs when you offer $170 for a VCR, specifying stereo, hi-fi, and four heads. The qualifying devices from Sony, Panasonic, and Toshiba become commodities with equivalent brands.

Software agents—blind to the brand—further undermine traditional thinking. Rather than the brand, you trust your agents. Sometimes called softbots, knowbots, or just bots, agents get to know your preferences and sense of style. These tireless little workers surf the Net day and night. They look for information, find the perfect chocolate chip cookie, evaluate movies, organize a personalized daily newspaper, communicate, try on various styles of jeans, and so on. In many areas, trusting agents will be synonymous with trusting experiences.

Our colleague Elliot Schreiber suggests that customers in a b-web will soon be able to customize a generic brand to be their personal brand: "I could create a 'Schreiber family' brand of products that has the attributes that I want to both own and convey to others."

Such developments will cause a change in the thinking among marketers from brand image to customer relationships. The brand matters, but as a measure of relationship capital, not as an image.

Thinking of communications as two-way is a tough shift to make. Consider the transformation of the public-relations function. Word of mouth has always been a powerful force. But how do you conduct public relations in a world where customers can freely communicate with one another, globally, in real-time, seven days a week, twenty-four hours a day?

In the spring of 1999, Lehman Brothers had just taken a company public. Two days after the IPO, hostile stock traders, disguised as independent investors, went on chat lines to denounce the newly public company. In the old days, Lehman Brothers would have called together a group of analysts in a controlled meeting to respond. It would then have monitored the resulting coverage, tracking anyone who wrote about the offering positively or negatively. They controlled an image. Now the emphasis shifts from creating an image and sending out unidirectional messages, to forging relationships. Public relations professionals will find that relationships, not messages, are the primary capital that they create for their corporation or clients.

To succeed, PR must shift from publicizing the company to managing two-way relationships. Many relationships are digital rather than physical, made with individuals, not the "public image" of mass society in days gone buy. Opinion formation will increasingly occur in cyberspace, not in industrial-age clubs, trade organizations, or mass media.

This is true for all communications and marketing as a whole. If Lehman Brothers had had a relationship strategy, then it might have avoided its fiasco. As part of that strategy, communications professionals participating in influential Web discussions would have spotted the saboteurs and taken effective action to discredit and isolate them.

The A, B, C, D, E's of marketing have replaced the four P's:

- *Anyplace, anytime, anyway shopping replaces place.* Companies must design integrated strategies for the marketspace and, if appropriate, the marketplace and marketface. Customers want convenience.

- *B-web customers drive revenue.* Relationship capital is reflected in a brand. Think of customers as part of your b-web and prospects as candidates for relationships, not as markets for your products.

- *Communication works, not promotion.* One-way media, like broadcasting, can be part of the marketing mix, but the customer decides whether—and with whom—to engage in a one-, two-, or multi-way communication.

- *Discovery of price replaces fixed price.* The days when companies unilaterally control prices are nearly over.

- *Experience replaces product.* Customers pay for experiences, not products. Products must be bundled with enhanced, customized services. The automobile experience replaces the product, as the vehicle becomes a platform for transportation, interactive entertainment, safety, doing business, and having fun.[13]

THE NEW MARKETING: EIGHT IMPERATIVES

How do you harness the power of b-webs to create relationship capital? Eight imperatives outline the actions critical to a new marketing approach.

1. Deliberately Plan Your Communications Strategy for B-Web Participants, Especially Customers

As with HR communications plans, business leaders need to drive communications strategy as strongly as business-model innovation. To begin, shift your resources from print, radio, and television advertising to interactive communications. If you view markets as ever-changing combinations of molecules, you'll focus on the accumulation of relationship capital, not the casting of messages. So far, marketers have not progressed much in moving to truly interactive communications. Initially marketers took the old model (the banner ad from newspaper or broadcast media) and applied it to the Net. But click-through rates dropped fast. If you think relationship capital rather than number of eyeballs, you see the need for a different marketing communications strategy.

Dell spends millions on traditional advertising. But it also invests in molecular marketing. More than 35,000 corporate customers use Dell's innovative Premier Pages, custom business portals on its Web site.

This rich information flow fosters new markets. Several customers have asked Dell to manage their internal PC operations, to become a services business. Michael Dell told us, "Many customers have said, 'We don't want to be in the PC business. We don't want to configure PCs, we don't want to install PCs, we don't want to support PCs, and we don't want to uninstall PCs. You do all this for us.' We become their PC and server department." Relationship capital has generated new businesses for Dell.

Establish a communications group responsible for relationship building. As the emphasis shifts from broadcast and print to interactive communications, this group should become *the* marketing department—spearheading all corporate marketing. This department should be staffed with people who understand the nature of interactive media. Often these are young people—the generation that naturally thinks two-way communications rather than broadcasting. Interestingly, they are also often women. Men dominated the traditional worlds of advertising, print and broadcast media, investor relations, and even public relations. The new business world emphasizes relationships, community—all characteristics in which women appear to excel.

Communications professionals must be "cyber-dwellers," Web-chat specialists and authorities on online culture. The interactive world presents many new challenges. For example, companies must guard against and filter the loudest customers' voices that may not speak for all, but that merit acknowledgment.

2. Shift Resources from Traditional Marketing to Product and Service Innovation

The Net provides new opportunities to evidence the true value of products and services. Real value is the precondition for relationship capital. Some readers will object that in the past, many innovative products lacked the marketing muscle to make them winners. Isn't marketing everything? they may ask. The answer is no. Low-value products and services will fail. Further, advertising will increasingly be an ineffective element of the marketing mix when customers control when and how they receive information.

For example, shoppers buying groceries from an Aggregation b-web like Peapod, Streamline, NetGrocer, or Webvan can ask for all the products in a category sorted by criteria such as calorie count or nutritional value. The most frequently used sort criteria are cost followed by fat content. Determining the healthiest peanut butter takes seconds; Skippy's mass marketing faces entirely new obstacles to the buy decision. Brand equity will correspond more closely to product quality, and products undifferentiated in value quickly become commodities.

In the old economy, R&D created goods and services, while marketing created brands. Many good products failed. And good brands weren't necessarily based on good products when they had the marketing muscle to establish the "word in the mind."

Now, lines between R&D and marketing blur. R&D increasingly contributes to brand. Tide can say that it washes whiter, but if it doesn't, consumers will find out—in thirty seconds. Agents and softbots, third-party rating systems, and discussion groups make clear which washes whiter. So P&G must redouble its efforts to innovate and have the best products.

Further, the services bundled with products will be increasingly important in branding, as relationship capital drives revenue. These may be the services bundled with Tide and delivered through the Net to various information appliances in the home—including the washing machine, the soapbox, even the white shirt—all containing chips that communicate with one another. P&G changes from a soap company to a relationship company that helps homemakers.

P&G must then base its revenue model on relationship capital: on the creation and exchange of true value. P&G must innovate even better products and services or create innovation b-webs that give rise to such products. Lousy products with great promotional campaigns will fail. Marketers must involve themselves in the creation of value itself, as services ground customer relationships. And communications programs must emphasize value.

3. Honesty Is the Best Policy

Candor builds trust. Trust leads to loyalty. Loyalty over time becomes relationship capital, which in turn enables innovation, revenue, and growth.

Trust is the sine qua non of the digital economy. With so many sources of information, new products and services, new product categories, and boastful hyperbole, whom do you trust?

The world of b-webs has few secrets, but finding truth adds cost. Companies can no longer claim that most people like them, that they have few complaints, or that their relationships are solid, when they are not. Corporations must walk the talk—achieve the standards that they set by their own words. You can't make garbage smell like cherry blossoms anymore.

Trustworthy behavior is a precondition to trust. When you have proven ethical behavior and good business practices, you can communicate candidly with customers about your behavior.

Mechanisms exist for establishing trust in each b-web type. Trust matters more in some b-web types. Some Agoras establish marketspace trust through authentication and openness. Everyone knows that the cost of violating trust is isolation. In exchanges, trust may be protected through the force of law. Aggregations establish trust through secure transactions, delivering real value and protecting personal privacy. Value Chains achieve trust through transparent access to information. When "everybody's naked" there is little room for deception. In Alliances, common self-interest galvanized around a mission enables b-web partners to work together well. Distributive Networks create trust through reliability.

4. Manage Attention as the Scarcest Resource in the Digital Economy

Everybody craves attention. The digital economy covets attention more than goods and even money, because it has truly become scarce. In 1995, Nobel laureate Herbert Simon explained that attention scarcity results from three simple truths: First, a day has only twenty-four hours. Second, the human capacity to pay attention is limited. And last, people are inundated with information.

The Net has increased the information overload exponentially. Every firm and b-web needs a strategy to break through the noise, to define and differentiate value propositions, and to secure mind share. Without customer attention, you lack relationship capital.

Traditional economics assumes that goods are scarce. Scarcity compels the consumer to buy more when it is cheap, less when it is costly. Scarcity motivates producers to produce more of a good when prices are high and less when prices are low. When the interests of producers and consumers intersect, a transaction takes place at an equilibrium price.

Attention economics works differently from traditional economics.[14] Consumers make rational choices to allocate their precious attention because the pool of attention is fixed. Producers compete with each other for customer attention by paying attention to customers. Equilibrium is the point at which a mutually agreed-upon exchange of attention occurs.

As a customer of Amazon.com, you pay scant attention to the company itself. But the company pays attention to you, collecting information about your interests or giving you opportunities to create value such as commenting on a book. You sign up, buy a book, and are greeted by name each time you return. With this share of mind, Amazon.com can turn your attention to CDs, toys, and just about anything that fits its business model.

5. Define the Price-Discovery Mechanism, Not the Price

The price is wrong. As chapter 2 suggests, dynamic markets and pricing challenge fixed prices. Managers should understand that price is now a function of many variables and that b-webs change the pricing context.

Dynamic pricing prevails when the interaction and relationship costs associated with real-time price negotiation are lower than the range of price uncertainty. Haggling over the price of a bottle of milk wastes time. But b-webs make it possible to force several supermarkets to compete over discounts in exchange for a shopper's long-term business.

As customers have more information about the actual costs of goods and services, their willingness to pay a high markup over actual cost declines. Inform your customer. Your competitors' pricing is only a click away. Successful companies provide reliable information about competitors' pricing, generating trust and relationship capital. The Progressive Corporation was among the first to do this, and customers were initially shocked to learn that an insurance company would divulge true price comparisons with competitors.

In a world of perfect information, price responds to demand. Anticipate or create demand, and dynamic pricing enables your firm to charge more—but only if you've adopted dynamic pricing.

Get ready for collective purchasing. Customer participation in a b-web can reduce costs associated with time, distance, and demand aggregation, all of which have restricted mass-market price negotiation. Would you reject an offer by a b-web buyers club to purchase ten thousand of your products because the margin is below the norm? Or will you set up a price-discovery mechanism (and b-web cost structure) to encourage and enable such purchases, taking market share and building relationship capital?

6. Provide the Context

In a b-web, the content of a value proposition (for example, a stockbroker service) is important. But if the brand is a relationship rather than an image, the context (the online environment where this stock service is provided) may be even more important. Brand strength derives from customer experience: the context.

Consider the impact of this change on a telecommunications provider debating how to handle the "last mile" to the customer's premises. As mobile data moves to the fore and users gain access to increasingly flexible mobile appliances, a battle looms over the consumer context. Will it be the telecom services provider (AT&T, Sprint), the appliance manufacturer (Nokia, PalmPilot), the interface designer (Microsoft, Symbian), or the portal (AOL, Yahoo!)?

Must you be a context provider to succeed? No, since every b-web can sustain only one or a few context providers. Countless firms participate successfully in b-webs in which someone else orchestrates the context. Ultimately, however, this is riskier. Many customer-facing industries of the past—in telecommunications, banking, insurance, stockbrokerages—will become infrastructure providers to others who own the customer interface.

If you are a bank, then this doesn't mean you should enter the grocery business to provide the context for online food shopping. You can provide commerce services to online grocers instead. But you should be seeking to provide the context for other financial services. For example, play a central role in bill presentment. When the customer pays for groceries, you should link to a financial services supermarket, where you set the context for a different value proposition.

7. Engage Customers in Many Roles

Customers are now often buyers/sellers, producers/consumers, employers/employees, strategists/auditors, investors/competitors—all in your b-web. Engaging them in multiple roles builds relationship capital.

Involve customers in defining value propositions and designing products. Enable customers to personalize products with their knowledge and tastes—from their personal version of the *Wall Street Journal* to the four-wheel, mobile, multimedia "infotainment" computing and communication center sitting in the driveway.

Involve them in setting and vetting short- and long-term goals, being careful, of course, not to jeopardize truly strategic information. This involvement goes beyond focus groups or visioning sessions and has the customers influencing marketing strategy on an ongoing basis.

View investors as b-web participants. Don't communicate messages to them. Build relationship capital. Volkswagen cannibalized its own stock in late 1999 by stonewalling investors. Rather than talk frankly to customers and investors, the company pitched products in a traditional way. When investors tried to get information about the company's performance, investor-relations executives showed less than total candor. Frustrated fund managers began selling the stock, followed by individual investors.[15]

8. Engage the Net Generation

Most observers think that the most important demographic change currently under way is the aging of the baby boomers.[16] Wrong. Instead, the boomers' children, the biggest generation ever, have arrived. This massive customer wave is already forcing smart corporations to rethink their marketing strategies. These kids have substantial spending money and influence a large portion of their parents' purchases. We estimate that American preteens and teens directly spend $130 billion per year and influence the spending of upward of $500 billion. As demanding and discerning consumers, these youngsters feel that they should have a large say in their families' purchases, from everyday grocery purchases to major acquisitions like computers, cars, and appliances.

They exert this influence with knowledge gleaned from the Web. They often know more about a product than their parents do.

Successful marketing to the Net Generation means targeting their unique personality traits. Net Generation kids love options—choice is like oxygen to them. If you want their loyalty, you must give them choice. Moreover, they won't accept being penalized for the wrong choice. If they don't like a new Web site, they just hit the "Back" button. The same should be true of products and services. McDonald's will need to figure out how to put a "Back" button on a hamburger.

Net Generation consumers enjoy customizing goods and services and like to try before they buy. The concept of the software or videogame demo is integral to their online culture. They are very critical of their environment, growing up in a world in which they must authenticate information, judge its veracity, and present and defend their views online. In their culture, you will find the new market and the new dynamics of marketing. Learn how to build relationship capital by involving them in your b-web. If you learn to market to them, then marketing to everyone else should prove easy.

Part IV

strategies for
business webs

9 how do you
weave a b-web?

Disaggregation and reaggregation may be powerful concepts, but how do you bring them to life? This chapter provides the answers. Step by step, we show you how to take apart the old value proposition, envision and structure a new one, and turn an industrial-age business into a digital economy b-web.

The first step of b-web strategy is to disaggregate the value proposition that the end-customer experiences. Focus on the *end*-customer, the person who really pays the bills and whose needs and appetites your b-web must meet. Think about the genuine customer needs that your product or service addresses, not just the "thing you (or the market incumbents) do" to get the business. And avoid preoccupation with the production or distribution channels that today stand between you and the real customer.

As we said in chapter 1, disaggregation frees you to generate entirely new kinds of value. It also encourages entirely new kinds of competitors. If you relegate digital technologies to flashy Web sites or short-term cost savings, you will likely fail. Begin disaggregation with the end-customer's experience. Dissect that experience in terms of your value proposition, as well as the enabling goods, services, resources, business processes, and organizational structures, into individual components. Honestly face the many weaknesses inherent in the industrial-age mind-set and tool-set. Challenge what you know, then redesign, build upon, and reconfigure the components to radically transform the value proposition for the end-customer's benefit. Imagine how networked, digital technologies liberate contributors to add new forms of value every step of the way—to each component. Then, creatively reaggregate a new set of value offerings, goods, and services, as well as the supporting resources, structures, and processes.

A business's value proposition differs from its products and services. The value that a customer needs—and that an effective business delivers—endures, regardless of the particulars. When a traveler needs to get from point A to point B, how he or she gets there matters much less than actually getting there.

A clear and precisely defined value space for your strategy initiative is vitally important. An inquiry on privately owned personal transportation, for example, may lead to very different conclusions from one on personal transportation as a service.

Identify opportunities to build human, relationship, and structural capital. Where do these capital reserves reside in the old business model? What are the gaps and vulnerabilities? What new forms of digital capital can we create to enhance customer and shareholder value? For example, consider how to convert human capital (wisdom in the minds of employees across the b-web) into structural capital (knowledge management systems and software-encoded business processes).

To describe, disaggregate, and reaggregate the core value proposition, the strategist should ask the following fundamental questions about the business system in question: Why does it exist at all, and should it continue to exist? Who benefits from it? What are its strengths and weaknesses from the customer perspective? How could we improve it? Who can help us, or who could improve it and kill us?

We have identified six steps for b-web strategy design:

1. Describe the current value proposition from the customer's viewpoint, that is, why this system exists.

2. Disaggregate: Consider the contributors and their contributions, strengths, and weaknesses. Compare the parts and capabilities of your business to those in other systems.

3. Envision b-web-enabled value through brainstorming and other creative design techniques. Decide what the new value proposition will be.

4. Reaggregate: Define what it will take to deliver the new value proposition, including processes, contributors, contributions, applications and technologies, and other success factors.

5. Prepare a value map: Design a visual map that depicts value exchanges in the b-web.

6. Do the b-web mix: Define a b-web typing strategy that will improve your competitive advantages.

STEP 1: DESCRIBE THE CURRENT VALUE PROPOSITION

Before envisioning a new future, assess the current state of things. For the marketspace in question, what value is offered, delivered, and consumed that justifies a business's right to exist? Three guidelines are useful in this assessment. First, focus on the essence, rather than a small, fascinating, or rarefied aspect of it. If looking at publishing, then describe the underlying value to the readers of the publication rather than the printed page or the table of contents. Second, begin with the end in mind, as in how to improve radically the value that the "real" end-customer receives from your business system. Nothing less will ensure your survival as a winner in the twenty-first century. Last, prepare and inform all steps of this process with an assessment of: customer, market, and channel trends; supply-side trends; competition; current and expected product and service innovations; industry use of human, relationship, and structural capital; business events (e.g., consolidation); environmental issues; and regulation.

We ask the following four questions to drive a "customer-down" approach to the current value proposition:

1. Who are your end-customers, as opposed to the intermediary customers such as the buyers and channels, of your products and services? Define the customer categories in today's market system and who else is serving them, regardless of value proposition.

2. What product and service offerings does the current business system provide its customers?

3. From the customer's standpoint, what value propositions can you attribute to these product and service offerings? List only the top ones that come to mind. Once you have listed several dimensions of the value proposition, construct a concise catch-all statement that accommodates all of them. This summary should nail your current business—its raison d'être.

4. From the end-customer's perspective, what are the main strengths and weaknesses of the value proposition and the enabling products and services? Who else delivers more value, and in what ways?

Consider the brokerage business transformation led by companies like Charles Schwab & Co., E*Trade, and TD Waterhouse Securities. Some might have described the purported value proposition of the traditional full-service brokerage industry in the mid-1990s as guiding customers in managing their investments through personal, knowledgeable advice and proactive customer service. In theory, an investment adviser at a firm like Merrill Lynch or Goldman Sachs develops an intimate knowledge of the goals and preferences of each individual client. Following a Value-Chain service model, the adviser integrates his or her firm's unique proprietary research with the client's personal strategy to provide customized service, particularly buy/sell advice at the critical moment.

Reality, of course, is different. Have you ever used a broker? If yes, then were you 100 percent happy with the relationship and service? If no, then join the club. Although many factors contribute to such disappointment, most traditional brokers make their money from maximizing the number of orders they process, rather than faithfully representing client interests. Many customers perceive that the quality of advice and service they receive does not warrant the fee structure. Table 9-1 illustrates how a full-service retail brokerage might have answered the above four questions during the mid- to late 1990s.

STEP 2: DISAGGREGATE

Disaggregation identifies the entities that contribute to the total value-creation system. We include customers in the model since they often perform work that contributes to the overall system value. Once identified, this work can be automated, eliminated, transferred to others, or left with the customer.

Where are the opportunities to capture digital capital? The grocery industry, as mentioned in chapter 3, calculates that customer effort represents 13 percent of the system's total value. Industrial-age grocers might argue that this labor is relationship capital (shoppers like to squeeze tomatoes); online grocers say that this labor is an obsolete form of structural capital (underpaid work), which online convenience turns to relationship capital ripe for the picking.

In conducting this analysis, look at the total value system—again, from the perspective of the end-customer. In securities markets, the broker is not the sole source of value. The broker acts as gatekeeper to the real "content" value of the system, which consists of access to financial markets, individual securities, and other investment instruments. The

---

TABLE 9-1   Current Value Definition for Traditional Full-Service Brokerage Firm

Customers	Product/Service Offerings	Value Proposition	Strengths	Weaknesses
• Retail investors	• Use of personal broker • Investment strategy advice • Proprietary research • Buy/sell advice • Transaction services • Portfolio/records management • Educational materials	• Counseling • Matching investment choices to customer needs and preferences • Quality and utility of research and analysis • Personal service	• Personalized advice and attention • Hand-holding • Quality of research • Professional management	• Costs • Restricted hours • Inconsistent quality of service and advice • Limited, often unpredictable access to research materials • Customers not in control • Some conflict of interest (broker income depends on transaction churn)

customer cares about asset growth, not the broker relationship. A useful disaggregation analysis of this value proposition, one with transformational potential, must look at the whole picture (figure 9-1).

Consider the five categories of value contributors that we introduced in chapter 1: end-customers, context providers, content providers, commerce services providers, and infrastructure providers. Each category typically includes several classes of participants; also, a single participant may play different roles in various categories. Cisco is the prime context provider for its b-web, but when KPMG and EDS integrate Cisco's

---

FIGURE 9-1   Five Layers of Value Contributors

Customers

Receive and contribute value to the b-web.

Context

The interface between the customer and the b-web. A context provider leads the choreography, value realization, and rule-making activities of the system.

Content

The core value—goods, services, or information that satisfy customer needs. Content providers design, make, and deliver value.

Commerce

Enables the flow of business, including transactions and financial management, security and privacy, information and knowledge management, logistics and delivery, and regulatory services.

Infrastructure

Communications and computing, paper and physical records, roads, buildings, offices, and the like.

solutions for customers, they become context providers. Cisco also adopts a content-provider role when it creates networking software for its products.

The economics of the system often depend on customer contributions. Some observers point to customer labor as a breakthrough innovation unique to electronic commerce. In fact, as the grocery industry illustrates, customers have been pitching in since the beginning of time. In the shift to b-webs, customers sometimes do less work, sometimes more. Web grocers like Peapod and Streamline reduce consumer labor. At eBay, customers do nearly all the work and shoulder most of the risks and costs.

The context provider is the interface between the customer and the system that creates the value. Because of this privileged position, the context provider dominates the b-web, orchestrating its choreography, value realization, and rule-making. The context provider manages, accumulates, and allocates (to b-web partners) digital capital assets. In the online world, context assumes even greater importance than before, since millions of customers can frequent a site in a day or an hour. Business-to-business aggregators like MetalSite and Chemdex derive disproportionate influence and rewards for providing industry contexts. And as portals like Yahoo! and Excite draw more visitors daily than do television channels, their influence and business value increase. Depending on b-web type, the primary context provider performs one or another typical role: Agora (auction or exchange system operator), Aggregation (storefront or portal), Value Chain (product/service designer and production manager), Alliance (setter of rules and standards), and Distributive Network (network services provider).

Content providers design, make, and deliver the core value—the goods and services—that ultimately satisfy customer needs. Content can be information (e.g., a TV show, an online publication, a personal health care record), physical goods (e.g., potato chips and computer chips), or services (air travel, heart surgery, etc.).

Commerce services providers facilitate transactions, exchanges, and the transfer of value. Their services include informational and financial transaction management, security and privacy, information and knowledge management, logistics and delivery, and regulation.

Infrastructure services include communications and computing, paper and other physical records, roads and transportation systems, buildings, offices, and the like. Commerce and infrastructure services often involve Distributive Networks (chapter 6).

As the preceding descriptions show, a business system usually comprises several layers of value creation. Disaggregation entails (1) identifying the key participants in each layer; (2) describing what each participant contributes to the system, and how they do so; and (3) pinpointing the weaknesses and opportunities for improvement in the current arrangement.

Wind back the clock, and imagine that you are a strategy adviser at Schwab in 1996 or 1997. At this time, full-service brokers act like Value Chains, integrating solutions for their customers—retail investors. What value do they give, and what do they get in return?

In days gone by, brokerage firms owned a monopoly of access to markets, few consumers engaged in personal investing, and many were naive and inexperienced. Back then, the traditional retail-broker model was a fair exchange. The customer gave the broker a personal profile, commission fees, and a set of investment objectives, and, in exchange, got tailored advice and the ability to trade.

But this model has a fundamental flaw. Retail investors do not and cannot yet receive the value commensurate with their contributions to the system. Retail investors are not mere customers; instead, they fuel the system from both directions, providing both financial liquidity (as buyers) and the "goods" (sellable securities and information) that make the whole system work. Other players, such as institutional investors and mutual-fund companies, may do the same thing—and have more clout due to their higher trading volumes. But the collective clout of retail investors—who in the United States represent close to 40 percent of trading value—is unrealized.[1] The deep weakness of this system is that the true contributors of value (retail investors) find themselves subordinate to self-serving intermediaries (full-service brokers) (table 9-2).

Couple this fundamental flaw with other weaknesses in the five categories of our value contributor model, and it becomes clear why online brokers seemed likely to succeed:

• Retail investors became knowledgeable and confident as the Internet provided them with real-time access to market information and transactions. The interested investor gained access to the industry's structural capital, acquiring knowledge tools comparable to those available to professional brokers.

TABLE 9-2   Current Value Disaggregation of Full-Service Brokerage Firms

Who	What Do They Contribute?	How?	Weaknesses
End-Customers			
• Retail investors (as buyers)	• Investment goals • Demand/liquidity • Fees	• Self-evaluation • Research • Analysis • Orders	• Disempowered by brokers and self-dealers despite providing both liquidity and content to the system • Increasingly knowledgeable and confident but disempowered
Context Providers			
• Full-service brokers	• Access to trading markets • Tailored personal service	• Personal contact, mostly via phone	• Untenable monopoly of access • Cost • Conflict of interest due to commission structures • Service quality uneven • Eroding credibility • Restricted hours
Content Providers			
• Full-service brokers	• Research reports • Advice • Trades	• Paper • Personal contact • Market access	• Advice and service often inadequate
• Media	• News • Opinion	• Print • TV • Internet	• Growing quality, timeliness, diversity of investment news educating investors and increasing self-sufficiency
• Retail investors (as sellers) • Institutional investors • Issuers	• Tradable securities and instruments	• Offers via broker channels	• Retail investor control not commensurate with contribution • Issuers bypassing brokers to communicate to investors
• Market makers and traders	• Price setting through bid/asks	• Floor trading • Electronic markets	• Insider self-dealing • Excessive transaction costs
Commerce Services Providers			
• Exchanges	• Exchange mechanisms	• Regulations • Facilities	• Pervasiveness of electronic trading • Emergence of alternative trading mechanisms (ECNs) • Feasibility of global 24×7 markets
• SEC and other authorities	• Regulation	• Regulations • Monitoring • Enforcement	• Monopoly regulatory models losing credibility
Infrastructure Providers			
• Exchanges	• Trading environments	• Physical trading floors • Electronic trading	• Obsolescent proprietary boundaries
• Technology providers	• Information and communications applications	• Computer/ communications systems	• Extending common infrastructure to all at low marginal cost

- Full-service brokers owed their privileged position as monopoly context providers who controlled access to financial markets to accidents of history in the securities industry. Their fee-per-transaction business model meant that many brokers were torn between maximizing turnover and ensuring the portfolio performance of their customers. Thus the industry's deployment of its human capital was flawed.

- As content providers (of advice and research), brokers failed to keep up their quality standards with the exploding market. Meanwhile, other media stepped in.

- The commerce services environment changed, with the shift to global markets and a growing trend toward continuous trading, twenty-four hours a day, seven days a week. Why should investors only trade during business hours? Why not any time of day or night? Why can't markets, too, be "live" all the time?

- As the infrastructure shifted from physical trading floors to cheap, ubiquitous networked computing, the transaction costs assessed by low-value-adding human brokers became unsupportable.

STEP 3: ENVISION B-WEB-ENABLED VALUE

Planners must step outside their day-to-day mental models to develop creative, discontinuous pictures of what they desire and can achieve. This activity draws on educated feelings, aspirations, intuitions, and hunches. Imagine a reinvented, hugely successful, and highly value-adding future three to five years hence. Suspend disbelief and consider several forward-looking questions: How will your value proposition change when the customer gains full control? What would you want if you were the customer? What might your customers' world be like five years from now? What could you achieve if there were no technological or organizational obstacles? What new business models—ways of creating, setting, and delivering value and of facilitating relationships with customers, suppliers, and partners—could you envisage? What could your competition do? What about new market entrants? What can you learn from innovators in other industries and other places? What is the state of the art in management thinking in the domains that affect your customers and you?

Revisit the original statement of your value proposition (like the full-service broker's "guiding customers in managing their investments through personal, knowledgeable advice and proactive customer service"). Modify it to reflect the new vision. This restated value proposition should inspire an original, competitive b-web strategy.

Consider the retail investment world that has begun to hatch. This, a different kind of full-service world, is cost effective and timely; the individual investor controls the inputs (information) and outputs (orders) of portfolio management.

Markets for all securities are live and directly accessible to individual investors worldwide, twenty-four hours a day, seven days a week. Investors can choose any media for conducting business—in person, online, wireless, or telephone. Technology has reduced the transaction costs that financial market intermediaries collect to below 5 percent of their former levels. Individual investors can participate directly in markets with a time delay approaching zero, so the price of the moment is the price they pay or receive for a security.

In a b-web-enabled investment situation, investors obtain advice from a variety of sources:

- Human advisers, motivated by asset value and growth rather than number of trades

- Automated alerts, triggered by investors' programmed threshold preferences

- Holistic financial planning tools that incorporate online research and analysis (as good as any available through full-service brokerages) and provide cradle-to-grave life-cycle planning

- Anytime, anywhere easy linkages to the consumer (wireless, intelligent agents, etc.) and his or her other financial activities (pay processing, mortgage, taxes, etc.)

- Investor communities, including online forums, chat groups, Web sites, and games

- Virtual advisers (software agents that provide real-time advice based on the investor's personal profile and portfolio management pattern)

• Analysis and simulation tools (to help investors understand why particular stratagems might work—or not)

• Aggregated real-time tracking of the most successful investor segments—what have the top 1 percent bought and sold today?

The investment industry builds relationship capital by designing its structural capital to suit the needs of the end-customer. This world is not here yet, but its outlines have begun to emerge. The restated value proposition for this new world could be Schwab's 2000 Statement: "Demystify investing and empower individual investors, providing them with the tools, access, and objective information they need to become better investors."

One technique that we have used to brainstorm and draw scenarios for the future is the e-business opportunity matrix (figure 9-2). The Biz.com quadrant in the figure includes opportunities to sell or deliver physical products and/or services using the Internet. The quadrant addresses the question, How can we provide value to the customer by moving our physical products and/or services to the Internet?

FIGURE 9-2   The B-Web Opportunity Matrix

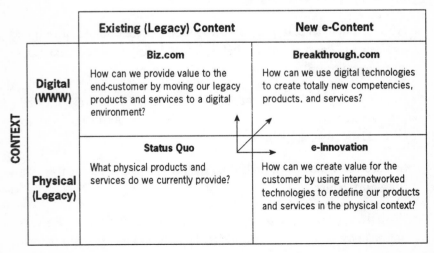

CONTENT (PRODUCTS AND SERVICES)

		Existing (Legacy) Content	New e-Content
CONTEXT	**Digital (WWW)**	**Biz.com** How can we provide value to the end-customer by moving our legacy products and services to a digital environment?	**Breakthrough.com** How can we use digital technologies to create totally new competencies, products, and services?
	Physical (Legacy)	**Status Quo** What physical products and services do we currently provide?	**e-Innovation** How can we create value for the customer by using internetworked technologies to redefine our products and services in the physical context?

The e-Innovation quadrant is for out-of-the-box strategies that contribute additional value to the customer for physical (often mature and commoditized) offerings. In other words, How can we use digital technologies to redefine, extend, or complement our physical products and/or services to create value for the customer in our current physical context?

Breakthrough.com represents the most spectacular opportunities: How can the Internet and other digital technologies help us create totally new competencies, products, and/or services?

The status-quo quadrant is no less important than the others. It sets the baseline from which further e-business opportunity springs forth.

Some examples further explain this matrix. Schwab.com moved the physical-world brokerage model online (i.e., a "Biz.com" step in the opportunity matrix). E-innovation opportunities include initiatives like delivering stock quotes and trade through wireless handheld devices. A Breakthrough.com opportunity might be anytime, anyplace decision support (tailored, real-time scenario and risk-return analysis).

STEP 4: REAGGREGATE

We have disaggregated the old value proposition, identified its weaknesses, and envisioned a transformed value proposition for the digital economy. Now we fashion a new b-web model for the reinvented value proposition.

This step entails repopulating the categories of value contributors and assigning contributions to the various classes of participants. The analysis defines the human, relationship, and structural capital on the supply side of the b-web.

Return to the earlier disaggregation analysis (step 2 above) and reassess the value contributions. Decide whether each relates to the new value proposition. If so, decide how to improve the value dramatically, who—in and outside your enterprise—should deliver it, and by what means they should do so. Think creatively about shifting responsibilities from one type of contributor to another.

For example, the full-service broker's value proposition typically includes tracking and researching the market. Schwab has disaggregated this task into a number of components and parceled them to three classes of b-web participants. A variety of content providers such as Big Charts, Quote.com, and First Boston provide market data, research, and analysis. End-customers identify and track relevant information and synthesize appropriate conclusions. Schwab itself aggregates and digests this content into an easy-to-navigate online package. Also, unlike many of its online competitors, Schwab also provides advisers, who, on request, help its customers decide what information best meets their needs.

Another task is to identify new value contributions that will enhance the customer experience and/or business performance. Assign these contributions to existing (or potential) b-web participants. Schwab's "live" telephone investment forums let customers interact directly with industry experts.

Expect and encourage polymediation (see chapter 3). Schwab uses portals like Excite and iVillage to drive traffic to its Web site. In addition, its AdvisorSource program reaches customers through some five thousand independent investment advisers.

Consider how a pervasive, application-rich, Web-enabled, internetworked infrastructure will support real-time, customer-responsive, integrated b-web communications and transactions. Assume that technology innovation will foster creative opportunities for improvement.

Think about the context provider as focusing on service or product strategy, relationship management, and b-web leadership, rather than on actual creation of "content." Assign "content"-oriented value-creating functions to the context provider when it makes sense for competitive advantage or cost effectiveness. In addition to organizing content from a variety of external suppliers (like Dow Jones), Schwab offers its own online training for new investors. Other b-web participants—including customers—will also provide content. Often, where the context provider delivers content, it invites competition from other content providers. Schwab offers customers its own mutual funds, but provides equal access to those of the competition.

Identify and engage a variety of best-of-breed participants to deliver other b-web value elements. Schwab has cultivated partnerships with leading information, product, and service providers, as well as community stars like AOL, Excite, and iVillage and site designer Razorfish.

Recognize and amply reward all participants, including customers, for their value contributions. Particularly diligent on this point, Schwab coddles its partners with great care. "I'm nervous of any deal where one of our partners doesn't seem to be making enough money," says Schwab's chief strategy officer Dan Leeman.

Remember that participants will both cooperate and compete within the b-web, itself a competitive marketspace. In Schwab's OneSource mutual-fund marketplace, companies collaborate to attract customers to the site while competing fiercely for customer business.

Anticipate public and government responses to your innovations, and consider how to maximize their support. Schwab and other online brokers led a successful public relations campaign for "booting your broker," including messages on prudently minimizing risk and protecting retirement nest eggs.

Table 9-3 is our depiction of Schwab as a b-web. Note the shifts in partners and roles from the current state analysis in table 9-2 to the one described here.

STEP 5: PREPARE A VALUE MAP

A value map is a graphical depiction of how a b-web operates, or will operate in the future (this technique is based on the work of our collaborator, Verna Allee).[2] We identify all the key classes of participants, including strategic partners, suppliers, and customers. In mapping, we view b-webs as complex systems in which the players exchange three qualitatively different, yet equally vital kinds of value:

1. Tangible benefits: goods, services, and money, including direct exchanges for paid services; the delivery of goods, services, contracts, and invoices; and the receipt of orders, requests for proposals, confirmations, and payment. Treat knowledge as a tangible good when it is part of a product or service for customers.

2. Knowledge: strategic information, planning, process, and technical knowledge that flows around value-creation processes.

3. Intangible benefits: other value and benefits, such as brand, community, customer loyalty, and image enhancement.

To visualize the new value-creating system, construct a value map. Include all key classes of participants and the most important value

TABLE 9-3 Schwab Reaggregation as a B-Web

Who?	What Value Will They Contribute?	How?	Key Success Factors
End Customers			
• Retail investors (as buyers)	• Investment goals • Research • Proactive portfolio management • Demand/ liquidity • Fees	• Self-evaluation • Online research • Online portfolio management and analysis tools • Orders	• Trust • Market literacy • Technology literacy and access • Agility, risk tolerance
Context Providers			
• Schwab	• User interface, integrated environment • Content selection and management • Access to trading • Real-time portfolio management	• Online environment • Personal contact (phone/office)	• Seamless, consistent, easy-to-use interface • System reliability • Partnering capability • Willingness to share rewards • Quality of tools and research
• Investment advisers	• Access to trading bundled with advice	• Schwab resources and channels	• Paid for overall service and results, not for trades • Special services for advisers
• Portals and other Web destinations	• Alternative access points and channels	• Schwab information and click-through	• Customer-appropriate interface and content
Content Providers			
• Third-party data and research companies	• Research and analysis	• Electronic • Paper • Personal contact	• Timeliness • Depth, quality, quantity • Ease of use
• Media	• News and views	• Real-time Net • Print • TV	• Selection • Brand • Quality
• Investment advisers (Schwab, third party)	• Personal advice	• Web phone/video • Telephone • In person	• Objective • Proactive • Tailored to customer objectives, interests, preferences • Congenial
• Other investors	• Shared perspectives • Advice • Community	• Online forums • Affinity group meetings	• Self-regulating dialogue • Segmented by interests • Forums for quality • Facilitation and monitoring

exchanges among them. Schwab's value map (figure 9-3) depicts the company's key relationships and value exchanges.

STEP 6: DO THE B-WEB MIX

In the digital marketplace, companies employ business models as competitive weapons. Business model agility can be the determining factor separating success from failure. David Ellington, president of NetNoir, says the company's business model has changed five times since he cofounded it in 1995: "Each model was absolutely right for its time and wrong for the next round of competition."

Every business has a core organizing principle that corresponds to one of the five b-web types: Agora, Aggregation, Value Chain, Alliance,

Content Providers (continued)			
• Portfolio tool developers, Schwab	• Portfolio self-management	• Integrated into Schwab site	• Seamless integration • Compatibility with desktop applications • Quality/functionality
• Retail investors (as sellers) • Institutional investors • Issuers	• Tradable securities, mutual funds, and other instruments	• Offers via online and broker channels	• Breadth of offering (mutual funds, IPOs, special offers) • Timeliness of deal closing
• Market makers and traders	• Price setting through bid/asks	• Floor trading • Electronic markets	• Less insider dealing
Commerce Services Providers			
• Exchanges	• Exchange mechanisms	• Regulations • Facilities	• Extended trading hours • Quicker and more direct access for retail customers
• SEC and other authorities	• Regulation	• Regulations • Monitoring • Enforcement	• Continuing, paced deregulation • Protections for individual investors
Infrastructure Providers			
• Exchanges	• Trading environments	• All-electronic trading	• Internetworking among major and parallel exchanges
• Technology providers	• Information and communications applications	• Internet/Web applications infrastructure	• Price performance • Ubiquity • New wireless/handheld appliances

FIGURE 9-3 Schwab Value Map

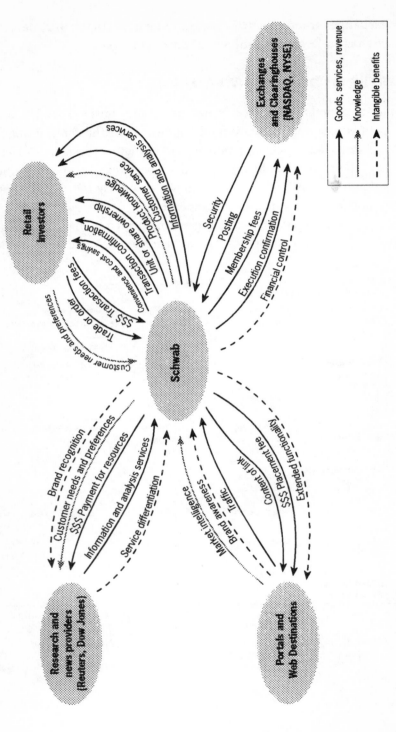

Legend:
- → Goods, services, revenue
- ⇢ Knowledge
- --→ Intangible benefits

Retail Investors
- Information and analysis services
- Customer service
- Product knowledge
- Unit or share ownership
- Transaction confirmation
- Convenience and cost savings
- $$$ Transaction fees
- Trade or order
- Customer needs and preferences

Research and news providers (Reuters, Dow Jones)
- Brand recognition
- Customer needs and preferences
- $$$ Payment for resources
- Information and analysis services
- Service differentiation

Schwab

Exchanges and Clearinghouses (NASDAQ, NYSE)
- Security
- Posting
- Membership fees
- Execution confirmation
- Financial control

Portals and Web Destinations
- Market intelligence
- Brand awareness
- Traffic
- Content or link
- $$$ Placement fee
- Extended functionality

or Distributive Network. Each type has further subtypes, which provide for a more precise business model definition: Agora eBay is a supply-side auction, whereas NASDAQ is an exchange. Beyond its core organizing principle, a specific b-web will incorporate aspects of other types in its b-web mix. eBay's online forums add the dimension of an Alliance discussion community to its value proposition.

In designing the b-web mix, consider how each type and subtype might apply to a creative package that enhances customer value, provides competitive differentiation and advantage, and reduces costs for all participants. Does the new business essentially create value, as in an Alliance and a Value Chain? Or does it distribute value, more like an Aggregation, an Agora, or a Distributive Network? This answer profoundly affects work design, competitive positioning, the definition of competency, and sources of profit.

As mentioned, a full-service retail broker is a Value Chain that provides a focused process of client interaction, market tracking, research, and analysis. Drawing on various resources, within the firm and outside it, the adviser comes up with just the right buy or sell recommendation at the moment of truth: the client conversation. To succeed, the broker must excel at customer intimacy and relationship development and know how to integrate information resources to reach conclusions and make recommendations tailored to the customer's interests and priorities. Brokerage firms face the challenge of attracting, motivating, and retaining professionals who genuinely possess these capabilities.

Schwab and other online brokers shifted the business model from Value Chain to Aggregation. Schwab customers expend the time and effort to determine their own investment objectives. They track the market and conduct their own research. On its Web site, Schwab assists the customer by aggregating and delivering current market data, news, and analysis. Such informational content aggregation is a revolutionary business-model innovation for brokerage firms—even (especially) for discount brokers like Schwab. The company's advertising makes much of this resource, seeking to boost investors' self-confidence and reduce their sense of dependence on traditional brokers.

(Arguably, Schwab also aggregates access to a menu of securities in which investors invest. In fact, the stock exchanges themselves aggregate securities directly. Schwab, in its discount-broker days, was the first investment firm to aggregate hundreds, then thousands, of mutual funds from dozens of different issuers—adopting an Amazon-like strategy long before the Web.)

Despite exponential market success, Schwab concluded early in 1999 that an Aggregation model—no matter how well executed—no longer sufficed. Through its retail branches and the telephone, Schwab had always offered some personal service to large account holders and others who wanted it. Now the company needed to extend a higher quality of personal service to a much greater proportion of its customer base. Schwab embarked on becoming the world's first full-service Internet broker, in effect, adding a Value-Chain dimension to its b-web.

E*Trade, the online discount broker pioneer, adopted a very different strategy. Rather than become an electronic full-service broker, the company broadened its Aggregation model to become a mid-market financial services portal with a variety of offerings, including a stock trading game, online community facilities, and a shopping mall. E*Trade also acquired ClearStation, a community of online financial forums. Rather than turn itself into a proactive "expert" online broker as Schwab did, E*Trade added a customer discussion and help community (an Alliance) to its b-web mix.

Schwab, positioning itself up-market from the E*Trades of the world, focused on its core business-model transition strategy. At the same time, it collaborated with mass-market portal Excite, a general-purpose Aggregation, which distributed Schwab financial content. Schwab sought to benefit from an E*Trade-like portal strategy while building professional and electronic advice into its online offering—a unique hybrid of Aggregation and Value Chain.

MAIN MESSAGES

The strategy for weaving a b-web can be summarized by the following points:

- Begin by disaggregating and reaggregating your core value proposition from a customer perspective, and be guided by your core corporate values. What are the vulnerabilities in the industrial-age deployment of human, relationship, and structural capital?

- Disaggregate in three main steps: (1) identify the key contributors in each of five b-web participant layers (customer, context, content, commerce services, and infrastructure); (2) describe what each participant contributes to the system, and how they do so; and (3) pinpoint the weaknesses and opportunities for improvement in the current arrangement.

- Answer these questions: How would the value proposition change if the customer were at the center and in full control? What "impossible" things could you do if technology-enabled capabilities were limitless, and there were no organizational barriers to change? What new business models—ways of creating, defining, and delivering value, and facilitating relationships with customers, suppliers, and partners—could you envisage?

- Define how the context provider will lead and add value by changing the rules, orchestrating the b-web, and facilitating the accumulation of digital capital.

- Creatively design your b-web, using the five categories of value contributors, value maps, and the b-web mix.

10 harvesting
digital capital

Managers must answer some gut-wrenching questions before they can plant b-web innovation and harvest the benefits of digital capital.

- What business should you be in? Briefly revisiting this issue, we discuss the new, risk-laden agenda of the automotive industry, which is now focusing on digital customer value.

- What's in and what's out? Who's in and who's out? How do you decide whether to learn, acquire, or externally source a capability? Drawing on research and the experience of leaders like Cisco CEO John Chambers, we sketch a road map to the next plateau on a never-ending journey.

- How do you protect the structural capital of business-model innovation— and your ability to innovate? Does patenting business models make sense? Focusing on Walker Digital, the business-model laboratory that invented Priceline, we discuss the pros and cons of this important issue—and present our point of view.

- Should you launch or invest in dot-coms, or has Wall Street grossly overrated—and overvalued—Internet companies? Here again we present our perspective, drawing in part on our own experience.

FOCUS ON VALUE

After twenty years of idling on the shoulder of the information high-way, the U.S. auto industry finally gripped the wheel, made some tough choices, and hit the gas. The day of reckoning was November 2, 1999, when both Ford and General Motors announced plans to create Value Chain b-webs. AutoXchange, Ford's stand-alone joint venture with Oracle, would offer supply-chain services to all comers, including Ford's competitors. Oracle said they might eventually take AutoXchange public. GM announced plans to work with CommerceOne, a competitor of Ariba, to set up an initiative called MarketSite. Unlike Ford, GM planned to limit MarketSite to itself and its own suppliers. Ford and GM struck again in the January 2000 Detroit Auto Show. They both announced plans for in-vehicle Internet services. Ford announced a major partnership with Yahoo!, GM with AOL.

How will these digital Value Chains benefit customers? Look for entirely new kinds of end-customer value propositions. Consider some of Ford's other initiatives:

- CEO Jacques Nasser said that his goal is to transform Ford into a "transportation solutions provider for the entire life of the vehicle."

- The company acquired Kwik-Fit, a European chain of two thousand service centers.

- Ford will collaborate with CD Radio to bring subscription-based digital satellite radio and commercial-free music to Ford customers.

- It initiated agreements with Priceline, Microsoft CarPoint, and Yahoo!, implicitly recognizing Web intermediaries as a first (and potentially the most important) point of contact for car buyers.

In a deal similar to its GM partnership, CommerceOne reduced British Telecom's supply-chain costs by 10 percent. If GM can achieve comparable results, it will cut costs by $8 billion—an amount equal to the company's profit. The company formed a new business group, e-GM, mandated to create a new class of applications for vehicles and related services, and to transform traditional automotive operations into a global e-business enterprise. Mark Hogan, vice president of the e-GM Group, told us, "In three years, e-GM will be GM!"

This is revolutionary for the auto industry. Buyers will specify a unique car configuration (more personalized than is now possible) and receive a built-to-order auto within two or three days. Instead of haggling with dealers over price, customers will pay a fixed, known surcharge over factory prices or just buy directly from the manufacturer. The car becomes a mobile information and entertainment system, with self-monitoring diagnostics and security. And further down the road, who knows what will happen as visionaries raise scenarios like pollution-free (thanks to fuel cell technology), self-driving vehicles, available to travelers and commuters on an as-needed basis.

The future may be exciting, but it is also unclear. What is certain is that these are the early days of a new era of radical customer value innovation. Clearly, these changes will threaten many established industry relationships—with dealers, employees, unions, suppliers, and adjacent industries like insurance. GM and Ford may not wish to admit it just yet, but they have surely recognized that they face harrowing leadership tests in the coming years. Why do the Fords and GMs of the world invest billions in b-webs? Because b-web-enabled digital capital formation is the only way to gain the agility and innovations they need to competitively deliver customer value in the digital economy.

REDEFINE THE BOUNDARIES OF THE FIRM

As we said in chapter 1, outsourcing is dead. Not because firms go back to industrial-age vertical integration, but the opposite. Strategists no longer view the integrated corporation as the starting point for allocating the elements of value creation. Rather, they begin with a customer value proposition, disaggregate it (chapter 9), and then reaggregate new value for b-web delivery. The context provider, like industrial entrepreneur James Richardson (chapter 1), might simply coordinate the activities of a collection of suppliers. He has nothing to outsource because nothing resides inside his firm.

The b-web revolutionizes partnering. It starts with a vision that the enterprise, like the Internet itself, is a Lego-like open platform. B-web participants provide value-adding capabilities that plug in as needed.

When an organization's membrane is so porous—and when transactions are fluid and nearly friction-free—how do you decide what resources a firm should contain and what it should draw from outside? Our experience with b-webs suggests that all is not a blur. Managers *can* make rational and thoughtful decisions about partnering and acquiring.

A business can choose from four mechanisms to gain access to a capability, each of which has implications for digital capital accumulation:[1]

- Go out to the *open market*, using an Agora or Aggregation mechanism, to find the best available cost/performance package, without necessarily seeking to amass digital capital over the long term.

- Develop relationship and structural capital through *partnerships*, such as contracts, strategic investments, and joint ventures: medium- and long-term arrangements for the creation of value.

- *Build* the capability internally through hiring, training, and capital investment: a human-capital accumulation strategy.

- *Acquire* the capability by purchasing another company and its human, structural, and perhaps even relationship capital assets.

In chapter 1, we offered Coase's law: *A firm will tend to expand until the costs of organizing an extra transaction within the firm become equal to the costs of carrying out the same transaction on the open market.* In other words, go wherever it costs the least. If the marketplace will cut you a better deal than your own firm can offer, then perform the transaction in the marketplace. As transaction costs approach zero, the question becomes, What other sorts of costs should managers consider when making the in-versus-out decision?

The economic theory on this issue begins with the costs of *opportunism,* which tends to arise when one party (which we call the "specialist") to an exchange gains the ability to take advantage of another (the "subject"). The specialist gains incentives to act opportunistically when the subject—often willingly—makes a big investment that depends on the specialist's services to conduct a critical transaction in a highly specific way (i.e., a transaction-specific investment). As Carl Shapiro and Hal Varian might say, the specialist "locks in" the subject.

For example, Amazon.com (the subject) based its start-up game plan for an online, no-warehouse bookstore on the capabilities of Ingram Book Group (the specialist), the largest distributor in the United States.

In January 1998, Ingram took the opportunistic step of agreeing to be purchased by Barnes & Noble, placing Amazon.com and other bookstores at their combined mercy. The U.S. Federal Trade Commission subsequently barred the deal because it would limit competition.

Other examples of opportunism occurred when industrial-age power and telecom monopolies exacted opportunistic pricing and delayed product and service innovations. Their customers (the subjects), with transaction-specific investments in their home and business real estate, had nowhere else to go. When deregulation came along, the tables turned. Now, power and telecom companies find themselves stuck with transaction-specific investments in a competitive marketplace. Customers increasingly became specialists in the eyes of asset-bound former monopolies, able to opportunistically demand better value for their power and telecom fees.

Structure provides a few ways to counter opportunism. One is through ownership: If you depend on a specialist company, consider acquiring it. A second approach is contractual: If you depend only moderately on the specialist, or the market has a few specialists to choose from, strike a long-term deal on price and quality of service.

Where the market contains many competing specialists, you need not worry about opportunism unless the specialists (like the oil companies) have put together a back-room oligopoly. Monopolies and oligopolies can fall to regulation, when the government steps in to prevent specialists from behaving opportunistically. Similarly, you can team up with other locked-in subjects and foster a new source of supply (like hydrogen or electricity). In all industries, deregulation, open standards, new technologies, and plummeting costs of market entry have broken the power of lock-in.

But opportunism is not the only issue that forces acquisition decisions; more often, you simply need to fill a capability gap. If so, why not build the capability internally or acquire it rather than source it from an external supplier? Companies have always done so, haven't they?

Answer these questions in four steps:

1. Decide whether having the capability inside your business is the right strategic choice.

2. Figure out whether you can ignore or offset the costs of buying or building. Jay Barney, strategy professor at Ohio State University,

points out that buying or building comes at a cost—often a prohibitive one.[2] Such costs grow as companies increasingly rely on fast-changing high-technology capabilities.

3. Consider the intermediate option: an internal venture fund.

4. If you still believe that you should acquire a target firm, assess whether you will succeed in integrating its capabilities.

The Strategic Choice: Inside or Outside

Cisco CEO John Chambers explains the importance of decisions about building internal capability:

The companies who emerge as industry leaders will be those who understand how to partner and those who understand how to acquire. Customers today are not just looking for pinpoint products, but for end-to-end solutions. A horizontal business model always beats a vertical business model. So you've got to provide that horizontal capability in your product line, either through your own R&D, or through acquisitions.[3]

Like outsourcing, vertical integration is dead. Horizontal integration lives. In a world of b-webs, firms should develop the digital capital that provides competitive advantages to their horizontal value offerings. Only acquire specialist firms that fit your horizontal slice of the universe. To avoid lock-in for the vertical capabilities that you need, cultivate the structural and relationship capital of alternative suppliers in your b-web, and promote deregulation and open standards.

The horizontal mind-set applies in every industry, but in new ways. In 1996, for example, American Airlines (AMR) formed Sabre Holdings as a horizontal reservations-focused subsidiary. Sabre, in addition to its traditional back-office services for travel agents and various airlines, started Travelocity, which quickly became a leading Web-based travel business. In 1999, Sabre announced plans to spin off its Travelocity slice, merging it with Preview Travel into a new publicly traded business called Travelocity. com. Built into the announcement was an exclusive distribution deal with b-web partner America Online. Then, in December 1999, AMR announced that Sabre itself would become a separate, publicly traded company, free to focus on technology outsourcing and Internet-based travel sales, and even to compete with American Airlines.

Amazon.com and (no doubt soon) Webvan redefine the horizontal slice of online retail. Each began in a narrow space—books and groceries, respectively. Amazon.com, which invested initially in relationship capital (brand and a portfolio of customization services), is extending its no- or low-inventory competency into other product areas. If Webvan succeeds with its very different distribution-centric model (a structural capital focus), we can expect this company to branch out as well. Both will be wise to focus on leveraging their core capabilities and to continue relying on b-web partners (like consumer-goods manufacturers) for other dimensions of customer value.

The Costs of Buying or Building

Where your digital-capital-accumulation focus passes the horizontal fitness test, should you build it internally, buy a company, or—again— source it outside because the costs seem too high? As all firms compete in e-business through technology, everyone faces such questions, because the costs and consequences of a strategic misstep can exceed those of the industrial age—and can be felt a lot sooner. On the other hand, in the digital economy, inaction can be worse than the wrong action.

Building new e-business capabilities can cost more in several ways. First, history and experience matter.[4] For example, a company that specializes in e-commerce Web sites or next-day order fulfillment goes through a learning process that can take several years.

Second, digital capital is *socially complex* to create and manage. For example, integrating human factors, processes, Web technologies, databases, and business acumen for a specific industry, whether health care or interactive entertainment, involves numerous disciplines and capabilities. Some companies excel at such integration more than others.

Finally, uncertainty has costs. Given the pace of change, how would you know that you are making the right internal investments? The reward should match the risks.

If these obstacles don't faze you, then maybe you should build the capability internally. If they seem daunting, then maybe you should buy a company that already has the capability.

This too can be costly. For one thing, uncertainty applies to acquisitions, too. If you've made a bad choice—as when AT&T acquired NCR during the 1980s or as when Mattel discovered in 1998–1999 with the Learning Company—then exiting the deal may seriously deplete your financial and digital capital.

Acquisition can reduce a firm's value, especially when customers value its independence. Publicis, a large French advertising agency, remained independent throughout the industry's consolidation of the late 1980s and early 1990s. Many of its customers, partially owned by the government, preferred to work with a nationally owned agency and might have gone elsewhere had it sold out to a global player.

With acquisitions, you can end up with unnecessary baggage. When America Online purchased Netscape, AOL was more interested in the technology skills of Netscape's people than in the company's money-losing browser. However, since the two are so deeply intertwined, AOL must bear the cost of supporting Netscape's browser in the marketplace. John Chambers has a simple approach to forestalling such problems: "Our ideal acquisition is a small startup that has a great technology product on the drawing board that is going to come out in 6 to 12 months. We buy the engineers and the next generation product. Then we blow it through our distribution channels and leverage our manufacturing and financial strengths."

Leveraging acquired capabilities can be difficult and costly. This common problem happens when companies fail to overcome differences in culture, approaches, processes, technologies, and so on. Citicorp and Travelers had a rocky start to their 1998 marriage. Turf wars and culture clashes plagued the newly formed Citigroup. Shortly after the merger, two key vice presidents resigned and business results weakened.

Conversely, several new factors favor partnerships. Reduced transaction costs make it easy to gain new capabilities through b-webs. Value Chains like Hewlett-Packard enjoy access to half a million software developers in India. Aggregations from eToys to Bloomingdale's can enter the online retail market and instantly acquire a logistics function from the U.S. Postal Service, FedEx, or UPS. And 3Com enlists thousands of digital Rotarians who unite in a self-organizing Alliance to create software for its PalmPilot. The Distributive Network Global Crossing linked telecommunications capabilities owned by others to win a bid for high-capacity networking across all of Ireland.

Partnerships often entail the risk of losing control over relationship (customers) and structural (business processes, product quality) capital. B-webs shift the risk/reward calculation toward partnerships. Firms can more easily adjust to partners. The Net provides a standards-based platform for collaboration; sophisticated b-web applications are easier to implement than traditional enterprise systems. Standardized inter-enterprise business processes facilitate collaboration and commerce.

Internetworking makes it possible to identify and isolate finer, more granular organization functions for deployment in new ways. Companies can achieve a better appreciation of their core assets and capabilities. B-webs may enable firms to genuinely implement, for the first time, the core competency concept to maximize return on invested capital.

The Intermediate Option: An Internal Venture Fund

Hundreds of businesses, from Amazon.com to Diageo (the food and drinks conglomerate that owns Burger King, Guinness, and Pillsbury), Nortel, and WPP (the advertising/PR conglomerate that owns Hill & Knowlton, J. Walter Thomson, and Ogilvy) have chosen an intermediate option: strategic investment.

Rather than build or buy, these companies have formed internal venture capital initiatives to achieve two goals. First, they take minority stakes in high-potential e-business firms. Second, they function as incubators for internally generated e-business initiatives.

Such initiatives provide good learning opportunities for the investor companies to accumulate digital and financial capital. Sometimes, as with Delta's stake in Priceline, these investments provide billion-dollar returns. The downside? They can divert investee company managers into focusing on their investors, rather than on customers and the competition. An early development Internet start-up may reach its potential more easily and quickly with relatively neutral, pure financial investment than with the strategic dollars of industry incumbents.

Strategic investment may be a way station on an acquisition path. In such situations, the strategic investment must not divert management focus and consequently reduce, rather than increase, the investee company's value.

Whenever such financial investments happen, ownership, rather than the "free will" of markets, binds participants together. Commitment is valuable, but, as we discussed in chapter 1, the Japanese experience illustrates how a *keiretsu* model based on permanency of ownership hampers agility. On the other hand, the venture capital firm Kleiner Perkins Caufield & Byers, for example, has consciously, and very successfully, injected Silicon Valley urgency into the *keiretsu* model.

The Integration Issues

Does your b-web strategy still lead you to buy a particular company? If so, then you must assess whether you will successfully integrate the proposed acquisition into your business. Integration is a two-way street.

Your business needs a policy framework and performance-management tool kit to ensure that when an acquisition occurs, both parties respond appropriately so as not to leech away the newfound human, relationship, and structural capital. Cisco measures and compensates responsible managers on how well they retain their acquiree's employees. It puts acquired companies through a structured, fast-paced hundred-day integration program.

Chambers describes Cisco's five rules of thumb for assessing the likelihood that a proposed acquisition will succeed: "Anytime you don't have all five, it's a yellow light. And where you haven't got at least three of the five, you don't touch it."

- Proof of a *shared vision* on where the industry is going and what role each partner should play in it

- Ability to create *short-term wins for acquired employees* (career opportunities, cultural fit, work satisfaction) for retention of human capital

- Long-term *strategic fit*, yielding wins for customers, employees, shareholders, and business partners—using structural capital to enhance relationship capital

- Similarities in *culture and chemistry* (perhaps the most important, according to Chambers)

- *Geographic proximity* to current operations to unite people and maximize efficiencies

When you get though all these hurdles, you probably have a valuable acquisition candidate. Otherwise, you have a potential b-web partner. Remember that Cisco, renowned for forty acquisitions in five years, has ten thousand partners in its b-web.

BUSINESS MODEL PATENTS: YES OR NO?

Ultimately, the way to defend digital capital is to continuously innovate—not just products and services—but business models. The old expression "If it ain't broke, don't fix it" has been replaced by "If it ain't broke, break it . . . before your competitors do." However, this new variant on an old slogan referred to product and service innovation. The new battlefield of innovation is in business models, which in turn drive all other innovation. Companies that innovate product and service offerings without innovating business models are pushing rope.

These days, you can also defend digital capital by patenting it. The U.S. Patent and Trademarks Office (PTO) now issues patents for innovative business processes: new designs for structural capital.

Priceline calls its price-discovery mechanism "buyer-driven commerce," claiming that it is a new and therefore patentable invention. The PTO agreed, and patent number 5,794,207 now protects Priceline's business method. Priceline sued Microsoft for patent infringement in October 1999 after the software giant offered a similar price-discovery mechanism on its Expedia travel site. (The suit also claimed that Microsoft had used confidential information, which Priceline had shared under a nondisclosure agreement.)

Priceline founder Jay Walker owns another company, called Walker Digital, which dreams up patentable business processes. Half its professionals are business-model innovators, and the others are patent attorneys. By mid-1999 the company had applied for over 250 patents, and won awards for a dozen or so. Examples include a prepaid telephone calling card valid only for numbers specified by the buyer, and traveler's checks that you pay for after using them instead of before. Many of Walker Digital's ideas make you wonder, "Now why didn't I think of that?"

Business and legal circles passionately debate the notion of patenting structural capital innovations. Some contend that patentability is a necessary incentive to innovators in a new economy; others say that patenting business processes and models stifles innovation.

Walker argues that he does not invest in developing new ideas to keep them to himself. He wants to put his ideas into action, and that means starting new companies or awarding licenses to other companies. Either way, new services enter the marketplace, the public benefits, and Walker Digital profits. This encourages the company to develop more ideas. From Walker's perspective, everybody wins.

Many observers disagree. Robert Kunstadt, a New York lawyer who specializes in intellectual property law, writes in *IP Magazine* that had this patent law been in force a couple of decades ago, "frequent-flyer points, infomercials, trading stamps and in-flight shopping all might have been patented by their original inventors as methods of doing business." Left unchecked, the new policy will lead to "large-scale disruption of U.S. commerce, as sharp operators move to patent business methods and assert patents against the unsuspecting." He calls on Congress to abolish the right to patent business processes before it spirals out of control.[5]

Walker's biggest idea is not any single patent, but Walker Digital itself, whose business model is patenting structural capital innovation. The digital economy is a new and fertile ground for such creativity. The company that systematically describes and patents the countless new ways of doing things now possible for the first time in history gains a corner on innovation that may come dangerously close to monopolistic practices. Walker often compares his company to Thomas Edison's laboratory. But where Edison's labs focused on inventing goods, Walker Digital invents new ways to run businesses and conduct commerce. If Henry Ford had followed the Walker Digital model, instead of merely using his moving-assembly-line concept to build cars, he would have patented it and forced potential competitors to stick with craft production. If this had occurred, would customers have benefited? Would GM have risen to challenge Ford and transform the auto industry for a second time?

The U.S. Congress has already set a precedent for striking down such patents. In 1996, it granted medical practitioners immunity for using patented treatment techniques without permission. The issue gained prominence when a surgeon patented a new cataract surgery procedure. A public uproar ensued when he sued another doctor to prevent him from using or teaching the technique.

Managers busily reinventing their business models ignore the patent issue at their peril. Consider this scenario: A wildly innovative b-web blind-sides your company. You spend tens of millions of dollars to compete. As you recover, your competitor announces that the government has approved one of its patent applications and it sues you for stealing its patented business process, demanding that you pay license fees or it will put you out of business. Even worse, it forces you to stop using the process. Checkmate.

In response to this situation, a flood of e-commerce patent applications has engulfed the PTO. Some companies even seek patents as bargaining chips for the legal wrangles of the future.

DIGITAL CAPITAL BEGETS MARKET CAPITAL

In light of the extraordinary valuations and stock market gains of many Internet and e-business companies, many observers have raised legitimate—sometimes anguished—questions about the durability of these changes. Consider the following comment by the editors of *PC Computing* magazine: "Stock-price feeding frenzy has returned to the Internet with a vengeance. Suckers all over the world are betting big on the next Sure Thing. Let's face it: Much of the NASDAQ is becoming a casino for imbeciles."[6]

Pundits have drawn parallels with the biotechnology stock mania of the early 1990s and the Dutch tulip frenzy of the 1630s, when speculators would spend a decade's wages on a single bulb. A reality iceberg is ahead, the pundits say, and Internet investors are like champagne-sippers on the *Titanic!*

Let's get a grip. The Net is not an obscure commodity like tulips and is more than an individual economic sector like biotechnology. The Internet is becoming the infrastructure for all business activity, the foundation of a new economy, transforming *all* sectors in the process. The *Titanic* metaphor does apply in one sense: Like the movie, the Net is making a lot of people rich. Doomsayers don't understand digital capital.

For example, has Wall Street overvalued eBay? Compare it to Wal-Mart, a brick-and-mortar retail leader. On February 15, 2000, eBay's market capital valuation was $19.2 billion. Its 1999 revenues were $225 million, with profits of $10.8 million (eBay has been profitable for a long time), and a stratospheric price-to-earnings (P/E) ratio of 1,856. In contrast, Wal-Mart had 1999 revenues of $166.6 billion and profits of $5.4 billion, a market cap of $253.9 billion, and a P/E ratio of a "mere" 49 (figure 10-1).

eBay's market cap was 7.6 percent of Wal-Mart's, though its profits were only 1.9 percent of Wal-Mart's. In other words, based on P/E ratios, eBay's premium over Wal-Mart was nearly 4,100 percent, or 41 times.

But consider sales and sales growth, rather than profit. If eBay—like Wal-Mart—operated physical stores and booked the value of all the goods that sold through its auctions, then its 1999 revenues would be some $2.8 billion—1.7 percent of Wal-Mart's revenues. Wal-Mart's price-to-sales ratio was 1.5, while eBay's (based on the $2.8 billion goods flow) was only 6.8. By this analysis, eBay arguably has a 453 percent, or 14.5 times, premium over Wal-Mart. This premium continues to increase. We performed a similar analysis in November 1999, and eBay's premium was closer to 3.5. Such premiums are significant,

---

FIGURE 10-1   Is eBay Overvalued?

	eBay	Wal-Mart	eBay/ Wal-Mart Ratio
Market Capitalization (million dollars)	$ 19,200	$ 253,900	7.6%
1999 Profit (million dollars)	$ 10.8	$ 5,400	0.2%
Price/Earnings Ratio	1,856	49	**3787.7%**
1999 Revenues (million dollars)	$ 225	$ 166,600	0.1%
1999 Sales (million dollars)	$ 2,800	$ 166,600	1.7%
Price/Sales Ratio	6.8	1.5	**453%**

but they are not totally out of the ballpark. And while eBay's growth accelerates, Wal-Mart's seems to be sputtering.

Compare quarter-over-quarter revenue growth trends for the two companies (figure 10-2) for the six quarters ending in late 1999.[7] eBay's average growth rate was 35 percent, and the rate was increasing over the period at a pace of 3.2 percent. Meanwhile, Wal-Mart's average growth rate was only 5.6 percent, which was in a 1.3 percent *decline* over the six quarters!

Will eBay forever enjoy the stellar growth rates of a start-up? In late 1999, eBay had announced plans to launch fifty regional sites and an entry into business auctions. Considering these plans, eBay still has lots of upside opportunity. Will Wal-Mart reverse its shaky perform-ance? Entirely likely. But could eBay scale much closer to Wal-Mart? We believe so.

In addition to these raw metrics, eBay has accumulated huge reserves of digital capital: networked human capital, networked relationships, and new business models (chapter 2). This digital capital further explains why investors pay a premium for the company.

The market capitalization of online auctions, bookstores, brokerage

FIGURE 10-2   eBay and Wal-Mart: Quarterly Growth

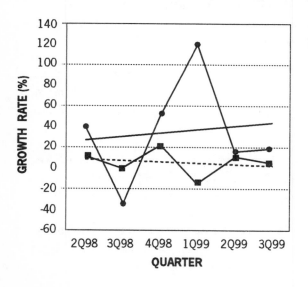
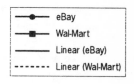

firms, portals, services, and technology enablers has eclipsed the titans of auto, steel, energy, manufacturing, and even finance. The pace of appreciation has already slowed, and many e-business experiments will stumble and fail. But these are the early days of digital capital. The Net has barely begun to hit. New business models call for new kinds of digital capital lenses.

When the steam engine came along in the nineteenth century, some people said, "No way, we're sticking with horses. There will always be a need for them." Others said, "Looks promising. We will invest in railroads, in the companies that build locomotives and make products shipped by rail, and in the new communities built in the new territories." Are you investing in stables, saddles, and blacksmiths, or in the emerging infrastructure?

THE E-BUSINESS FUND

In 1998, we worked with colleagues to design and advise a new mutual fund that draws on the perspectives and frameworks in this book. In its first fifteen months, the "Altamira e-business Fund" nearly quadrupled in value—appreciating by 239 percent and building an asset base of C$415 million.[8] It was the best performer among some 3,000 Canadian retail mutual funds (including many U.S.-based funds which were sold in Canada).

The fund builds on a simple idea: A balanced e-business portfolio should include three types of companies:

- "Pure play" new b-web leaders; high-risk, high-reward companies including Agoras like eBay, Aggregations like CommerceOne and Amazon, Value Chains like Cisco, and Alliance players like Red Hat, a Linux services business

- Traditional bricks-and-mortar companies shifting to b-web innovation, such as Time Warner (both an Aggregation and a Distributive Network), Ford (Value Chain), and FedEx (Distributive Network)

- Internet infrastructure and technology builders, such as Nortel, IBM, i2, and Descartes

THE POWER OF B-WEBS

Pioneers of the twentieth-century corporation—people like Henry Ford, Frederick Taylor, Alfred Sloan, William Hearst, and Thomas Watson—had no idea what would become of it, nor how it would change the world. How could they have predicted the century's global upheavals, how the car would transform everyday life, or the rise of the computer? How could they have known that this institution, rooted in hierarchy, command-control cultures, and "scientific management" would turn into its opposite—a place where success depends on letting go, on teamwork, and on trusting the wisdom of front-line employees? Perhaps the most visionary of these pioneers had such inklings, but the world took one hundred years to get there.

We are again in the early days of a new corporate form. The business

---

Many of the fund's investment criteria draw on the concepts in this book:

- Innovative business models that transform existing value propositions, leading to discontinuous change in an industry

- Strong relationship capital across the b-web, with solid branding, loyalty, customer value creation, and the capacity to attract, retain, leverage, and effectively manage financial, distribution, and technology partnerships

- Superior human capital—not just traditional good management but networked intellect, management of knowledge, and active engagement of many individual participants inside and outside the firm

- Context leadership through prime mover effectiveness, standards leadership, and/or rapid growth

- "Scaleability"—the ability to handle explosive growth and the inter-network effect (chapter 1)

- B-web leadership—expertise in managing partners, coopetitive culture, pace of change, deal making, curiosity, technology, uncertainty, new ideas, and leadership rather than bureaucracy web, rooted as it is in the modern enterprise, is perhaps not quite as revolutionary as its predecessor. But the evidence suggests that it differs enough to demand new ways of thinking, behaving, and being.

For many, learning to live and work effectively in a world of b-webs may pose the most gut-wrenching change of their business lives. For others, because of youth or temperament, a b-web is already the only livable kind of work habitat.

We all have much to discover as this new tale unfolds. As one of the authors' daughters, Amy Ticoll, likes to say, "Nothing you imagine is absolutely impossible."

notes

1 Value Innovation through Business Webs

1. Peter Guralnick, *Last Train to Memphis: The Rise of Elvis Presley* (Boston: Back Bay Books, 1994).
2. International Federation of the Phonographic Industry, quoted in "Music Piracy a $10 Billion Industry," Bloomberg News, Special to CNET News.com, 10 June 1999.
3. Herbert Simon, "Theories of Bounded Rationality," in *Decision and Organization,* ed. C. B. Radner and R. Radner (Amsterdam: North Holland, 1972).
4. Don Tapscott, *The Digital Economy: Promise and Peril in the Age of Networked Intelligence* (New York: McGraw-Hill, 1996); Larry Downes and Chunka Mui, *Unleashing the Killer App: Digital Strategies for Market Dominance* (Boston: Harvard Business School Press, 1998); Thomas Malone and Robert J. Laubacher, "The Dawn of the E-Lance Economy," *Harvard Business Review* 76, no. 5 (1998): 144. These works featured Coase's ideas prominently and provided insightful analysis of the implications of his work for the new economy.
5. Ronald Coase, *The Firm, the Market and the Law* (Chicago: University of Chicago Press, 1990), 44.
6. Joel Kurtzman, "These Days, Small Manufacturers Can Play on a Level Field," *Fortune,* 20 July 1998, 156.
7. Adrian J. Slywotzky, *Value Migration* (Boston: Harvard Business School Press, 1996), 4.
8. Robert Sobel, *IBM: Colossus in Transition* (New York Times Books, 1981), 78.
9. James T. Womak, *Race for the Future: The M.I.T. Report on the Coming Global Revolution* (New York: HarperPerennial, 1992), 45.
10. Tapscott, *The Digital Economy,* 28.

11. Robert L. Cutts, "Capitalism in Japan: Cartels and *Keiretsu,*" *Harvard Business Review* 70, no. 4 (1992): 40.

12. See David Akin, "The Next Internet Revolution," *National Post,* 11 January 1999, <http://www.canada.com/cgi-bin/cp.asp?f-/news/nationalpost/stories/20000111/173407.html>; and Tish Williams, "Seeding the East Coast," *Upside Today,* 10 November 1999, <http://www.upside.com/texis/mvm/daily_tish?id=382883640>.

13. William H. Davidow and Michael S. Malone, *The Virtual Corporation: Structuring and Revitalizing the Corporation for the Twenty-First Century* (New York: HarperBusiness, 1993).

14. Steven Goldman, Kenneth Preiss, and Roger Nagel, *Agile Competitors and Virtual Organizations: Strategies for Enriching the Customer* (New York: John Wiley & Sons, 1997). Emphasis added.

15. James Moore, *The Death of Competition* (New York: HarperBusiness, 1996), 26.

16. This figure is based on estimates by Forrester Research, 15 January 2000.

17. Adam M. Brandenburger and Barry J. Nalebuff introduced this term in *Co-opetition* (New York: Doubleday, 1996).

18. Hubert Saint-Onge and Leif Edvinsson's collaboration set the foundation for understanding these issues. Saint-Onge developed the three-type view of intellectual capital. Edvinsson, one of the earliest and most influential thinkers on the topic, developed the concept of structural capital. He drew on the work of Karl Erik Sveiby, author of *The New Organizational Wealth: Managing and Measuring Knowledge-Based Assets* (San Francisco: Berrett-Koehler, 1997). Thomas Stewart describes the three-type approach that was adopted in his book *Intellectual Capital: The New Wealth of Organizations* (London: Nicholas Brealey, 1998). Saint-Onge collaborated with us in the early 1990s and has greatly influenced our thinking.

19. *Encyclopedia Britannica,* 11th ed., s.v. "agora."

20. Others apply the term *dynamic market* to these situations.

2 Agoras

1. Charles Smith, interview by Alan Majer, Alliance for Converging Technologies, December 1998.

2. The main exceptions are liquidators, who usually take title to the goods that they resell. However, they arguably function as surrogate principals for goods with uncertain or declining value. Also, liquidators often must buy large, diverse lots of goods; they do not get to pick and choose what they wish to sell out of the supplier's catalog.

3. U.S. Department of Commerce, Bureau of Economic Analysis, Industry Economics Division, November 1998. Source: <http://www.bea.gov.doc>.

4. Hendrik Bessembinder and Herbert M. Kaufman, "A Comparison of Trade Execution Costs for NYSE and NASDAQ-Listed Stocks," *Journal of Financial and Quantitative Analysis* 32, no. 3 (1997): 287.

5. Alan Majer, "Financial Markets: The Original e-Business Community," *Inside e-Business Communities* (Toronto: Alliance for Converging Technologies, 1999), 5.15.

6. Jeffrey Ricker, interview by Alan Majer, Alliance for Converging Technologies, December 1998.

7. These are our projections based on 1999 third-quarter revenues of $142 million.

8. Named after 1996 Nobel prize winner William Vickery. His work deals with the impact of various auction designs on economic efficiency.

9. Michael Fix, interview by David Ticoll, tape recording, Toronto, August 1999.

10. Martha L. Stone, "The Classifieds Conundrum," *Editor & Publisher*, 15 September 1999, 6–8; Leigh Muzlay, "Online Ads Stiff Competition for Newspapers," *St. Louis Journalism Review* 30, no. 220 (October 1999), 10.

11. These numbers are based on a comparison of the Business 2.0 Index, a listing of fifty Internet companies (August 1999) and the 1999 Fortune 500 companies. All data was collected from <http://www.hoovers.com> on 17 November 1999. Institutional holders include banks, insurance companies, and mutual funds with equity assets over $100 million.

12. Marc Lackritz, the president of the Securities Industry Association at the trade association's annual meeting in Boca Raton. Quoted from Jack Reerink, "Nearly One-Fifth of U.S. Investors Trade Online," *The Industry Standard*, 4 November 1999, <http://www.thestandard.com/articles/display/0,1551,7419,00.html>.

13. Charles Smith, *Auctions: The Social Construction of Value* (Berkeley: University of California Press, 1990).

14. Robert Kagle, quoted by Michael Wilson (chief technical officer of eBay), in interview by David Ticoll, tape recording, San Jose, CA, March 1999.

15. Cited in Julie Landry, "AuctionWatch Aggregates $9.6 Million in Funding," Redherring.com, 12 August 1999, <http://www.redherring.com/insider/1999/0812/VC-auctionwatch.html>.

16. Leigh Buchanan, "Seller Door," *Inc. Online*, 15 September 1998, <http://www.inc.com/incmagazine/archives/19780621.html> (14 November 1999).

17. Anne Perlman, interview by David Ticoll, tape recording, Toronto, 2 June 1999.

18. Jay Walker, interview with Alex Lowy and Mike Dover, 8 January 1998.

19. Priceline.com, "Priceline.com Delivers Savings for Flexible Travelers in Side-by-Side Price Comparison," <http://www.corporate-ir.net/ireye/ir_site. zhtml?ticker=pcln&script=401&layout=7&item_id=34023>.

3 Aggregations

1. Andersen Consulting, Consumer Direct Cooperative Consumer Research, "Early Learnings from the Consumer Direct Cooperative," January 1998.
2. Brent Johnson, "Chemdex: The On-Line Market for Bioscience," *The Scientist* 12, no. 14 (6 July 1998), <http://www.thescientist.library.upenn. edu/yr1998/july/tools1_980706.html>.
3. Charles Shih, "Rapid Revolution: How E-Commerce Is Changing the Plastics Industry" (Toledo, OH: Roman Peshoff, Inc., 1999).
4. Carl Shapiro and Hal R. Varian, *Information Rules: A Strategic Guide to the Network Economy* (Boston: Harvard Business School Press, 1998).
5. Bobby Lent, interview by Dave Cosgrave, Alliance for Converging Technologies, tape recording, 28 October 1999.
6. Barbara Kahn and Leigh McAlister, *Grocery Revolution: New Focus on the Consumer* (Reading, MA: Addison-Wesley, 1997), 49.
7. Don Peppers and Martha Rogers, *Enterprise One to One: Tools for Competing in the Interactive Age* (New York: Currency Doubleday, 1997).

4 Value Chains

1. The concept of shops is also described in Charles B. Stabell and Øystein D. Fjelstad, "Configuring Value for Competitive Advantage: On Chains, Shops, and Networks," *Strategic Management Journal* 19 (1998): 413–437. Our thanks to Doug Neal of Computer Sciences Corporation for drawing our attention to this work.
2. Michael E. Porter, *Competitive Advantage: Creating and Sustaining Superior Performance* (New York: Free Press, 1985), 49.
3. Ibid., 48.
4. Teri Takai, interview by Natalie Klym, Alliance for Converging Technologies, tape recording, 16 June 1999.
5. Phil Hood, "Cisco Systems: The Network Is the Company," in *Inside e-Business Communities* (Toronto: Alliance for Converging Technologies, 1999), 1.3.
6. Don Listwin, interview by Don Tapscott and David Ticoll, tape recording, September 1999.
7. William Diem, "Magna, TRW May Build Cars," *Detroit Free Press*, 9 July 1999.
8. Michael Dell, interview by Don Tapscott and David Ticoll, tape recording, 28 May 1999. Unless otherwise noted, all quotes from Dell are from this source.

9. Michael Dell, interview by David Ticoll, tape recording, 22 October 1999.
10. Don Listwin, interview by Don Tapscott and David Ticoll, tape recording, September 1999.
11. Dell's rates are from Michael Dell, interview by Alliance for Converging Technologies, tape recording, 28 May 1999. Other companies' rates are from Adrian Slywotzky, "How Digital Is Your Company?" *Fast Company,* February 1999, 94.
12. Michael Dell, interview by David Ticoll, tape recording, 22 October 1999.
13. Phil Esling, quoted in Phil Hood, "Cisco Systems: The Network Is the Company," in *Inside e-Business Communities* (Toronto: Alliance for Converging Technologies, 1999), 1.19.
14. Art Mesher, interview by David Ticoll, 28 May 1999.
15. Baer Tierkel, interview by David Ticoll, 25 May 1999.
16. Marty Tannenbaum, interview by David Ticoll, 28 May 1999.
17. Rob Haimes, "RosettaNet: Plug and Play Value Chains," in *Inside e-Business Communities* (Toronto: Alliance for Converging Technologies, 1999).
18. "When Companies Connect," *The Economist,* 26 June 1999, 19.

5 Alliances

1. Michael Learmonth, "Giving It All Away," Metro Active, 5 May 1997, <http://www.metroactive.com/papers/metro/05.08.97/cover/linus-9719.html> (14 November 1999).
2. Bill Gates, *The Road Ahead* (New York: Viking, 1995), 63.
3. Howard Rheingold, *The Virtual Community: Homesteading on the Electronic Frontier* (New York: HarperPerennial, 1994), available on the Web at <http://www.rheingold.com/vc/book/>.
4. John Hagel and Arthur G. Armstrong, *Net Gain: Expanding Markets through Virtual Communities* (Boston: Harvard Business School Press, 1997).
5. Carl Shapiro and Hal R. Varian, *Information Rules: A Strategic Guide to the Network Economy* (Boston: Harvard Business School Press, 1998), 175.
6. Robert Metcalfe is the former CEO of 3Com and the inventor of "Ethernet" networking technology.
7. Shapiro and Varian, *Information Rules,* 184.
8. Kevin Kelly, *Out of Control: The New Biology of Machines, Social Systems and the Economic World* (Reading, MA: Addison-Wesley Longman, 1994), 121–127.
9. D. R. Hofstadter, *Godel, Escher, Bach: An Eternal Golden Braid* (New York: Basic Books, 1979), cited in John Holland, *Emergence: From Chaos to Order* (Reading, MA: Addison-Wesley, 1998), 81.
10. See the "Halloween Documents," leaked by Microsoft internal reports, at <http://www.opensource.org>.

11. Eric S. Raymond, *The Cathedral and the Bazaar* (Sebastopol, CA: O'Reilly and Associates, 1999), available on the Web at <http://www.tuxedo.org/~esr/writings/cathedral-bazaar/cathedral-bazaar.html> (14 November 1999).

12. Gary Hamel, "Killer Strategies That Make Shareholders Rich," *Fortune,* 23 June 1997, 70.

13. Actually, there was one plug-compatible alternative to the IBM 370, provided by Amdahl. But this was the exception that proved the rule. In any case, IBM sold 95 percent of the 370-type computers. And it had several other product lines, all of which were incompatible with one another.

14. Peter Kollock, "The Economies of Online Cooperation," in *Communities in Cyberspace,* ed. Mark Smith and Peter Kollock (London: Routledge, 1999), 221.

15. Eric S. Raymond, *Homesteading the Noosphere,* April 1998, paper available on the Web at <http://www.tuxedo.org/~esr/writings/homesteading/homesteading.txt>.

6 Distributive Networks

1. Charles B. Stabell and Øystein J. Fjelstad, "Configuring Value for Competitive Advantage," *Strategic Management Journal* 19 (1998), 427, citing J. D. Thompson, *Organizations in Action* (New York: McGraw-Hill, 1967).

2. Enron's water business, called Azurix, was formed in January 1998. Azurix made its first big investment in July 1998 with the acquisition of Wessex Water, a British utility.

3. Enron Communications, "Enron Communications Introduces Global Bandwith Commodity Market" (press release 20 May 1999).

4. Utility.com is an Idealab spin-off company.

5. Some commentators pointed to the irony of the merger, suggesting it could herald the rebirth of the vertically integrated industrial-age conglomerate in the digital economy. Others have astutely warned that AOL's "dated strategy" is a major risk. Today's leaders, one analyst pointed out, have learned that "melding a sleek, fast-growing organization with a big established enterprise is the quickest way to slow growth and smother creativity." See the January 24, 2000, issue of *Business Week* for details of this discussion. In particular, see "The Great Irony of AOL Time Warner," editorial, 188, and John A. Byrne, "Is This Baby Built for Cyberspace?" 40 (the quotes in this note are taken from the Byrne article).

6. Rick Roscitt, interview by David Ticoll, tape recording, October 1999.

7. U.S. Federal Reserve System, Board of Governors, Flow of Fund Accounts, 1960–1997, <http://www.bog.frb.fed.US/releases/z1/current/data.htm>.

8. Information shares this property with money. In fact, unlike money,

information is infinitely leverageable; it can be replicated a thousand times without being diminished in any way.

9. Our thanks to Doug Neal of Computer Sciences Corporation for this example.

10. John Hagel III and Marc Singer, *Net Worth: Shaping Markets When Customers Make the Rules* (Boston: Harvard Business School Press, 1999).

11. Ibid., 19.

7 People: The Human Capital in the Business Web

1. Peter F. Drucker, *Post Capitalist Society* (New York: HarperCollins, 1993).

2. Saint-Onge was among the first to recognize that networking changes intellectual capital when, in 1966, he wrote the following with Peter A. C. Smith:

> Computer-telecommunications networks most effectively facilitate the designed connectedness that enables the Evolutionary Organization to develop its most potent collaborative infrastructure, and provide the current through which knowledge can travel instantly across the organization. The [organization's] identity and purpose are embodied in the network for all to access and fashion dynamically. . . . These networks can be extended to include not only employees out to the periphery, but also the customers and suppliers; in this way customer capital is enhanced. It has a unique capability to restructure operations and hardly a single aspect of business is not touched. We believe changing tools changes who we are.

Peter Smith and Hubert Saint-Onge, "The Evolutionary Organization: Avoiding a *Titanic* Fate," <http://www.knowinc.com/saint-onge/learning/>.

3. Thomas Malone and Robert Laubacher, "The Dawn of the E-Lance Economy," *Harvard Business Review* 76, no. 5 (1998): 144.

4. Ibid.

5. The auction was never completed, and the team withdrew.

6. Thanks to Stan Davis, author of *Blur: The Speed of Change in the Connected Economy* (Reading, MA: Addison-Wesley, 1998), for inspiring this scenario.

7. See <http://www.interbiznet.com/ern/archives/000102.html>.

8. Eugene Polistuk, interview by Don Tapscott, tape recording, September 1999.

9. Jeffrey H. Dyer, "How Chrysler Created an American Keiretsu," *Harvard Business Review* 74, no. 4 (1996): 42–56.

10. In *The Digital Economy: Promise and Peril in the Age of Networked Intelligence* (New York: McGraw-Hill, 1996), Don Tapscott described customers as prosumers, arguing that the divide between production and consumption was blurring. Subsequently, others like Patricia Seybold, in *Customers.Com*

(New York: Times Books, 1998); Regis McKenna, in *Real Time* (Boston: Harvard Business School Press, 1997); and Peppers and Rogers, in *Enterprise One to One* (New York: Doubleday, 1999) have all recast customers as economic units involved in production.

11. For a good summary of proposed measures of intellectual capital see Thomas A. Stewart, *Intellectual Capital: The New Wealth of Organizations* (London: Nicholas Brealey, 1998), 223–246.

12. Riel Miller, *Measuring What People Know: Human Capital Accounting for the Knowledge Economy* (Paris: OECD [Organization for Economic Cooperation and Development] Publications, 1996), cited in Don Tapscott, *Growing Up Digital: The Rise of the Net Generation* (New York: McGraw-Hill, 1998).

13. Thomas A. Stewart, in *Intellectual Capital,* was the first person we know of to suggest that firms should treat employees as investors of intellectual capital.

14. Michael Hammer and James Champy, *Reengineering the Corporation: A Manifesto for Business Revolution* (London: Nicholas Brealey, 1993).

15. The term *Net Generation* was introduced in Tapscott, *Growing Up Digital.*

16. Tapscott, *Growing Up Digital.*

8 Marketing: Relationship Capital in the Web

1. Thanks to David Carlick, formerly of Poppe Tyson Advertising, for the inspiration leading to this scenario. Says Carlick, "Instead of having one feature that suits many people, you can have many features that suit one person. Interactivity allows that one person to explore products and services according to their own interests and find out what is important to them."

2. John Sviokla, "The Price Is Wrong," *Context,* July/August 1999, <http://www.contextmag.com/archives/199907/DigitalStrategy.asp>.

3. Jeffrey F. Rayport and John J. Sviokla, "Exploiting the Virtual Value Chain," *Harvard Business Review* 73, no. 6 (1995): 75. The article explains how information and services can be added to products. Rayport and Sviokla coined the term *marketspace.*

4. An OECD report, *The Economic and Social Impact of Electronic Commerce: Preliminary Findings and Research Agenda* (Paris: Organization for Economic Cooperation and Development, February 1999), <http://www.oecd.org/subject/e_commerce/summary.htm>, projects 1 trillion dollars in digital marketspace sales by 2003—already a proven conservative estimate. The United States, Canada, the Netherlands, Australia, New Zealand, Singapore, and the Scandinavian countries are early candidates for this prediction.

5. Customers may or may not contribute value to the actual product (as discussed in chapters 7 and 8), but increasingly, they invest their time—say, to customizing a portal to meet their unique needs.

6. Sun CEO Scott McNealy describes a car as a "Java docking station."

7. See, for example, <http://www.saynotothirdvoice.com>.

8. John MacDonald and Jim Tobin, "Customer Empowerment in the Digital Economy," in *Blueprint to the Digital Economy,* ed. Don Tapscott, Alex Lowy, David Ticoll (New York: McGraw-Hill, 1998), 206.

9. Thomas A. Bass, "The Future of Money," *Wired* 4, no. 10, (1996), <http://www.wired.com/wired/archive/4.10/wriston.html>.

10. For a good discussion, see "Death by a Thousand Clicks," *The Economist,* 4 December 1999, 21. For an eloquent defense of the banks, see Lloyd Darlington, "Banking without Boundaries: How the Banking Industry Is Transforming Itself for the Digital Age," in *Blueprint to the Digital Economy,* ed. Tapscott, Lowy, and Ticoll, 113–139.

11. John Gallaugher, "Challenging the New Conventional Wisdom of Net Commerce Strategies," *Communications of the ACM* [Association of Computing Machinery] 42, no. 7 (1999): 27.

12. For a thoughtful discussion by two PR leaders on the Intel fiasco, see James Barr and Theodore Barr, *The Pentium Bug War Ends PR as We Know It* (Providence, RI: Omegacom Inc., 1994).

13. For a full discussion, see Joseph Pine and James Gilmore, *The Experience Economy* (Boston: Harvard Business School Press, 1999).

14. See Michael Goldhaber, "Attention Shoppers," *Wired* 5, no. 12 (1997); and the Alamut Web site at <http://www.alamut.com/subj/economics/attention/attnt_economy.html>.

15. Scott Miller, "VW: Investor Ties Pressure Stock," *Wall Street Journal Europe,* 16 November 1999.

16. Baby-boomer stories dominate the media, while their children's generation is called diminutive names like the boomlet. Public policy discussions focus on the aging of the population rather than what's really happening—a bifurcation. See Tapscott, *Growing Up Digital,* 1–45.

9 How Do You Weave a B-Web?

1. Households held 39.9 percent of the share of total equities outstanding at the end of the second quarter 1999.

2. Valve mapping is a variation of Verna Allee's holo-mapping modeling technique. See Verna Allee, *The Knowledge Evolution: Expanding Organizational Intelligence* (Boston: Butterworth-Heinemann, 1997).

10 Harvesting Digital Capital

1. Jay B. Barney, "How a Firm's Capabilities Affect Boundary Decisions," *Sloan Management Review* 40 (Spring 1999): 137–145. Our discussion in this section draws extensively on Barney's analysis.
2. Ibid.
3. John Chambers, interview by John Daly, in "John Chambers: The Art of the Deal," *Business 2.0*, October 1999, 108–116. All references to Cisco and Chambers in this section draw on this interview.
4. Instead of *experience*, Barney uses the more rigorous term *path dependency*.
5. Robert Kunstadt, "Opening Pandora's Box," *IP Magazine*, January 1999, <http://www.ipmag.com/monthly/99-jan/kunstadt.html>.
6. Wendy Taylor and Marty Jerome, "The Net Is a Casino for Imbeciles," *PC Computing*, 21 January 1999, <http://www.zdnet.com/zdnn/stories/comment/0,5859,2190580,00/html>.
7. Ian Ainsworth of Altamira Investments suggested that we examine this point. Note that eBay and Wal-Mart have slightly different reporting periods.
8. The Altamira e-business Fund is managed by Altamira Financial Services Ltd. We advise the fund through Intelligent Enterprise Corporation, whose CEO is Paul Woolner. Michael Miloff is managing partner.

index

about the authors

DON TAPSCOTT is Chairman of the Alliance for Converging Technologies. He is also President of New Paradigm Learning Corporation and an internationally sought consultant, speaker, and authority on information technology in business. Vice President Al Gore described Tapscott as one of the world's leading cyber-gurus, and the *Washington Technology Report* called him one of the most influential media authorities since Marshall McLuhan. Tapscott is the author of seven books, including *Growing Up Digital: The Rise of the Net Generation*, which won the first Amazon.com nonfiction bestseller award in 1998, and the bestsellers *The Digital Economy: Promise and Peril in the Age of Networked Intelligence* and *Paradigm Shift: The New Promise of Information Technology*.

DAVID TICOLL is Managing Director and CEO of the Alliance for Converging Technologies. A global authority and consultant on business strategy and frequent, in-demand speaker, he was the first to describe a taxonomy of business webs, the new platform for wealth creation in the twenty-first century. Ticoll established the Canadian program of the Gartner Group in the early 1980s. He now leads private engagements and multiclient research on the impact of the Internet, wireless computing, and e-business on competitive advantage, organizational effectiveness, digital supply chains, and the future of government. Ticoll is a contributor to the *Harvard Business Review*, *Business 2.0*, *tele.com*, and *USA Today*, among others.

ALEX LOWY is Managing Director, Research and Programs, of the Alliance for Converging Technologies. He is the primary leader of the

Alliance's research initiatives, groundbreaking investigations into e-business innovation. He is also a preeminent consultant and educator specializing in the creation of innovative work, learning, and information systems to achieve high-performance results. Lowy has contributed award-winning articles to journals including *Training and Development*, the *Journal for Group and Organizational Studies*, and *Business 2.0*. A frequent conference speaker, he promotes the application of high-performance b-web design principles in firms around the world.

Tapscott, Ticoll, and Lowy are cofounders of the Alliance for Converging Technologies, an international research and consulting group that advises corporations and governments worldwide on strategy in the digital economy. They are coeditors of *Blueprint to the Digital Economy: Creating Wealth in the Era of e-Business*.